T0197200

SATORI
MOMENTS

Awakening Life & Guiding Fearlessly
from Fight to Flight & Beyond

JONI KIRBY

All Proceeds Donated to Dr. Loh's Childhood
Cancer Research in Honor of Smilin Rylan

BALBOA.PRESS
A DIVISION OF HAY HOUSE

Balboa Press books may be ordered through booksellers or by contacting:

Balboa Press
A Division of Hay House
1663 Liberty Drive
Bloomington, IN 47403
www.balboapress.com
844-682-1282

Print information available on the last page.

ISBN: 979-8-7652-3506-5 (sc)
ISBN: 979-8-7652-3508-9 (hc)
ISBN: 979-8-7652-3507-2 (e)

Library of Congress Control Number: 2022917972

Balboa Press rev. date: 10/17/2022

Contents

Introduction

Always Begin Within, and Life Flows

Happy New Year 2021. Happy new now. May each moment be in love.

I choose to start writing my *soul-full* words of love on this first day of a new year and a new beginning. Every moment is a new beginning, so as I wrote that statement, a nudge of Om warmed my heart.

Moving to this tiny home in Cambria, California, on December 23, leaving Hanford, the home we had for many years, I begin my life after the third of my three (two men, one Smilin' Rylan) heartstrings took flight on July 16 of last year. What an amazing year 2020 was and continues to be as our energy at times remains stuck there.

What if we had an agenda we came into this beautiful play of life to accomplish?

What if being brave or being a hero didn't play into our decisions? If fear weren't even a knowingness but rather a dreamlike state of mind made up to bring contrast to the desire of moving forward?

What if we just had an inner knowing, a desire to help extend the humanity of humankind, bringing more kindness into this play of life?

I'm going to be sharing some acts of bravery, all stemming from the choice to love and choose life, through to flight and beyond.

I felt an inner calling to begin this writing at this present moment and then go to a nowhereland that is no longer real but that has left me with the realization of the preciousness of this moment—this present moment as I begin sharing with love not only for myself but also for any people who have felt cancer was taking their lives as spouses, family members, friends, or caregivers, or for whom cancer has been a part, an intimate part, of life.

I had never been close to anyone going through cancer, so as I was turning fifty, I had the next ten years (and more) caring and loving "cancer" as my husband, dad, and heartstring grandson, Smilin' Rylan, began their adventure (and therefore mine, as I was a companion) toward flight and beyond.

I will write of how I believe my life's dress rehearsals, and all the many characters performing in the different acts, the parts of my life's play, helped me to return to the I Am that I am, delivering me back to my whole self. Not that I believe I was ever *not* whole—what I believe is that who I really am became covered up with layers of, yes, s——. I would often use the example of lugging around suitcases full of manure that we collect from our choices in each present moment, and before we realize it, we are exhausted from the loads we carry and the accompanying smell.

Through my words, you will understand that as I write, I experience an overwhelming sense of fluttering, warming butterflies throughout my body, often beginning in my heart and spreading from there.

Having moved from my home of forty-five years, Hanford, California, to a beautiful coastal town, Cambria, after the last of my two men and super Rylan had taken flight, I was now ready to begin again by the sound and feel of the ocean. Back to where I was born, close to the waves. And as I watch the waves, I am reminded that we all will return to the one. I have heard that even as we rest our heads on our pillows at night and drift off to sleep, we return to the oneness, and there we continue learning and growing. Or not—our choice, ultimately.

I just knew it was time; moving from a beautifully spacious home of 2,700 square feet to a magical, simple, less-than-1,200-square-foot manufactured home was and is just perfect. It is January 1, 2021, and I am stepping out from my tiny home in Cambria, looking at all the green trees and seeing a stream forming right below my porch. I am thinking of all the little yogis and of my baby sister by another mother, Naomi.

The year 2020 was definitely a life changer for (I believe) all of us. The New Year celebration of 2020 was filled with anticipation of hopes and dreams.

Especially with all the children of Smilin' Rylan Kids Yoga. They really missed coming to class and learning to be (I should say *remain*) in each moment.

My husband was an optometrist, and I managed the office for more than thirty years. I enjoyed every moment! I was sincerely excited every day I walked into the office to serve others. A gift.

After my husband's second diagnosis of prostate cancer and subsequent selling of the practice, I began teaching kids (as well as adults) yoga in honor of Rylan, my grandson, who had barely taken his flight from the physical.

Reflecting back one year ago, on enjoying coming together, embracing each class while beginning our lives on the mat, and allowing stillness and silence to be present.

Now I am presently bringing them to my heart's space energetically, through energy of love, all the while remembering their spirits and feeling their love.

This past week has been an emotional roller coaster for me. I've lived enough in my present life to know deep in my heart that this, too, shall pass. This is true for the joys and heartwarming moments as well as the challenges. I am reassured, blessed, and filled with gratitude with the knowingness that moments come and fade. What is real is this moment now—leaving the past and believing the now is magical and just perfect.

Believing the now is a blessing. I release any expectations or judgment. It's my life in this moment. For me, I choose love. The most challenging for me is to let go of the moments and memories, avoiding the comparison ritual.

Not so difficult for me is allowing the bad or harder moments to dissolve, evaporate as mist. More challenging are the beautifully loving memories. So as not to become stuck, I try to avoid comparing past memories with the present.

When I am aware, I understand how important it is to live in the now, in this amazing present moment, allowing the space required to enjoy the memories but not becoming stuck in them, not allowing them to take up residence.

As 2021 becomes the year of new realities, giving birth to new ways to both show and accept what is, may we all feel the blessings that are real in the presence of now. As we are living the moment with whoever, whatever, is present with us, may we choose to share love and appreciation for life. Finding peace with the knowingness that challenging times have unforeseen rainbows of blessings and miracles, may we choose to feel the fear during times it attempts to take over and allow our awareness to bring us back into the now, moving through the mist as best we can. Remembering we are the cause of the feeling, and have the choice of focus, of love or fear, which are you willing to choose? Who are you willing to live in this moment with? Perhaps you may be called to choose to bring peace within the frustrations of this moment and give yourself the love that heals.

*Nicolas, one of the amazing Smilin' Rylan little yogis, with a
kindness note for the delivery service during lockdown.*

Choose to remember to live the moment. Truly, what other time do
you have?

Satori Moments: A Sort of Brain Surgery, Awakening to a New Paradigm—One of Love and Acceptance

Darrell and Satori.

I debated using *satori* in the title. Over more than twenty years, I have met only a handful of people, at most, who know and understand what that word symbolizes. I encourage you to continue reading—you will not regret it! If you picked up this book, you are meant to travel the awakening satori moments from the beginning to the end, enjoying every step, allowing the words to lift your consciousness into a place of new birth. This is my wish for you. Take a deep cleansing breath, and believe life is about to get even clearer, deeper in meaning, and more magically real *now*.

One of my childhood labels was *sickly*—"Joni is our sickly child"—and boy, did I live up to it. Asthma, hospital stays with pneumonia, shingles at age five, mononucleosis in third grade, and the list goes on. I believe my very cells were listening to my mind, to the script it was hearing from family and friends, and they were doing exactly what they were called to do. They were not going to make a liar out of my mind's request. For those who know me, you just don't believe it. It has been years since I have been sick. Well, read on, because part of my satori moments led me to become strong but flexible—full of spirit and living life with no referencing of my age. Why do we allow our birthdays to dictate how we are supposed to feel or what we're supposed to look like? I am forever young, at least in my heart's space, where I take up residence most of my moments now.

Of course, back then, I also found a pathway to attention, and I remember telling one of my sisters when we were older that I used the label. Of course, when I was a child, it was not that obvious to me. It was my way of escaping from the expectations that were placed (innocently) on me as a child. I know that was one way of surviving.

I have vivid memories of my childhood. I still take the time during meditation and wrap my arms around that child, the fearful, scared, desperate little child. I remind that child that I am forever filled with gratitude and appreciation. Why? Because she was the cause of my amazing love for her and me, my self. I loved being a child. I remember, though, being told often that I was "just too emotional." Believing it, I soon welcomed that label as a truth. The more I tried to hide it, the sicker I became. And unconsciously, I used it as a way to survive, becoming sick.

I choose to remember her and to be reminded to look ahead, out of the past, into the present, toward the lights now being lit—how perfect it feels. The satori moments would just download like a tidal wave of love. So much joy and love I hold for her, that little child within me. I'm forever filled with gratitude for the clarity I would come to uncover, for the role she's had in this life and that she's now playing as I venture moment by moment, reunited with my self.

I giggle as I write this: I was told I was shy, too sensitive, sickly, but I came to realize others just didn't know or understand—they were unaware that my inner child was preparing me to live the rest of my life as a child rejoicing, dancing, whenever and wherever, without a care about who's watching. Singing in the drop of a moment and loving with all my heart, I can only pray that those I have hurt have been able to move through and forgive my naive, at times selfish, wrongdoings or any wrong choices that have caused them pain.

I grew to love and forgive, to shake any and all guilt (and all the drama that rides its shirttail) I allowed to cover up my true self. The guilt that was unloaded on a small, delicate child who believed in what she was feeling and hearing and all along the way knew the real truth that was being pushed down. The guilt and drama that come from not living your truth. I believe and choose not to blame others, parents, family, or friends, who are only living through what they believe to be the way it is or should be. Their actions and beliefs are born from their perceptions and the paradigms they are looking through on their journeys, or in their own plays of life. I do not believe in holding on to anger, blame, or any fear-based emotions. I am a true believer of surrounding my self with practices through love.

Satori moment—another aha moment, or awakening. This was a big one for me: When I am able to deeply and completely forgive who I think

I am, I am brought into the present moment. In that present moment, I am able to forgive others. Well, sometimes it has taken a little longer, but I can't think of one person over whom I have held on to hurt or anger because of a situation (or a situation I *perceived* to have happened).

I discovered, uncovered, many years ago that if I am not able to let go and not be so hard on who I believe my self to be, there is little chance I will extend that courtesy to others. I will remain judgmental and find reason to blame. I do not like the yucky, mucky feeling I get at those times, and it is very, very seldom I experience them. Life becomes so free and fun when we choose to let go and be.

Butterflies and their journey have been part of my journey since I was very young. A repetitive journey, to spread my wings and fly, but it was not like that when I was a little girl. I disliked caterpillars with a passion! They were furry, ugly, creepy worms. And where I lived in Long Beach, it seemed they would find me. They'd be crawling on sidewalks as I walked across the street to kindergarten or on the playground, taking their time, often grossly crawling up a tree or a leaf. Very much how I have felt about my life, my journey.

Ironically, that was the same early years during which I was teased relentlessly because of my speech and inability to hold in my sadness, the growing hurt I experienced from feeling I was different and less-than. I had nothing inside of me to attack back, to tell anyone, to just be, and the being was sadness. I look back to see and feel how I felt as the caterpillar, but how soon I would move through the beautiful journey and find my cocoon breaking open, my self taking flight and never looking back. Those struggles, challenges, brought change and fueled my determination to spread my wings and fly, soaring to rediscover me.

I still remember a day I had a satori moment! Again, back then, I would never be able to explain it; I could only live it in the moment. While my amazing, loving kindergarten teacher was reading a book to our class about the flight of the caterpillar, my entire attitude about caterpillars changed.

There was the satori moment, even though, as a child, I had no official name for my awakening, but they seemed to come often, and I accepted them as normal.

I still remember Ms. Wagner. She also would take flight as she sung to us every morning. Those who know me often hear me sing to kids (or really whoever—sometimes to the wind!), "Today is Friday, today is Friday. Is everybody happy? Well, I should say yes." Krisi would sing that song to both her little boys as she would go into their room to get them up, ready to start a new day, just as her mommy did with her. Craig, my stepson, still recalls my singing voice as I would come try to get him out of bed. Since he came into my life as a teenager, he really did not appreciate my voice or the cheerful song in the morning. But, as a father of four, he soon came to appreciate the song and singer of love.

Through the years, many have blessed me with tributes to my metamorphosis of love. Unique gifts of butterflies fill my loving home to this day. When it is my time to take my final flight (from the physical), my loved ones will find boxes and boxes, as well as, hanging here and there, kindness gifts, butterflies, flying in remembrance of my life. I trust that my final flight leaves a residue behind not of acquired cocoons of my life— things, possessions, labels—but rather of the butterfly flight times I brought and left through moments of kindness and love.

How many of us stay in our safe cocoons instead of breaking through and taking flight into who we really are, possibly because of fear of what others may think of us if they found out who we really are? I can understand. It can be scary, but the takeoff gives birth to magical moments and just-right alignment, and life becomes light and nondependent on external surroundings.

Can you just imagine going within, into a shell, and allowing who you really are to be covered as you heal and rediscover (embrace) and then break out of those barriers of fear, ultimately spreading your wings, taking the flight of freedom, and feeling free to just be? What would that look like? Feel like? Be like?

Would it possibly bring feelings of uncertainty? Fear of what that might move you to? Perhaps you'd no longer feel comfortable hanging with the friends or acquaintances you are now spending your moments with. You'd possibly feel the desire to make changes in your life. Perhaps your job? I still to this day tell anyone who wants to hear, or heart listen, that I would be the same Joni regardless of if I was still loving being a part of Dr. Kirby's office, teaching yoga, or selling hot dogs on the street corner. What is inside me does not change depending on who, what, or where my body is at in any given moment. I will add that I choose differently, though, how and with whom I spend my time.

How long do we spend in our cocoons, struggling through the comfortableness, perhaps even unsure of who we really are? Could it be perhaps that we are afraid of what we may find within? What that realization would move us into becoming? Once the layers have been broken through, what is left? My experience has been a peace, a oneness within, of layers dropping—layers of what and who others think or thought I am—and my becoming who I am. Who I really am.

I have moved through many a cocoon, and it is so freeing when I become comfortable taking flight into my life and expressing the moments, leaving behind a clear message of what my life is about—not what I do or have acquired, not even the form, but rather a deeper residue of who I really am, not what others may have thought I was or perceived me to be. Now I feel free to let go of all layers and accept the change into authenticity.

A caterpillar, a cocoon, and then a flight forward into who I really am—magical and precious. So let's get out of our cocoons and lift off, enjoying the moment and feeling the wind beneath our wings as we prepare to take flight.

Once I was able to begin the journey of excavating within myself, I naturally found the space in my heart to forgive others. Being truthful gives birth to the rainbow of reassurance of peace and serenity, validating the blessings of letting go. Powerful yet so beautifully freeing and light.

I am going to share one of my many collections of moments in which my practices guided me gracefully toward breaking through another cocoon of bondage and once again embarking on a flight of freedom to be my self.

Story: To this day, I continue to wear the plastic heart earrings (my favorite is the pink) that one of our longtime employees gave me more than nine years ago. It was an employee who was found stealing from us, our practice, our hearts. An audit uncovered that more than $40,000 (estimated three times that amount) was embezzled through the years.

It was not so much the money. It was the heartbreak of uncovering that for six or more years that she worked with us, she was lying and using us to front her unhappiness and fill her pockets. At least that's what I thought at the time. It took my remembering the forgiveness I had given myself, feeling the love I continue to choose through forgiveness, to open enough to begin the journey of forgiving her. I deserved that peace.

Possibly you're wondering why I mentioned that I continue to wear the plastic heart earrings she had given me. Well, I will do my best to explain what I didn't really realize at the time I was doing. It was after some time that I felt, knew, and embraced the intentions I was previously unaware of. Those plastic earrings helped me find the love in my heart's space to forgive and to understand she was hurting. Every time I would feel a hint of sadness or anger welling up, I would find myself choosing to feel the heart earrings on my ears, and to this day, I still choose to send her love, forgiveness, and courage.

Of course, this didn't happen right away, but eventually, I saw through the turbulent waves, choosing to see past the storm, allowing the rainbow to appear, reminding myself that she was broken. I still wear those plastic hearts, and I still send her family love. I loved her family; I loved her kids. I still do and wish them so much happiness, peace, and forgiveness.

Maybe, just maybe, we can all choose to forgive—beginning by being still, going within, and listening as our hearts send just the perfect messages we are meant to receive. As we become still and allow our minds to rest in the moment of now, we can possibly start our dances and songs by calling or writing that one person we now know we can forgive and setting ourselves free.

Set sail and fly in peace.

Before you head to the next chapters, here is a little background on how my trainings of over thirty-five years came to be called *untrainings*. (Though I have to admit I was tempted to just allow you to figure it out as you read the following untraining chapters.)

Untrainings versus trainings—big difference, in my book! We don't need to be trained to *be*. For most of us, we have had years of training in what other people wanted us to be. Labels unintentionally found homes in our lives, in our subconscious. And we just acted them out day after day, developing patterns, habits. We've acquired many dysfunctional labels, expectations we have rehearsed over and over from scripts handed down to us, not ever allowing ourselves to voice an opinion. Our monkey minds made sure of it.

"This is how it has always been in our family." "This is how our family always has done things." "This is just who I am."

I could go on and on with so many handed-down scripts others have shared with me that became part of their robotic lives. Of course, this doesn't apply to *everyone*—although most of us, if we are honest, have been programmed from an early age and have not taken the time to question this programming even after several unhappy life experiences. Through subtle nudges, our hearts indicate our deep unhappiness and softly (and sometimes not so softly) call us to change and to return to who we really are. There is a feeling, a knowing, deep within that we have it all within ourselves. A soft voice from the heart's space summons quietly to them, you, me. Now we choose who will live out our plays—who we really are or actors?

You will read in more detail about my husband, Darrell, and his first diagnosis of prostate cancer; my dad's journey with lung cancer (the day after my dad's flight, news came that Darrell's cancer was back with a vengeance); and Smilin' Rylan's journey of dancing through cancer, helping to remind all of us that life is love and we must live fully each moment.

In each love-filled experience, my dad, my husband, and my grandson (my life's gift of satori moments) prepared me as if my soul communicated from a very young age what I would need to be of service, fully present.

Well before *cancer* was ever a common word in our family, I was being prepared. After the passing last year of my husband (the last of the three to take flight), it even became more apparent that I was called to share with as many people as possible. We all have a gift of inner knowingness and a desire to use our moments for (first) uncovering our selves, and we must begin from within and start the excavating to uncover all we are meant to be.

Then we must use our rebirth of who we always were and have been to move through life with grace and appreciation for ourselves and all others. Love thy neighbor as thyself. I grew to love myself again and haven't looked back. I live more in the present and leave the past as a no-longer-required road map to discovery.

Full circle: it all just becomes a no-brainer. You desire your newfound (but always available) awareness. You desire to be present and there for others. We all have so many practices we are presented with—practices to keep us in alignment with our spirits (or call it Holy Spirit; I call it my inner self, my real self, the I in the background watching).

You will come across certain words throughout the book, including *now*, *awakening*, *awareness*, *presence*, and *enlightening*, that are just typed words, but their meanings have come to be the inner view of my life's play. They really are my book. I hope you will not become complacent reading those words, as they are the heart and theme of my book, my life. You could call them all within the awakenings of my satori moments. Be patient and allow your heart's mind to open.

The next seven chapters will take you on this journey, the satori journey of reawakening—RYLAN'S untrainings:

1. Remember Who You Are
2. You Are Energy
3. Love the Moment, Live the Moment, Learn from the Moment, and Laugh Often
4. All Is Well: All Are One
5. Nothing Can Still Your Joy
6. Space: Breathe in the Space of Stillness between Thoughts
7. Seeds of Intentions: Plant Your Life's Garden

Remember Who You Are

Free to Be Me

June 21, 2019

Super Rylan and I saving the world of now.

"Who am I?" While attending an amazing retreat ("Seduction of Spirit") at the Chopra Center in San Diego, we were asked to begin our meditation with that question, followed by "What do I want?"

Just last week, as I guided a meditation leading with the question "Who am I?," I was asked by a little yogi in our Smilin' Rylan Kids Yoga class what that meant to me. He was having a challenge answering, or finding the answer he felt was correct. We seem to feel we need to answer and that there are right and wrong answers. Perhaps judgment. Why? I feel at times we move our children (innocently) into always feeling they need to come up with an answer—"Answer me."

I have noticed when children are left to feel free to choose whether or how to answer, they will naturally know the answers from within regarding who they really are.

For me, when I allowed the question to just sit, feeling no need to come up with an answer, to solve it, my meditation became magical. The second question, "What do I want?," really opened my heart's mind (which I will be referring to as *my heart's space*). With time, my crazy monkey mind would lose its urgency to interrupt my journey, and I would fall into a deep, peace-filled awareness of who I am and, most important, who I am not. There's a space, a falling awake, and it is a wonderful way to explain this beautiful meditative experience.

Years ago, a spiritual teacher, Anthony de Mello, woke me up—another satori (aha) moment! I was only in my early twenties.

He said something along these lines: "Once a child is told the name of a bird, the child no longer sees the bird."

I am reminded of this every day, especially in nature—to really look at each tree not as a tree but as if I am seeing it for the first time, unnamed. This way, there's less likely to be a lot of needless mind chatter.

Oftentimes, unaware, we put people, things, events, and places in boxes. Once a name is uttered, we begin losing the beauty of the moment and fail to experience the bird as if we're seeing it for the first time.

Who Am I?

What are your answers?
*I am a teacher, mother, father, woman, man, teenager ...
*I am lazy, energetic, ugly, tall ...

This is not about right or wrong answers—in fact, it's not about answers at all.

What Do I Want?

This question sends many of us deeper. We see the bird without the label.

I know I did! I started questioning my answer to who I am when I answered what I want with quiet feelings of emotions from my heart, my heart's space.

Not my mind. As I often say, use your heart to filter the mind. Now perhaps answer "Who am I?" For me, there are no words to describe.

"What do I want?" Once again, allow the question to just be. Now, as my heart's space is now taking over, my answer put in words would most definitely be love-filled moments of joy, peace, and aliveness!

Our Childhoods and a New Habit

June 5, 2019

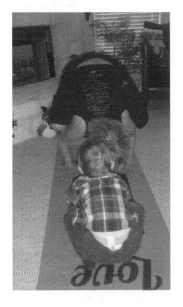

I never had to ask Rylan whether he wanted to get on the mat and practice yoga. Rylan wanted to do a balancing pose called *crow*. Rylan, Mom, and Dad gave me my Love Yoga mat for Christmas! Perfect!

When our lives are in balance—and for many of us it's not as often as we would like—we give ourselves permission to live fully, allowing the inner child to travel back to childhood days. Days when we laughed often, criticized seldom, and rested when need be. But soon life happens. Habits begin to be instilled, and though many are good ones, many perhaps would have served us better if we'd left them as fleeting thoughts.

When we are taught, or when we choose, to carry out an act or engage in a specific thought process time and again, day after day, repetition gives way to habit. Habits are programs that continue to run in our minds without us even realizing it. Before we know it, we're living a program and not life.

Watch children—when left alone, they choose to be in the moment, most often living life to the fullest! It is such a joy to be around children and watch the miracle of beingness.

The wonderful news is that we can develop new habits. Yay! It's not easy to open that door back in time. Being open to spending time with children, instead of bringing them into your programmed habits of life, allows them to bring you back in time to enjoy more laughter, calmer moments, and perhaps singing and dancing a little more than usual!

That was a huge relief I began acknowledging as I left my childhood scripting, which included "Don't be silly," "Stop messing around," and "Someone is going to get hurt"—and heaven forbid we laugh at the dinner table.

Again, it is not a time to blame our parents; they were only carrying on the torch of learned scripting from their parents, who'd learned it from

3

theirs. When was the last time you let loose and danced and sang or didn't give a second thought to what others may think? I was just a child who really was oversensitive and wanted to please my parents, so I made sure to be silent more often than not. Again, if you start blaming anyone, you are missing a blessing of returning and uncovering who you really are, and you remain stuck. So put on those dancing shoes and bust a move.

I just had a new neighbor tell me she admires that I am a free spirit (I took it as a compliment), and one of my favorite neighbors from Hanford texted me that she missed my singing. So funny, because I know my voice is not a pleasant sound, but I love to sing. So perhaps use earplugs if I am your neighbor.

Question: Would more people sing, dance, and laugh loudly if they really didn't worry who was there, who could see or hear them? My new neighbor—I really love her—accepts my craziness of talking to myself, singing constantly, and laughing hard! Just a suggestion, but how about we all start practices that bring our selves back to the front lines of our lives, letting the scripts that have carried us this far yet not served our souls blow into the wind, and we begin again as children.

Many still talk about remembering back to when Smilin' Rylan was teaching us the secrets of living a joy-filled, in-the-moment life. We are reminded not to take things so seriously and to instead smile more often, dance more freely (wildly), and fill each day with gratitude.

Smilin' Rylan has a website that many still visit. My guess is they revisit to remember who they really are and to return there as often as possible—returning to the innocence of childhood, taking in each moment as they live each moment, celebrating the child within, and allowing themselves to return to the innocence and freedom of being themselves.

If we're more open to changing daily routines, then our actions will become more aligned with what we truly desire. When we let go into pure nonjudgmental play, we allow our spirits to be in the moment. We allow our to-do lists to contain fewer items—or we expand the lists, but we make sure to do so with chores more aligned with past childhood days of living in the moment!

Diagnosed with leukemia at age two, Smilin' Rylan helped many let go of the idea that kindness has to be earned. And when people are kind, it doesn't mean they are necessarily expecting anything in return; it's all about the intention. Rylan was a pure example of kindness.

Until we (Joni and Naomi) started a new chapter in our lives, we played together many years at Dr. Kirby's office, now called iCare of Hanford. We enjoyed our days serving people and helping them see better. So here's the secret: what we really did was use our service for serving others with kindness. Now you know. You thought we wanted to help you see twenty-twenty, and all the while, the main thing was to keep the main thing the main thing, and the main thing was a service of loving care, with the bonus of your seeing better.

Serving Is Beautiful / Remember Service Is Not Self-Sacrifice

Serving others is a beautiful place to be. In my experience, when you start feeling depleted or you're feeling as if you're sacrificing yourself, the energy behind the serving is most likely not coming from your loving heart space.

We are, or should be, our own greatest teachers as well as our number one students, ready to learn from our selves at times when resentment has driven our service, perhaps making us irritated and leaving a bitter taste in our mouths.

At the office, we would talk about this often. By the end of the day, if your body is feeling tired but full of loving energy, you know you have done your service through your heart space and not from your ego.

When our selves are not top priority, our own best friends who we love to nurture, the ego will take over the driver's seat.

Self-care for me: yoga time with a bestie.

Naomi and I Zooming for others during lockdown. Note to self: our spirits, souls, cannot be locked down.

Those times when I have felt depleted, I have learned and continue to learn through satori moments to be proactive and to keep myself at the top of my friendship list (you'll learn more about friendships later through a helpful analogy), staying self-full so as to become selfless and serve from my inner heart space.

It's a night-and-day-different experience of my life. I continue to choose light! The moments I lose who I really am, I often will be found with my mat rolled out, reconnecting with my breath and becoming present once again, or I take a walk in nature or, at times, just a time-out to sit and breathe in stillness.

During those moments, I feel no resentment, entitlement, or need for a returned thank-you from the recipient. I am being my inner self, with no attachments. My giving is my receiving. I feel energized with appreciation of just being.

When you end your day feeling emotionally and physically depleted, most likely you need to revisit how you are, first serving your self, taking care of you, and making sure you are filling your self full enough to be of the service energy that truly serves another soul. Or you must at least choose not to be in a position where you are feeling pressure to give to someone of your time and energy. Of course, I feel that if you are found there, it's best to choose with a knowingness that the energy you give will return to the world one way or another. Choose your actions.

You cannot give in and through love if you are not full of love yourself. Yes, it's there, just covered up for the time being, in need of self-care.

So just a thought: Contemplate ways you can provide self-care physically, mentally, and spiritually. It is so very healing and proactively preparing you to be present for others. Those are the times I feel I am connected with all.

Another playshop goal about how we speak to others and ourselves.

When you serve others and give from your self through your desire to serve, your heart space of love, your actions speak proof of your intentions.

Take a pause and ask yourself what your actions are speaking. I believe I am choosing to serve most of my moments—if not myself, then nature, others, fur babies, and so on. I have learned to be much more aware, asking myself whether I am serving with absolutely no conditions or no strings or expectations attached to the service. Hopefully the answer is most often yes! I hope that, for most of us, the answer is yes and we enjoy giving and receiving kindness. I do believe that's what we are born to do.

Serve and receive in love. When giving and receiving, know no difference. But seek to understand vampires—those who do their best to suck the life out of givers; who, when confronted with the choice to give, more often than not will do so only for a price, a return; and whose actions speaking so loudly you aren't able to hear the words they express to the contrary. Which sort of giving do you believe in?

Journal: Do I keep score? Do I believe giving is receiving and receiving is giving?

I believe we are giving back when there is a natural flow of love and gratitude. It is just so beautiful—amazingly beautiful! The ocean's rhythm is a current, a circle of love.

Hugs are a constant for my self: COVID may have tried to win, but we are the only ones who lose when we allow distance to cause love to become less present—less touching within the heart's space. Love knows no boundaries!

I am reminded that when I become gentle with me, I naturally become gentler with others. So be patient and gentle.

Remember you are perfect within your self. There's no question that when we go through our day naturally serving, we are not sacrificing our inner selves. We do not serve to gain or add to who we are. We have no need to jump on a train of thoughts trying to convince us otherwise—just be and feel the hugs.

The challenge at times is the mind chatter, and boy, does the mind like to chatter, often causing feelings to rise as a current of ocean waves crashing through. And as the ocean demonstrates, beneath the active surface is a valley of calmness if and when we want to dive in and experience it.

In a turbulent moment, what we can always count on is that a decision awaits of returning to the one calmness, which observes softly, waiting patiently for us to return. We, too, in this moment can remember we are all one, striving to live as one in peace. I choose to believe in that as truth. How about you?

Now back to our fun time at the office called Dr. Kirby's for almost forty years.

We often would dress up as superheroes in honor of Smilin' Rylan.

Although at times, on their first visits to our practice, some would accuse us of being fake or unauthentic, of course that didn't change us from being real and authentic. We always understood it was their suspicious fears, their perceptions because of where their hearts (really their minds) were in those moments. And yes, it only happen once in a while—sarcastic tones with words meant to hurt—but when it did, we knew that most likely, those people found it hard to be genuinely kind unless there was a motive, or they'd been mistreated in the past and didn't feel worthy of being loved by others, especially someone they'd just met.

Many returned and, as they opened their hearts, would see, having changed the lenses they were looking through, enough to rediscover their joy and kindness. Most often, they'd end up being our most loyal family. Love always prevails—if not initially, then eventually through the miracle of the rainbow awaiting in the distance.

We became like family—not just our staff but every person who entered our office. Many families returned through the years, including grandchildren and great-grandchildren. As promised, the rainbow appears.

It was not uncommon for us to sing, dance (yes, we had a flash dance), laugh, and cry (of sadness at times of loss), but we choose kindness and will always choose love over fear.

Rylan did, and if a young soul could with all the treatments and needles and still smile and choose to live life to the fullest, well, why shouldn't we?

No, I Am Not Patty Hearst, but I, Too, Love Fur and Nonfur Babies

September 3, 2021

Love and Faith, and who is that with them?

And life: I am blessed and so calm and peace filled as I walk in this masterpiece we call beach, nature, paradise. A passing breath of fresh air as I am driving with the window down, a smile from a stranger, a possible angel brushing by my self at the grocery store, eye contact that speaks unspoken words of love—so many miracles just waiting to be felt, seen, through our awareness.

A few days ago, I was walking my fur babies, Love and Faith, during our morning beach time, as we're blessed to live close to the beautiful beach across from Hearst Castle. My girls are really well trained and stay close by and come when I call them—of course, I have their favorite treats. This particular morning, a man watched us intensely as he walked toward us on the beach.

When he was close enough for me to hear him, he asked, "Are you Patty Hearst?" To make a long story short, I guess she now is common around this area and raises, as well as trains, dogs (fur babies). He told me he was there for a conference and there was talk that she roamed the beach with her dogs.

When I replied no, his whole demeanor toward me changed. He was still of course kind, but he was not interested in continuing a conversation, or perhaps it was my energy of distraction with the girls and the surrounding beauty. I smiled as usual and continued walking and playing with Love and Faith. My daughter, Krisi, said I should've kept the man guessing, telling him, "I don't know. Maybe"—an answer I'm sure he would have taken back to his conference-attending group for conversation.

Once again, I praise the play of life. Beyond my mind, there are attempts to find words and attach labels to moments, experiences, and people. I continue to be in awe of the now, where there are no boundaries or labels. All are one.

This is where (actually in the nowhere) once again I am reminded of, brought back to awareness of, and feel who I really am ("No," I said and smiled. "I am not Patty Hearst."), and I fall completely in love with my self. Once again, I am filled with the desire to love others with no prejudice, no boundaries that indicate who is worthy and who is not, even with those nonhuman.

I continue to pray that I am able to become even more willing to leave behind labels, prejudices, and conditions. I feel the difference when I experience the day (moment) with my mind in the background (I like to say it takes the back seat to the inner light of I) and I'm present once again in the moment of now.

OK. I will also have to share this—and my close chosen friends and family know it already: I will try to save any alive crawling or walking body. The little yogis would be so sweet if a spider was joining us in the yoga room (many knew that Rylan loved Spider-Man, and we would often say it was a message from Rylan). We would do our best to usher the little guy outside. Whatever the outcome, though, everything becomes just right, a deep trusting of this beautiful mystery of life.

Thinking back on *not* being Patty Heart, I reflect, asking a what-if question and bringing a vision to my heart's mind within. How beautiful it would be if just for a day everyone looked at one another and saw their selves? No labels, no cultural or religious identity, and no judgment—everyone was on the same soul-full ground? What if we saw within our inner selves our selves reflected in those we are present with? Reflections of our selves in others, allowing space for the knowingness that what we see in others they can see in us.

I remember reading once that the Dalai Lama believes that if every eight-year-old in the world is taught meditation, we will eliminate violence from the world within one generation.

"Peace begins with me."

Wow, in such few words, hope of peace on fire. What is so sad now but was so beautiful back in the moment is that when Naomi and I taught Smilin' Rylan's little yogis meditation, they took to it right away. "Peace begins with me." As they would sit, eyes closed and each finger leading the spoken words slowly to silence, continuing the words in their heart minds, they were as fish are to water. It was so beautiful, so hopeful. We would talk about the energy, and they could feel the energy. And they loved it!

You may be asking yourself, "What's so sad about that?" Well, I find it disappointing that it's not included in all schools, that not all children start at an early age, even for five minutes, to become still and begin with those four simple words—"Peace begins with me"—every day! I know I would have jumped on board at age five, six, or seven or even in my teens. The younger the better. Rylan and I would meditate when he was not much older than three, opening the porthole so as to welcome as much peace during the teen years and onward.

Now, just for fun, let's revisit my late teens and early twenties and consider who that young woman was and what might have been if she'd continued on the path she was exploring. A path lined with self-involved labels and self-absorbed ideas of life, in which she reached for everything external to her and seldom went within. What if she hadn't begun awakening, hadn't welcomed satori moments with so much openness or allowed her inner child to resurface and be heard? What an array of storms and beautiful discoveries, rainbows, light, and miracles just waiting.

It was a period of time when so much of life connected to the material world of things, status, and labels. You know the old phrase "Keeping up with the Joneses." So that you have my soul-full honesty, know that my costumes, so to speak, changed often, and there were many. Remember we all have the I witnessing in the background, waiting patiently for the satori awakening moments.

I believe, for most of us, as years come and go, we become tired—tired of the challenging and sometimes downright hard times. They finally bring us to begin within and explore the deep, dark, heavy, stinky baggage we're carrying around. And it becomes enlightening. Acceptance begins as our moments turn to stillness, peace, and joy, rather than fear, frustration, and blame. Our lives become lighter.

Hopefully we have not become so used to the adrenaline associated with drama that we accept it as life and become almost numb to real emotions. Mind chatter that reaffirms the scripting of "It is what it is" would be a good if it led to movement toward peace, calmness, and love. Often the idea of peace is a foreign thought but sounds rather nice.

First things first: begin within. We are truly all the same deep within. We must become honest, allowing the I of who we really are to be present, moving to the driver's seat of the soul.

You must accept that although at times it may not be easy, with faith, it will become so real, and before you realize it, the me personality will feel more open and comfortable climbing in the back seat, enjoying as the journey begins again—the journey to get to know the real you under all those layers. You'll discover who you really are, leaving the labels, titles, and material stuff on the sidelines, and get to know just how wonderful the real you is.

Yes, we are. Just that thought warms me, and it guides me at times when I'm having a tough moment believing that a person, event, thing, idea, or comment is or will be a blessing. When we look to feel and see the good in one another, all is well. The knowingness that we all are together on this journey, connected at the seams—we truly

We are the face of God.

are all a part of a beautiful tapestry of love. I personally believe it is about not only people from our lifetimes but everyone, past, present, and future, as well as all breathing entities.

I know you probably already picked up that I am a little "not normal." What if I'm very normal? Or giving permission for people to be not normal? Naomi makes me smile, and she asks, "What's the Joni-ism now?" I accept I am not everyone's cup of tea, and that's OK by me. As long as I continue with intentions wrapped in love, I am at peace with that.

I see and I feel love in my self, and I love my self. When I do feel that connection, a circle of love continues, and it flows outward to others.

During untrainings, I would ask those in our group to look in the mirror. I share this often, but it is worth hearing, reading again, and for several minutes repeating love messages to the self while staring deep into the pupil of the eye (and finding the I). I never recommend or suggest things that I don't myself do.

First thing in the morning, I look in the mirror and tell myself, "I am the face of God. I hold so much love within. I love you. All is well. You are a blessing to the world." Messages change a bit day to day—some days I may use *I* and other days *you*—but regardless, I feel an overwhelming love for my self and others. More often than not, tears will make a trail along my cheek, at times a small stream, and I feel enlightened.

I remember that I am just perfect in all the imperfections of life and all is well.

Do not give up. At the beginning, you may start turning away from your I contact—your mind may start telling you all the normal criticism, such as "What are you doing?" and "That's crazy." I'm here to tell you it's beautiful. So beautiful.

Now look at others. As you feel the same, they become part of my self, your self—perfect in all the many judgments of imperfections of life.

I do believe we are all part of the reflection, the face of God, whatever that represents to you and your self. My mirror conversations change in words but not the energy of love. Looking deep into the pupil of the eye, for several minutes, at the beginning was a challenge, but now it is me. I.

So perhaps this Friday, as we move into the weekend, we will choose to awaken and our first moments will be brought to one-on-one eye conversations with our selves. We will once again uncover who we truly are, beginning our days with love for self and others. Look into the face of God.

Namaste. The light in my heart's space connects and rejoices with the light of your heart's space. Together we shine that much brighter!

Where Am I Going? Where Are You Going?

July 6, 2021

Rylan at his fifth birthday. Every day is a celebration of Rylan!

Happy birthday, Smilin' Rylan! What a gift you continue to be!

You were (still are) an example of living in the moment. Thank you for that reminder.

Probably for most of us, we acknowledge how time is just moving faster—flying by—as birthdays seem to come way too quickly. For many of us, maybe we would rather see less of them. Happy to just watch them come and go?

What if every day, every moment, was a celebration of your life? A birth moment to rejoice and play? Something to be opened—the present moment, to be unwrapped with excitement? And what a gift! There becomes the priceless birthday gift! Open it as often as possible and celebrate.

When we allow ourselves to stop, become present, be here in the now, and watch children, we quiet ourselves and listen with the moment's freedom of breath. Contemplate the fact that children get so excited and count the days down to their special day. Having put that in writing, I want to add that until the stress of life's race begins to be their story, when they're often duplicating what they've listened to and witnessed, children seem to enjoy

17

the moment they are in now. They're often excited and playful but willing to wait.

At what age does that seem to begin to fade? They seem to grow up way too fast, taking on many of the adult's stresses in order not to fall behind in the race. Where are they going? Where are we adults going? What are our actions preparing children for? Speaking to them?

Perhaps we should slow down and breathe in the moment—breathe in the joy of life and the mystery of it all. We should open our hearts and embrace what we already have, rediscovering that we have all we need in this moment; this present moment is our lifetime. Like newborns, we must truly embrace the newness and wonderments of life.

Yes, I know we can do a list, approach this as mature adults being real. And where has that gotten most of us? We just have "no time," we say, and it becomes our mantra: "I will just keep working harder. It will get better …" The story continues, and the words remain the same—and so does the ending.

What is the ending of your story? How do you desire your last chapter to speak about your life? I know that for me it has nothing to do with external materialistic things. Rather, it's about how I served, what I gave through my love and received from love. Of course, intentions are the wrappings that the gifts come in and through. Amen.

I know for that Rylan, his lifetime was each moment. The chapters ran together as one. He lived each in the moment of the now, unaware of any time other than the present. It was so magical.

Thank you, Rylan, for that gift.

To already be home with my self and to know with all my heart that's where I find my peace, my joy, my life. Always simply right here. Nowhere to go, nothing to do—just be.

Satori (Aha) Moments Can Save Your Life, Birthing Peace from Sorrow

March 25, 2021

When I began my journey of excavating my inner self—actually, I think I began long before I knew it to be real—I enjoyed the hollowing out of energy blocks, the blocks my soul already knew did not serve me. I started having aha, or satori, moments. *Satori* means "awakening"—and I was doing just that!

When I decided to name my fur baby Satori, honestly, people thought I was crazy. After my husband's first diagnosis and treatment, he was ready for us to bring a fur baby into our lives (I am always ready).

My husband, Darrell, was used to my Joni-isms, and he knew there was no arguing with me. She was my birthday gift from him, and I was going to name her what I wanted to name her. I laughed because her favorite trainer would call her Tori.

Satori and I walking in Cambria, a vacation place for us for years, now my home.

19

What started off as a regular "What's her name?" became a topic of conversation that would lead to cleansing. Questioning why I chose to name my fur baby Satori was always meant to be. It was a wonderful way to open conversations about what a beautiful name Satori is and what the term means. And, even more beautiful, Satori saved Darrell's life and who knows how many others, but that's for later in the story.

To this day, Satori is a legend to so many. An earthly angel in fur, she was a regular greeter at our office for six years. People came to understand the name Satori and the meaning it brings birth to. Some would stop in just to see and pet her. I am hoping to create (perhaps several) awakening moments as you read the blessings written on the pages of this satori book.

Have you ever forgotten something? I hope all you're nodding, because if you aren't, you should probably just go ahead and stop reading at this point. Car keys? Glasses? An appointment? Your child's name? If we are all honest, the list goes on. I laugh because I told my mom to stop boiling eggs for me. Many of you know that boiled eggs wrapped in hot tortillas are one of my favorite things to have in the morning. Yummy! But I felt she would forget them and perhaps start a fire. Other family members had similar concerns.

As life is so generous and eager to show us, remind us, I had an aha moment as I was boiling eggs and forgot to turn off the stove top myself. What a mess and what a satori moment (and how stinky my house was for hours!).

My satori moment—one that I used often at untrainings, opening up space for many to share one or more of theirs—was a common one, conveying that we need to be careful and listen, really heart listen, to the advice we so openly give to others. When we feel the inner calling to recommend, guide, advise, and share with another, we must first make sure we have our ears turned on and opened up so we, too, can take in the words coming out of our mouths.

And even more important are the actions that speak loudly. The satori moment applies not only to listening but also to being heart-fully aware and present

I am going to take it to another, deeper level, so hold on. Have you ever put something in the oven and forgotten about it? I don't know about you, but I have. Only once or twice has the fire alarm gone off—and only after smoke filled the house. What if? Just what if you left something in the oven and decided to run a quick errand, which turned into meeting people and getting caught up visiting? What if a fire started?

Can you let go of the ego (edging God out) long enough and feel, perhaps imagine in your mind's eye, the possibility? Of course, you can make this scenario even more intense and tragic by adding animals or people.

Can you imagine going to bed with something in the oven? This is where you release and allow a loving mind (one of the gifts, inspiration to imagination) to guide you to awaken your self-awareness. We must understand we are human and remember who we really are: loving, forgiving children of God.

Yes, if you're not aware, or you're feeling defensive, please allow me to explain. We all make mistakes. Yes, you too! Take a breath. When we begin to forgive others, we are able to extend inward acceptance, opening space for forgiveness toward the people we sometimes have the toughest time being kind to: ourselves.

This is one thought to meditate on, and I often do. I do believe that when we are hard on others, it is because we are so hard on ourselves. I also feel that when we begin forgiving and being there for others, we find even more space to open to see within ourselves the hot spots awaiting healing.

Do we at times put the cart before the horse for a while, struggling, as we go deeper, to figure a better way of traveling on this road of life? I believe so, but as our road begins to become smoother, less rocky and jolting, the ride becomes even more enjoyable and adventurous. A mistake, take two, and learn to forgive others as well as yourself.

So this is worth repeating: when we awaken, we are able to forgive ourselves, and we feel more openness to extend forgiveness to others. It doesn't always happen in the moment (in fact that's very rare), but we can choose to begin. Isn't that what God wants us to do?

After Darrell's second diagnosis, he spiraled into depression. Pain can do that to you. I've had only minor pain, and I can imagine, but I cannot even come close to feeling what he must've been feeling.

I experienced firsthand, watching Darrell, my best friend, the years of pain, the buildup anger over fear—fear of lack of control. He was desperate to escape from his reality. I don't care what I or the counselors would say. He felt anger, hopelessness. He lived his own reality, so it was indeed real to him. But it was still painful for me to watch.

I remember one of the many returning car trips from UC San Francisco after one of his surgeries. Of course, he was miserable, holding back tears

21

(he didn't like to cry). He asked me why I didn't try harder to get him to understand the untrainings I would present. He felt the joy as I would give and receive, preparing and delivering the message of love, and the residue of love that stayed with me after and continues to stay with me. The satori moments continue to flow, untraining our years of training into what we felt we had to be. The awakening allows us to understand we are not our roles, what we do to make a living, what cars we drive, what houses we live in, how much money we have in savings, or how we look to others.

Naomi and Satori at the office on Halloween.

We are much more yet much less, if you get my message. We are much more of nothingness that makes us complete in the everythingness of who we really are!

Satori, my fur angel, and me.

How many of us have had surgeries for which we've been prescribed pain pills? I'm building this so that you can hopefully release any judgment (in any direction) because that is not what this is about.

Darrell had become very addicted to pain medication. He felt relief for a short time, but the sad thing is it wasn't Darrell. Where was Darrell—the real Darrell I knew? Little by little, the pain pills were taking him from me, from himself.

One of my satori moments—I believe there were a lot of little ones that led up to my huge awakening—was (and is) that I cannot be there for anyone else if I allow myself to step into that person's emotions, or into the person's shoes, so to speak. Empathy, yes, but I can't allow it to paralyze me. (This was really emphasized to families of patients during our time at Mayo Clinic.)

I knew that, but it certainly wasn't easy. I wanted to be there for him with 100 percent of myself. For me, that meant continuing to be in alignment of love, caring for myself first and foremost.

I had to choose and to take care of myself, my spirit, so that the dark times would not have a chance to cloud over the love and care I could give him when he needed it. I can't control another person; you can't control another person. All we can do is be there the best way we can. We must protect our loving energy and nurture it from moment to moment. Accepting and releasing is at times the best and healthiest way to peace for all.

So I take a cleansing breath and continue another chapter of life where I believe everything is meant to be and already set in motion.

August 1, 2014. I was preparing a luncheon at my house in honor and celebration of friends.

Darrell took Satori to hang out at the office. I never saw my sweet fur baby after that. I still remember my last words to her. She came running into the kitchen with her usual beautiful energy as I was preparing the luncheon, and I told her go with Daddy to the office. I think— no, I *know*—she knew what was going to play out and was saying goodbye to me and not to worry.

Darrell forgot he had Satori in the car. It was 106 degrees.

He went into the office to visit. Three hours later, intense moments would play out.

What's the satori moment? Does your mind instantly go to blaming someone? I've heard blame in all directions—the doctors for prescribing him the medication, Darrell for leaving her in the car, me for allowing him to take her. There were even a couple of people who asked, "Didn't the staff know Satori was coming to the office?"

So the blame was like a wildfire. I would hear it from all directions. And that was one of the hardest things for me to forgive—the judgment from others. During this sad time, how could people feel the need or desire to judge? It tragically happened and was now in the past. My satori moment? Forgive all, for they know not what they do.

I pray that as you take the time to read this, you begin to use your self-awareness and watch your mind. What it may begin to tell your heart—what you'll know with all your heart—is that forgiveness is the only choice, the only way to receive peace. Your heart can and will find forgiveness through even unbearable situations, often moving you to share with someone who is going through a difficult time. Forgiveness will be welcomed. Love and forgiveness can also spread like wild beautiful fires lighting the way out of darkness.

To this day, I still at times find myself (actually my mind) questioning my heart, asking, "Did I show Darrell enough love?" Was I present enough when he was in pain? And then I quickly choose to remember my heart's own words, the wisdom of my heart, and I bring my self back to me, the one who knows I cannot be fully present in this beautiful moment carrying any baggage of fear. I once again choose love—a choice I make moment to moment.

Another hopeful satori moment: please never hold back from asking for help. On August 1, I immediately asked for help. As was in God's plan, I could not kick my friend Cyndi out of my house; she insisted on helping me clean up after the luncheon, and I'm so blessed she was there. So when the phone call came from Naomi—and to this day, I can't even imagine how hard that call was for her—I was immediately blessed to have one of my chosen sisters drive me to Hanford Veterinarian Hospital. There was a beautiful circle of people waiting for my arrival: the doctors; office family; and Satori's longtime friend, mentor, and trainer, Marcie, with open arms.

The tears flowed as I walked in the room and went up to Darrell to console him. He would never come to forgive himself.

Once we arrived home, the loving-kindness flowed. Darrell's colleague and good friend Dr. Jeff White came right over (thank you, Susan Drew, for contacting him). Darrell's therapist, his medical doctor—so many people who helped to get him to Mayo Clinic in Minnesota. That was the beginning of the saving grace to come.

I truly feel I would have lost him completely (in 2014) if that Satori miracle had not happened. I believe Satori was born for that day, that moment when she sacrificed herself for Darrell. It did not stop there. Miracles came from that dreadful day of sadness. One of the immediate miracles was that I felt forgiveness toward Darrell right away. That was me remembering who I really am and God reminding me who I am. I felt it all that day, and every day that memory slides back into my moments.

A victory of amazing grace was Darrell accepting the long road of drug-addiction recovery, beginning at Mayo Clinic in Minnesota. Of course, it was every day, a choice to stay clean from the oxycodone that had become his partner in life. It was a moment-to-moment decision for him to choose to love himself enough to go through this journey within. Yes, he received a lot of support from others, but this was an inside job of returning back to his self.

I, too, was blessed to spend a few days there at the end of his treatment for a week of family counseling. One of the healing requirements was that Darrell talk in front of the group. Wouldn't it be wonderful if we all could share openly and honestly in a safe environment knowing that no one was judging us? If we had our own stories to tell and came to honor one another's challenges with open hearts of support?

I pray for all of us to have a circle of human kindness and unconditional love surrounding us. More important, I want to ask the question, Are you one of those kind individuals who would be there for someone in nonjudgment? Forgiveness? Would you just be present totally for that person?

I choose to not blame anyone (including myself) for what came as another beautiful example of hidden rainbows and miracles birthed from that day—a day that some would still find unbearable to go through.

From that moment, I knew—felt in my heart—that my sweet Satori's purpose, and the reason I named her Satori, was to sacrifice her life and save

Darrell's. And really, I believe the experience saved many in ways we will never know. Who knows what might've happened?

My hope is for others to perhaps lovingly learn and grow with the knowledge that blaming, not forgiving, serves no one. In fact, it births only darkness. Why would we not choose loving light, the option to see the beauty right before and within our own selves?

I miss Darrell every day, but I visualize "the Loving Pack" at the Rainbow Bridge: Darrell, Rylan, and Satori, as well as other playful souls. I imagine Wyland joining in for fun times, playing Frisbee. Yep, that's what I know to be real, as I was in meditating in Savasana the day he took flight and watched in my heart's space while Rylan, Wyland, and Satori joyfully played Frisbee.

Believe there is a satori moment waiting just at the right moment. Claim it, and feel the peace.

Wow—so much easier to read, type, and speak than it is to truly remember who we really are.

Untrain the Habits That Do Not Serve Your Heart, Your Soul

July 25, 2020

Continuing on our journeys, innocently we repetitively react to moments, and soon those reactive behaviors are habits—habits that become so much a part of our daily lives that often it's not until we become so unhappy, finding ourselves desperately blaming our outside existence for our own choices and inner beingness and our lives becoming pretty messy, that we are ready! Ready for what? You guessed it. Another satori moment!

I find it comical at times to look at my past. I was sharing with my chosen granddaughter Alissa yesterday as she was asking me (again) how many times I have been married. She so wanted to solidify that Darrell was my real husband. I told her thirty-five years I dedicated my heart and soul to that man, explaining that we were not halves completing each other but rather each whole and becoming one in a moment-to-moment decision to love. That it is not always easy, but for me, the feeling of peace is always the indicator.

I try to keep it educational (wisdom) as I hopefully show and tell with my love and actions as well as with words that I am able to look back, share the choices I made, and see the miracles and rainbows that came from those choices. I'm thankful the marriage lessons were quick and came when I was very young and, by choice, led me to the miracle as I confronted the person I thought my self to be. The wisdom poured out. It's as if I was in fact blind and then everything became so much clearer—and it had nothing to do with Darrell being an optometrist.

The truth, the real realization for me? That in every relationship you have, there is only one common denominator, and that is you, so if you continually have the same issues, the best place—the only place—to point the finger is back at yourself. Look closely in the mirror. For me, this was a huge satori awakening.

Habits become who we are (the person reality), not who we really are, and, often unconsciously, we blame, point fingers, and hold resentment, all the while wondering how people can possibly feel life is joyful, happy, and wonderful.

But if we get miserable enough, we may discover a gift within the unhappiness and venture on an exciting journey within as we begin excavating, using our own response-ability, unwrapping the truth that happiness is *really* an inside work of love. What we soon begin rediscovering is that all that is truly real is within our selves.

As I continue my journey excavating, I myself find it magical and inspirational. So get out your loving shovel to begin again digging through the layers and remembering, rediscovering by uncovering, who you are— *really* are.

As you venture on, there may be times or awakenings that feel very dense, where it would be easy to return, fall back into excuses, and perhaps place blame over why your life is hard. I encourage you to take a breath and continue on, unearthing layers that will begin bringing a lighter presence, at times even excitement and relief, as you bring them into view.

Yes, what an enlightened awakening when you begin to view yourself watching your in-the-moment movie, with awareness being the lens you look through as you step outside and watch your actions, listen to your thoughts, and experience fully (or at least a lot more clearly) your choice of actions. Use the Replay button, enjoying the labor of love! Who you really are is in there! Keep digging, excavating, and enjoy the journey, the exploration of self.

So here's the thing regarding habits. We hear and read words. We then put the meaning—feeling—to each word. Most often, we're told, beginning at birth and continuing to the present day, what that word should mean to us.

Well, I object! It was another satori awakening when I started realizing that I desired to birth meaning, feeling, to my words. And I choose to bring them to life, into my moments, with love and faith. Bringing meaning and feeling in this way serves my soul and therefore all.

Love and Faith, at peace no matter where they lay their fur-baby heads.

One of the reasons I named my fur babies Love and Faith: tied up at a shack in Tulare is where my beautiful niece, Ashley, found them for me! They were meant to come into my life just at the perfect time, reminding me that with Love and Faith anything is possible.

So take the word *habit*: I have learned (I'm offering this to you in case it resonates with your heart's mind) through many satori moments that when we develop habits—habits that do not serve our inner selves, our inner knowingness—it's not so much about developing another habit to replace the old one but instead about going within, meeting your self, and knowing who you really, truly are.

For me, habits fell away as I began the courting of my self. They were not part of my uncovering. Well, they were, but they became part of my baggage. I know it sounds crazy. As I reunited with my self, my choices were not categorized according to whether they were *habits*. My moments began to just flow. This may be hard to understand right now, but continue on. I did continue using the word *habit*, but the meaning was totally turned upside down, inside out, and all around. The meaning I associated with *habit* was not what it once had been.

It most often does not happen overnight, but I would not have had it any other way. As you remove layers of stuff, unloading the years of baggage, revealing the truth of who you really are, you begin to discover that your life is beautiful, just perfect with all the chaos and craziness of imperfection. You begin making different choices—*habits*? Yes, you can put that wisdom under the category of *habit* if it helps you, if it serves your inner beingness.

As for me, when I bring awareness to my moments, I feel the knowingness of who I am. There is no right or wrong way to convey that we would be developing a new habit. Again, these are just words, and individuals attach their own hearts' meanings to words, as well as feelings. For instance, *love* may mean different things to you and me; we may feel different connections to that word.

When you find and choose peace in the unlearning and becoming, you have uncovered the gift of wisdom, even if it is fleeting. Little by little, you begin to live your moments with a clearer meaning of life and return even for just a moment to who you really are. The word *habit* and its meaning for me became nonexistent. Well, it's probably best to say that when you are coming from the place within you, then your thoughts, actions, and therefore feelings flow from the presence of now. I know that even writing this, I have to reread it. It is from that space within. Allow it to resonate within your heart's space.

For this sharing today, we will keep the word *knowledge,* if it's easier to understand, learning the idea of replacing a habit that we have recognized as unhealthy for our spirits and developing another habit (or simply choosing a different choice in the moment) that serves who we truly are.

When you continually feel unhappiness, believe me—it's soul-searching time. It's a journey of looking within and not without. It's exciting, and becoming close with like-minded people provides you space to share and laugh at some of your old paradigms. It truly is revolutionary!

The little yogis are doing yoga to a song that features the phrase "a revolution of love." We must join together and celebrate the love inside one another. Mirror it to one another!

You could say a bad habit becomes a good habit when it gives birth— wakes us to miracles of wisdom, the deep knowingness (or knowledge) of wisdom that lives within who we really are. These are the satori moments that move us into space where we naturally take a deep breath and flow into life.

Friends and Family Do Not Keep Score; They Choose Love and Forgiveness

September 25, 2020

Rylan and me in the moment.

If we would all come to the knowingness within, we would not value ourselves according to the way people treat us. When we value our selves, we will value others, and there's no need for earning.

How often do we choose to measure how valuable we are by the way we are treated? Please don't allow yourself to get into score keeping. I'm talking both ways—with yourself and with others.

What I know to be true in my heart's space is that we hear from the subtle soft voices of our hearts' minds that we are valuable because we are. We don't have to earn in order to feel accepted or approved of. Believing that our value is fleeting or debatable is stressful and draining and never gives birth to happiness. Amen!

If anything, perhaps step outside of yourself (your head) and, with your awareness view, feel what lies within you by how you treat others. Yes, perhaps reread the previous statement. Remember the current of waves I write about? It's amazing how easily we can fall into role-playing, following a handed-down script that doesn't tell the story of who we really are. We rehearse and rehearse until they become who we think we are.

This is perhaps a good time to rewrite your soul's mission. What is the vision of your self? Ask your self, and listen softly to your heart space's answer. Feel it.

I believe there would be a lot less anger if we went within ourselves to rediscover our own happiness instead of internalizing or measuring ourselves by how others treat us. What other people say about us is not our business. Truly, what business is it what they say or think of us? If we are being our true selves, why would we care? We are our own best friends, hopefully. I told the little yogis (some of my chosen grandchildren) yesterday that you get up with yourself and you go to bed with yourself. I want to fall asleep with my loving, kind self, not a person I'm unhappy with.

I was saying, "Love yourself. You are the one you are always with." It opened up a wonderful conversation: Maximus, ten, said, "We're not *always*—sometimes we are with other people." I just smiled, and it opened up a beautiful channel to a deeper fun conversation. It ended with the agreement (self-awareness) that, yes, we can be with other people (in space) but we're always within ourselves.

You could feel the satori moments. It is so wonderful to witness how young people aren't so quick to argue with an insight offered to them. When do we as adults start arguing, often just to be contrary, becoming very defensive, hiding behind layers of scripts and labels that may be threatened if we open our minds to change? When do we rule out the possibility of changing the paradigms, the lenses we're looking through, or at least cleaning off some of the smudges of the past that are clouding our vision and blocking the light?

Ask yourself who you're spending time with. How often do we spend time with our best friends? How often do we spend quiet time getting to know ourselves, truly, deeply, as if we're spending time with our best friends? We must arrange for times of solitude so we can become still, sit quietly, and ask ourselves about our visions for our lives. See it and feel it. Ask yourself, "Who am I?"

I believe—I know this holds true for me—we could all do a better job of remembering who we really are by taking time in silence, with our inner selves. Perhaps time in nature? Feeling the wind, hearing the birds, listening to ourselves within. No computer, phone, or TV distractions. Breathing in the stillness, really, truly taking the time to get to know the deepest parts of ourselves.

We must remember "I am enough, with no desire for score keeping," embracing every moment as a lifetime to love and to choose, because love truly does bring us back home.

Please take the time to watch the following video (on YouTube) and decide to choose love: "Smilin Rylan Kids Yoga - I Choose Love 9/23/20," https://youtu.be/FHuVMRknN-w.

From Transferring to Transforming, Humbly, Willingly Present

August 7, 2020

We must rejoice in knowing that we are who our thoughts *are passing through*—we are not our thoughts. We must be open to or acknowledge the thought that we are also not our actions. We are so much more than that. And even when we feel we have beautifully given to the world through an action, we are still not that action. We are who we are deep within. We are who the action is passing through. We are not the action, good or bad. This is, or can be, so freeing. The giving and allowing space for us to take seriously that we choose each moment—that it is in fact a choice—I love that.

OK. Take a breath, and choose not to allow your thoughts to become reactive to the preceding paragraph. Give yourself space to just marinate with the idea of it.

We have been talking about habits and how they form, or how we have been taught they form. When we become humble and willing to ensure the best for our children (both biological and chosen), perhaps we will at least be open to the idea that what we are transferring onto the younger generation can and does make a difference.

Also—very important—I have recited this for many years: "Quiet. Your actions are speaking so loudly I am not able to hear your words." Children watch what you do, not so much what you're repeatedly saying to them. We oftentimes just don't realize how our actions are in fact what others, especially children, "listen to."

All of this makes a difference not only to that child but also to every person that child comes into contact with throughout life. Why not start transforming old habits *now*? It's a much better choice, a proactive alternative; it changes lives instead of transferring habits on to them (possibly for generations). We must begin to choose differently.

As I've mentioned several times—but it's worth mentioning it again—I look forward to the satori moments, and I continue to celebrate them, though sometimes it takes a while. In my early years, they were rampant. I will even be so bold as to say they were *epic* in my late twenties. I remember one of my heroes saying, "You need to be your own hero in the story of your own life."

And so my new journey began and continues. Early in life, I became tired of experiencing the same yucky feelings every day. I went through major satori moments, and I am forever blessed.

I decided I wanted to be able to look at myself each morning as I opened my eyes and each night before I closed them in a presence of peace—at peace with the person I was and the person I am. I wanted to be at peace with the person I was rediscovering choice by choice, the person I knew I was (and am), and I realized (though it was challenging to accept at times) that it really doesn't matter what other people think about me, their opinions. It's about what I know about me.

It was and continues to be such an inspirational journey of returning to who I really am when I feel the disconnection, and it is met with an excitement to return. It is a returning, my knowing myself as if the me—the person—were never separated from the self, or the I-ness within. The I that is always present, waiting patiently in the background. No worries—all is well.

I started realizing these words of wisdom: our words do matter, but what *really* matters are our actions. But again, we must not beat ourselves up, because we are not our thoughts and we are not our actions; we are so much more. However, we are responsible for our actions. We have a choice of what actions will spring from our thoughts. Celebrate that acknowledgment, and begin transforming with energy of love for yourself and others. Don't get attached to either one, thought or action.

People who know me also know I love butterflies, and those close to me understand that I have thought of myself as a caterpillar off and on throughout my life. I embrace the metamorphosis times of my life as moments of rejoicing, as I go through another excavation into flight, only to return as a caterpillar at any given time. Through the years, the metamorphosis has become so comfortable to me, helping me understand not only my release of guilt but also my ability to forgive myself and others.

I am hoping that by the time I take my final flight, I will fly with grace and ease of knowing that all is well before I surrender and let go.

Maximus, Alissa on my lap, Braden, and Rylan.
One of my favorite places to be present.

Number one for me was taking the time to sit with children and communicate heart to heart, learning to say "I apologize" and "I am sorry." What a gift to give children, and never ever, ever follow up the apology with a *but*—one of my satori moments that I live by today.

Remember that we are never the caterpillars, in a sense. We were and are always the butterflies. We must acknowledge that the metamorphoses, or the cocoons we find ourselves in, are part of the miracle of taking flight. The freeing feeling of birthing, breaking open for satori moments—allow the moments life, and allow them to continue! Be present and enjoy.

So today, begin and continue breaking open (more often) through your awareness—in my opinion, one of the most precious of the four gifts given at birth. And do not push the gifts to the back to collect dust. Use them. Have fun unwrapping and playing.

Humbleness Is the Strength of Knowing Who We Really Are

October 16, 2020

Yes, I believe words have different meanings for everyone, and sometimes communication (if you can call it that) can become very intense because of a failure or refusal to understand another person's perception, experience, and paradigm.

What if we all took the time to truly listen? Each of us does have two ears and one mouth. Perhaps then we would become humbler without even defining what that word means to us. It just *is*. It is then given birth as we choose to feel how wonderful it can be to listen twice as much as we speak. It doesn't mean we have to agree; we can choose to agree to disagree.

Being different is not bad or dangerous when we remember we are all the same: we are all human beings having our life experiences.

At times, we can become stuck striving to live up to the labels we have taken on. What are your labels? What would happen if we all just dropped the labels—those projected on us as well as those we plaster on other people?

What would it look like—better yet, feel like? What if we just let go and decided to simply be? I realize that sounds crazy to some, but what if? No attachments, no labels, just the present moment, as if we were children seeing and hearing the beautiful ocean for the first time? If each moment were fresh and new, with no attachments? Just take a moment, feel, and ask yourself what if.

How about we accept who we are and therefore have the openness to accept others? Wouldn't that be miraculous?

I have heard and witnessed people shy away from being called humble for fear of being labeled weak, compromising, or unsuccessful. It's amazing how quickly we get into boxes with the meanings we associate with labels that we have put on ourselves as well as others.

Self-awareness can help you to reexamine the value of labels. Breathe and feel the retrieved understanding through peace. Release as you become aware and view the baggage. Drop the baggage and feel how light you become. Letting go of the labels we have put on ourselves and chosen for others, we begin reconsidering their value.

*Rylan loved to play doctor, mimicking what he was
so familiar with. He was a kind doctor.*

Being humble is quite the opposite. What I have found (and therefore what informs the meaning I associate with the word) is that humble people are those who envelop wisdom. There's a knowingness that when we are self-full (love), we become selfless and others are us, just simplified (or more complex) in a different set of life experiences, paradigms, and perceptions of moments lived.

Humble people—and I really don't like labeling others—*accept*, and therefore they are more likely to be able to handle stress and seem to be living in the moment and enjoying more of their moments. They are grateful, caring, and self-full and feel their energy sending out peace. They radiate diversified love. I enjoy time spent with humble friends. There is such a beautiful atmosphere that fills the space, inside or outside, and most obvious is within.

Humble friends understand balance. They seem to have an innate knowing that there is a time to lead and a time to follow. They practice nonjudgment of themselves and others. They naturally synergize, understanding that when you can take two (or more) who see (perception, paradigm) opportunities or situations differently and bring them together to communicate and discover (*uncover* may be a better description) a third alternative, that's better than either one alone. It is just so liberating and freeing, and the outcome is so much more diversified and productive, not to mention so much less stressful.

I can feel humble people's energy of kindness, their desire for the betterment of all involved. Not all the time, but for the most part, I choose to share my time with friends who through time have come aboard. Yes, another adventure of friendship. All aboard? Or not. It's a choice each one of us is free to make.

These types of friends do not panic in uncharted territory and jump ship or throw other friends overboard. They weather the storm, humbly encouraging open communication, at times choosing to agree to disagree.

When the storms do come, and they will, the sun soon brings the rainbow of reassurance, a bow that ties the value knot we all feel for one another. Solid friends do not abandon ship when the weather becomes rough.

Mother Teresa, one of my heroes (it's sad to me how often the young ones don't even know who she is) was our topic during yesterday's funshop (so much more soothing than *workshop*). The little yogis were engrossed with stories about her. As we shared, there was a silence of peace. They were so captivated by her spirit of humbleness.

May we all find our Mother Teresa within and celebrate the freedom of the moment when we embrace in a loving humbleness of the now.

To Gain Knowledge, Study; to Embrace a Satori Moment of Wisdom, Observe

July 7, 2020 (This truly brought me back in time as I was putting together the manuscript of blogs. This was nine days before Darrell took flight.)

When I asked our little Smilin' Rylan yogis what the title of this blog meant to them, "To be me" was one of the little yogis' answers. The full-of-wisdom little yogis were a breath of fresh air to listen to, share with. This is not saying *not* to go to school to learn to read and write and study all the subjects that are taught in school. They are very important. Knowledge is important—and I did remind them of that fact. But their minds did not even go on the defense as we talked and shared about wisdom and the small, soft voice within.

What does this mean to you? What does your heart's mind speak when listening to this statement? When you silence your mind (which is in itself a journey of observing, discovering), are you able to fall into the meaning behind the words and feel the quiet answers of wisdom speaking softly, comforting your you? Softly speaking to your personality? That's a wonderful opportunity for a meditation.

Years ago, I changed the name of the trainings I offer to simply <u>un</u>*trainings*. Then, of course, Rylan inspired me to start calling them *Rylan's*

Rylan and me being ourselves together, breathing in the moment.

untrainings because he lived so much of the wisdom that I believe we are naturally born with but, little by little, forget as amnesia sets in. Here's an opt-out for ourselves that our play of life inadeptly covers up. We begin learning to adjust who we really are to a label, who we think we are supposed to be, often for approval of others, and life happens unconsciously. We study, and at times, knowledge hinders our ability to open to our wisdom present within.

When awareness started to be front and center in my life, in my midtwenties, I started to receive—to feel waves of the true, real me. It was like I knew, and I excitedly began digging. I wanted to keep the feeling of alignment, the true feeling of being myself. It didn't come without sacrifice (blessings in disguise), and it continues as life continues.

It was amazing when I welcomed wisdom to lead me. I started realizing how, for much of my life, I just wanted to please. At that time, it was mainly family, but there were also some close relationships (husbands) and a few (superficial) friendships. I don't even know if I want to use the word *sacrifice*, as losing artificial, vampiric relationships was not a sacrifice in the long run, but at the time, it was tough. Still challenging is managing my family's disappointment regarding who they wanted me to be, or my not living up to their idea of my highest potential. I will say it again: my family truly felt they were (and feel that they are) doing the best for me. The satori moment, the downpour of wisdom, soon gifted me feelings of lightness—as if the chains were now releasing me, allowing me to breathe and become more present so I could start rediscovering my self, holding space for me.

I feel it's up to us to begin digging through the layers, excavating, finding our buried treasures, with no desire to blame and no need to point fingers. We must discover a feeling as if each moment were a fresh start, at times a knowingness that a more level, balanced foundation is needed. We should be excited for the construction, as each moment is an opportunity to be present, and using our newfound wisdom, we can truly begin again, living authentically who we are. For me, this is so rewarding as I continue rediscovering my wisdom within.

So may we continue our school of unlearning in the comfort of our souls. Happy excavating!

Be Your Own Hero

February 4, 2020

Rylan will always be a hero to so many of us. Children provide such an example of living life to the fullest. Often, we admire the strength, courage, and kindness of others but find reasons not to see these qualities in ourselves, possibly feeling pressure, or that we'll not live up to our interpretations or visions of what it means to be a hero. For me, having a hero who I look up to and learn from helps me discover the hero within myself.

Many of us have people we call our heroes who can help us aspire to a deeper sense of who we truly are—that part of us that is unchangeable, unaffected by the outside play of life. That hero is in all of us. Yes, our heroes can be you and me. Thinking of ourselves as our heroes just isn't an option for many of us, but why not?

Or maybe our heroes are unattainable to us: Perhaps we imagine a hero as a pro athlete or an award-winning actor or actress? Perhaps a fashion model? Someone with the look of success through material items, such as cars, homes, and power via job or title. Of course, added to other aspirations, those temporary material things can be wonderful, but they will change and eventually leave. They're fleeting—unlike the unchangeable qualities of the heroes I aspire to be.

We asked the little yogis to make cards to give to heroes in their lives. Of course, as always during our funshop, we begin by talking about Rylan's untrainings and what it means to them to be a hero. What are some qualities a hero possesses?

They addressed their envelopes to their chosen heroes in the moment and were challenged to be the kinds of heroes that they shared their heroes were to them. What qualities did their heroes have that they looked up to or felt safe with or that brought them joy?

Do you know not one of them brought up someone because of status, fame, or money? It was Mom and Dad, aunts, uncles, and friends. Why? Because of who they are, not what they *have*.

So here's a question for all of us: Why do we get so excited to see someone of status (what society has labeled)? Fame? I have had friends who talk about getting to meet a known person from TV, a celebrity, or, nowadays, a social media "icon" and becoming starstruck. I'm not saying I wouldn't get excited—I would love to meet Oprah—but I have found in my life that there's an Oprah in all of us. And I have to say all the years of practicing yoga have brought me a real sense of what I believe a hero is.

One of the beautiful traits (I believe) of heroes is living the change they say they want to see in the world—Gandhi is one of my heroes. Often, that means not being passive when you feel the need to act. There have been several times when taking initiative, standing up for what I believe in, has brought me to stand alone (well, with myself) through the years. At times, the ego tries its best to talk me into going along with someone, something, just to fit in or to avoid upsetting someone.

Some of Smilin' Rylan's yogis with their hero cards.

Choosing acts of kindness, giving—and often it's the giving of a thought into an action at the time it enters my mind (live in the moment), without allowing it just to fall back into a crowded arena of past thoughts that become forgotten or to just settle somewhere in the back of my mind. For me, often, it's about taking action in the now, sharing with your heroes in the moment! Let them know! Be in the now. As I often share, do not allow a kind thought, word, or action to be left within your heart. Spread it. Often!

For years, I have truly lived my belief to bring a kind thought about someone to life and express it outwardly, bringing life to the person's light—the light that person brings to the world, our world! I've tried not to hold back, as I often did years ago, because of accusations of being fake or having alternative motives (sounds so crazy to me now when I hear it). Now I let comments just go as a wave: no energy given, only the energy toward the act of kindness, the energy of love.

I soon discovered I did not feel authentic allowing others to reflect their own thorns toward my acts of spreading kindness. Rather, it was sharing

thoughts through words, or giving—whatever my soul was nudging me to do, I just did it. I choose to feel the freedom to be my own hero and therefore give others space where they feel safe to do the same.

Each time we shed light, ours and theirs, the world shines that much brighter! So let's all give of our own light and allow others to do the same, even encourage it. May we all look within and find the hero. Together our light will be so bright nothing could dim it. Have fun shining.

Jovie—what a kind, fun, loving yogi.

You Are Energy

Walk for Life

October 14, 2019

Team Smilin' Rylan's Walk for Life, 2019! Yes, another year, another walk in honor of my hero. Leukemia and Lymphoma Light the Night, Saturday, October 12, 2019.

RYLAN WAS NOT ABLE TO ATTEND OUR FIRST WALK, AS HIS BLOOD COUNTS were too low, but his energy was high, and he was filled with love. He was only two years old, and they lived in Texas. That walk was so powerful for me! I remember feeling so sad for some of the teams who were walking in remembrance of a young child or adolescent who had not made it through the walk toward cancer freedom. I had no worries at the time because Rylan was 94 percent curable! We were blessed that his prognosis was wonderful, so with no doubt, we walked for the cure, unaware that on his last visit for his treatment, that would change.

Rylan relapsed October 2014. Both he and his parents would be at UCSF hospital, but the walk would go on. Naomi and I made twenty-five awesome posters, with pictures of Rylan on front and back.

The support was overwhelming. It was a truly beautiful Light the Night. I like to say Walk for Life—and Smilin Rylan's Walkers for Life led the entire walk that night! It was amazing, breathtaking, to look back and see all the lit lanterns extending past our view and to witness the parade honoring heroes that evening. The groups of people walking in support of a cure for cancer as *one*! We are all truly one, and that night proved to be a testimony to that truth!

Once again, another year, we walked the steps that we never anticipated, this time carrying the energy of love regardless of the fact that Rylan's physical body had been set free. No longer here, his energy continues to walk with us.

Krisi, Jmom (me), Jason, and Grayson (in blue car).

"You Are Energy," from Rylan's untrainings—I am reminded of how much energy played in Rylan's life. Well, it plays in all our lives.

So here's something to contemplate: Be responsible for what vibrations you carry into any moment. Are you able, aware, to feel for the energy you carry from this moment to the next? How often do you justify why your energy is low, even bad—yucky, as the little yogis would say? If we are honest, we all unconsciously, sometimes even consciously, justify our choice to embody energy that is less than kind, loving, and centered. Bottom line: the truth is we choose.

Krisi and I were just talking about how amazing it is that out of all the doctors, nurses, and hospital employees who interacted with Rylan, 99.9999 percent had loving, caring, energy! (One of his favorites was Nurse Kelli.) My guess is all of them could have resorted back to reasons not to be in the present moment, but time and again, it was obvious they filled each moment with loving care.

I can only guess that they laid (and continue to lay) their heads on their pillows at night feeling at peace, their hearts centered and rejoicing in another day's end. When was the last time we chose to totally set aside a tough moment filled with sadness, fear, and anger and replace it with a moment filled with gratitude? We must practice this, allowing the fragrance of loving energy to pour out and fill the room, our surroundings, for all to feel and breathe in. Such is the magic of wisdom.

You will probably get tired to reading this, but the redundancy is worth the recognition on my end to allow it: I believe we move from one moment  to the next with the choice of our energy. How are you feeling? If it's not bringing a smile inside your heart's center, decide to move toward a new beginning, because each moment is a new beginning.

I know—I can hear it—we "can't just always be happy." People have said that to me more times than I can count. Sometimes that belief can keep us from accepting the possibility that we are able to choose a new thought, a new action, to lighten our moments. How about beginning a gratitude list you engrave in your mind's eye for times of struggle?

Nurse Kelli at UCSF children's hospital was an angel.

It helps me at times to remember that I cannot be brave without fear. Allowing fear to be the catalyst can bring magical moments—but when we allow fear to take over, well, we lose. But the loss of that moment, when brought to light, can be replaced with even more light, more energy! Then we remember who we truly are, and we rejoice in that moment of enlightenment—a moment-by-moment choice to enjoy our daily walks for life!

Our dear neighbors and friends of twenty-five years,
Trish and Jeff (and Beanie, fur baby).

Are You Right Where You Are Being You? Accepting You? Or More of a Chameleon?

July 23, 2021

I will start by saying that I'm not one to change my colors depending on who I'm with. Yes, there were definitely plenty of times I would find myself wearing a mask, feeling it would serve myself as well as others. Is that really that bad? We can only answer by first reflecting on the way we feel during and after these moments.

For myself, I choose myself. Taking on the labels of mother, Jmom, yoga teacher, and person, I welcome others to be who they really are, because in my heart, I understand that when they are comfortable with who they really are, they can wear labels and those labels don't take away from them. The labels are wrapped in love. That is what changes the world—the beingness that creates the doingness into wonderful moments of change. You are energy. What is your desire?

Now, I do at times listen more and find silence in the moment, almost in a meditative state, yet I'm present with whomever I am physically with at the time. I find at times it's a healthy way to be around people. I am only sharing what my heart is speaking.

When I began to truly love myself, I began enjoying spending time with my self, becoming my own best friend. I then realized I could be anywhere yet be in my inner space of nowhere and feel just right in the comfortableness of my self. I will say that I choose quickly to change my physical location when I'm ready to move into a more comfortable environment. No matter where I am physically, I'm aware that I, not outside conditions, make my presence.

Also, it's so wonderful when I'm in a group or with a person who I feel the connection (oneness) with, or who I belong with in that moment—where the energy is that of liberation, the feeling one of safeness, and I'm being exactly who I am, free, with no rules or labels to live up to and no need to change hats in order to be accepted. I reflect at those times; it's as if there is no time. Every moment is lived with such enjoyment and lightness. I know you have experienced what I am talking about and sharing here. I have these moments often, and I celebrate in the realization that we are all in this beautiful play of life together. Let us celebrate together.

The joy of anticipation when I'm having a rock-painting get-together for a little one is so dear to my heart. I can feel the love as the kindness rocks are being created, painted with hands of energy expressing excitement, and I imagine to whom or where these love messages will be delivered. I begin with thoughts of expectation but slowly and lovingly move toward acceptance of just what will be.

With time, little by little, the habit of expectation no longer takes residence as thoughts in your head, in your mind. It remains only as a reminder—a reminder that of course your awareness becomes the lens you look through from your inner heart's space. Not from your mind, if the energy is, as we say, of the monkey mind.

This is going to sound oxymoronic, a paradox. You no longer become aware that you are in fact aware; you are just being aware. No thoughts, no judgment—you just are.

Children seem to naturally live there most of the time. I feel us grown-ups move them away from that birth gift way too soon, often with them resisting. Instead, perhaps it would serve everyone if we spent time learning (relearning, unlearning) from children that it is beautiful when we are in the moment, absent of any expectations. It's a freedom that all is well and we just are—enjoy it fully.

Like a child, you came into this beautiful play of life, so enjoy more of the moments with a child, as a child.

Yes, begin again, reborn, and choose to return to being you no matter what situation you are thrown into. There will be times where we can't predict what our next moment will bring to us. But when we know who we really are, without all the conditions, we can step into the moment and live it fully. Get ready!

So many satori moments come from the very young. The beginning chapters of life continue and (hopefully) evolve into the climax of a beautiful physical ending to flight and beyond.

Alyvia and me painting kindness rocks to deliver to neighbors.

I am continually reminded how freeing and peaceful it is when I am me (the I-ness of who I really am), with no thought of having to please someone,

51

which seems to come—no surprise—as I naturally want to be of service and spread love and joy through acts of kindness. We aren't even realizing it, aren't aware of it—it just is. No gauge or concern or worry, we are simply being.

Be you, and have fun in each moment.

Be with the ones you choose, and enjoy all other moments knowing and believing that, in the end, all is well. Sometimes I can forget where I am meant to be and accept that it's where I am now. I begin to get way too much into my mind about the need to do more. For example, children and the elderly, as well as fur babies, are tender to my heart. The situations for some children in other countries break my heart. There are children here, too, who are struggling and encountering hardships—children in need of love, who are thrown into situations by no means of their own doing. As are fur babies and many elderly.

I know I have shared in past blogs one of my spiritual teachers (I believe it was Marianne Williamson, more than twenty-five years ago) saying that you can talk all you want about the horrible things happening in the world (there truly are many more wonderful things) but that what helps alleviate that talk and the sadness is *doing something*! Breathe, and then make the decision to do something to help solve the situation, hardship, or challenge.

I know from experience that the action of love heals the ache and the mind once again quiets down. I have to add that guilt is from the mind. When I release and listen to the soft voice from my heart, that's when the energy turns my love into action. I desire my love to bring the act to life, providing service that brings change.

I was twenty-eight years old when I first started sponsoring a child from World Vision. I have watched, witnessed through so many children, what a few dollars a month can provide for not only them but the larger family. At times, I begin to feel hopeless about my little donations. Yes, sometimes that ego voice inside my head starts lecturing me that I need to do more. Darrell used to say that when he passed away, I would join World Vision or some missionary and be perfectly happy.

I am here because I feel—I know—that here is where I am supposed to be, and I know deep within that my heart will give me loving nudges when or if the energy summons me elsewhere. I feel the perfection of so many imperfections of my life, and I love it. I love following the nudges from my heart and where they lead me, even if they simply lead me to smile at a person, a stranger—yet friend. Miracles happen ...

Of course, it still is hard for me to watch commercials, read emails, or look at mail sharing what is going on in different parts of our world, but I also don't allow these moments to harvest crops of sadness in my heart, to the point where they paralyze me, keep me from taking action. When we live in each moment of each day, we have every opportunity to reach out and touch a heart.

I feel no need or desire to sit and talk about the sad stories when I'm spending my moments of life in alignment of love. If each of us would do a small act of kindness, can you imagine how it would grow?

There are wonderful organizations. Of course, together we can do our part right where we are now, with our own organization of the Me and We Movement.

I seem to just naturally gravitate toward people who want to make a difference. They don't sit and complain about the world; they act. They do things and make a difference, though not with anger or a need or desire to point a finger of judgment at the homeless or other people or situations they don't understand; they just act through kindness of nonjudgment. Why make it wrong to be homeless? Would you seriously choose it? Stop with the judgments. Just listen quietly, and respond if your heart calls you to. And if not, then, in love, choose to just walk away. Allow kind acts to be, with no judgment either way. Don't allow guilt to birth anger, where you feel you must justify your choice. There should not be judgment of anyone's decision. There is not a single one of us who really knows what's going on in someone else's life. We think we do, but we don't.

Rylan being airlifted. He thought it was so very cool!

Regarding children with cancer: I hear people talk all the time about it just not being right or fair. Well, it is hard to watch, but I do have faith that there's something deeper—deeper seeds planted to bring the growth of some beautiful love branches into the world.

When I hear people in conversations, I share about ways to donate. Or, perhaps when buying a gift for someone, go to and through MD Anderson's

Children's Art. Or why not adopt a child through World Vision to help hunger or just pick whatever your heart's impulses lead you to?

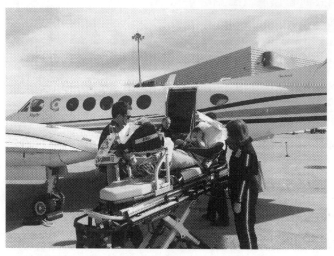

Rylan's flight to Maryland for T cell research.

But please go within your heart, and when you start the judgment, be aware of it, stop, take a breath, and center yourself in an energetic surrounding with people who come up with some beautiful ways to extend acts of loving-kindness through monetary means as well as service. Please don't underestimate the small impulses from your heart. Small is still big!

I believe there is so much love in the world. As we come once again to the end of the week and lead into the weekend, may we all choose to live each moment releasing all expectations of what others think we should be and do and just be who we really are, because we are in fact energy. What does your energy speak? Filled with love and kindness ... magical!

Best Gift to Give Your Loved Ones? Be You, Be Happy, and Be a Love Light

Our favorite thing: to be happy! Rylan is a love light.

A love light? Rylan was and is a love light. He lit up the room with his energy and laughter. What energy do you bring to any given moment? Are you even aware? When you are as bright as a love light, as you breathe in awareness, your family, friends, and acquaintances may not perceive or receive it as a gift; in fact, they may view it very differently. Perhaps they'll think that you're high on something or not really living in reality. Yes, I know the feeling of catching others' under-the-breath comments—which I actually grew to love to hear. How others view who you are is only their perception through the lenses they're looking and feeling through. And that's OK. Let it be.

Laughter is contagious. Love to catch it, but choose to be the carrier.

Nevertheless, it truly is a hidden gift to those who are present. Most enjoy the presence. Perhaps felt yet not clear twenty-twenty eyesight. But, as if it were an actual material gift, it is received quite a bit differently. You're not visiting any thoughts of what you're giving or receiving. You're just being— no expectations in return. Your love light is not affected either way. As it is lived through satori moments, it becomes simple, another aha moment that becomes a natural way of being. That's a gift to others, whether they choose to open it and enjoy. Let's go on.

What's so beautiful about being a love light? Well, you're not only a gift to those ready to receive; you're a gift to yourself, by being you, your self. You're not concerned with meeting other people's expectations. Just being present. Yes, I know, there are times of challenges, times when it may feel easier to fall back into old scripting, defensiveness, judgment, and stress, when your love light dims or even turns off and your inner self fades to the back, drowning in the mind chatter yet always observing, waiting patiently for you to return.

This is where journaling offers such insight, especially when you practice going to your journal and writing when your monkey mind has taken over. Just do it. I so enjoy looking back to my journaling and smiling. I often ask myself, "Who was that?" Such a powerful gift—awareness, as well as the other birth gifts to guide you back to self. Here's a reminder of your other three gifts: listen for the soft voice in the heart's space; use your inspiration to imagine, see, and feel back, forward, to who you really are; and act from your freedom to be!

Breathe, become still, and listen softly as your heart nudges quietly, reminding you as you feel, and take in the contrast. Remember the oneness as you reconnect and return to your self, if only for just this moment in time. That's all that matters: this moment in time.

I am here to be me and shine my love light. That is home to me, where I find my inner self and peace. There's the place I feel at home, answering the calling deep within, with love and faith that I may return a gift or be a gift to the world, or even to just a handful, before I take my final flight.

I am guilty—oh yes—of taking in their words and feeling the need (well, desire) to change *their* words of wisdom, their doubt, unhappiness, and justifications regarding the reasons why their lives are tough, miserable, or scary. I felt the need to change what they view as wisdom on staying clear and safe from misery, as well as on what must be part of success. It's as if they believe that to receive any great thing in life, a person must struggle, sacrifice, and endure much pain. I guess it's people's personal definitions for words and how the words tell the stories of their lives. The harder, or the more drama and unhappiness, the more interesting and exciting. I remember that feeling of sharing and the residue—the yucky feeling after—yet I was so used to it. It was what I knew to be real, and that's what I marinated in for years.

I have heard this often: "How can that person be happy (calm, still) at a time like this?" How can I not choose calm when my inner self is so much more lovingly effective through my beingness to my doingness, extending out, when I am happy? Once again, being happy does not mean that you are going around smiling and laughing all the time. Happy, to me, means you are choosing to see and feel all the beauty within and surrounding you in any given moment. It means you sense a smile present within your heart's space, a smile of happiness over just being present in the now.

I do understand, though, how we become stuck in the handed-down scripts, the words and actions of our perceived wise adults, carried down with so much authority—their words of reason to doubt with suspicion the stories of any happiness not earned through hard work or outside rewards. As if it's unnatural and unearned, or we're unworthy, when we look for happiness within and through simplicity. It's often perceived as an easy way out of hard work.

Why? I believe that, for many of us, we connect happiness to conditions of the outer world, making happiness so temporary, fleeting. I am only explaining what I have come to realize through years of untraining, sharing, caring, listening, and journaling every day. And, again, this is not about blaming our parents, teaches, pastors, or other authority figures. They live through their scripts handed down to them. But we can choose to change those scripts that no longer connect with our spirits, our souls, who we really are. And we can hand down our handwritten, newly revised scripts to our children, both natural and chosen, and to others who connect with us.

I had bought him his Super Rylan outfit, and he wore it as much as possible. We had and still do have so many happy times. I miss my physical time with Rylan, but he still brings me happiness unconditionally.

Regarding rescripting: there seems to be lack of belief that happiness doesn't have to be earned. People may not use these words explicitly, but so many of us witness this messaging. But happiness is not earned; it is a residual form of being in the space of peace, awareness, presence in the now.

When you do feel such a freedom to be, you want the gift for so many other people to experience, knowing, remembering, that no words are needed. "Quiet. Your actions are speaking so loudly I am not able to hear your words." Rather, may we choose to just be. It truly is so freeing.

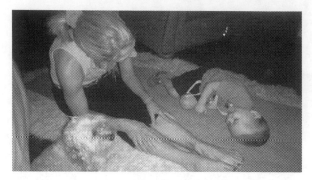

Just be.

Otherwise, there's where my love-light switch can be turned off. That's not my business. I still fall into that hole. And when I do, I feel like I'm falling into sadness quicksand. My heart just aches. And then what do I do? For me, I choose to do a practice that will bring me back into alignment, returning me to my self. My energy returns to calm, patient, and, yes, happy. Well, at least most of the time.

It may take a few minutes, at times hours, and sometimes days. I yearn to be back to me (actually my self). I do my best and let it go. All is ultimately well, and I know it even before I feel it.

What are you filling your days and moments with? We cannot control the outside, but we can influence it through our inner selves. Shine your love light, your loving energy. The only thing you need is your energy, your light.

Life has ways of teaching us, if we are ready and open to learn. When I let others go free and I am in my space of freedom, I feel no need to be approved, and I am so open to welcoming and loving others wherever they are.

Breathe in the love and exhale the judgment. No one says you have to take their words, bring them to your heart, and give them birth. It's an ongoing journey—a journey of release, a journey to flight. I love it!

Look for the rainbow, but breathe in stillness during the storm.

Here's an activity I enjoy: Allowing your feelings to be your pen and the paper a canvas, write or paint words or pictures to tell the past story, because it is now past. Watch as the wind picks it up, and visualize the past floating to the heavens above. So what will your future moments present? What will be your gift?

Truly, the best gift we can give our loved ones, whether they know it, is to be happy, to truly be a light of love, a love light. We can find a way, spreading love out to all.

What Is Your Heart Saying? Someone Is Listening and Feeling—Speak from Your Heart

May 19, 2020

(I am adding this as I am reading through the pages, after seeing the preceding date. The date that the blog was published [not written] was the day Darrell was taken by ambulance two months before I was to bring him home for his last five days into his flight, free from pain. His birthday was meant to be the day he would begin another ending, the beginning of his birth into the beyond.)

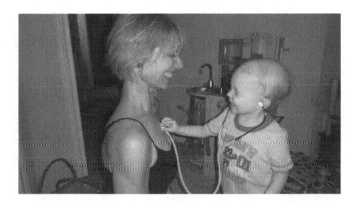

Yoga on my mat guides me to open, increasing heart energy as my mind quiets in the background through my breath. After moving through poses, ending in Savasana, and rolling up my mat, I step into my life off the mat, embracing each moment with an excitement for life. My heart is filled with energy of love extending out, reaching, connecting, as if communicating heart to heart with others. Yep, the butterflies begin to warmly swarm, fluttering from my heart out.

When I feel I have lost my alignment and am once again operating on autopilot, I will move into the space of acknowledging I am not present and take time to re-center. I feel so often we all have in our minds the nagging voice that tells us we should just push through. I can say I have never regretted taking time with my self, and I open to share with others why.

Choose to take some time for your self, and welcome others to do the same when needed. Start with young ones, communicating with children so that they keep the precious gift of being present. For example, I recommend that instead of initiating a negative time-out, make it positive. Allow children

59

to see and feel you when you make the decision regarding a time-out. Rejoice that you are taking care of your self, therefore being there wholly, fully, for others. Your children will understand more than you think.

Journal or meditate: What is your life communicating through this vehicle, this body, you move through and travel in? What are others hearing or feeling from your energy? Just let your pen guide you to write from your heart's mind. Do not allow your mind to start a conversation, telling you what to write. Your heart's intention will be pure and without judgment.

For years, I have been athletic, participating in sports from gymnastics, dance, and cheerleading to basketball, volleyball, and softball throughout grade school and high school and continuing with related roles in my adulthood: Kings Athletic Club fitness director and IDEA-certified aerobics instructor (yes, this really ages me). I also jumped rope for years. But never did the breath of awareness, the meditative aspect, of any of those speak to my heart as yoga has these past fourteen-plus years.

You already know my story about starting yoga for my husband to benefit his health and relaxation and falling heart over mind (head over heels) in love with life, a deeper knowing, never stopping to look back, only forward, in exhilaration for life. It was another avenue into deepening my faith and belief.

There are so many heartfelt adventures and discoveries that rolling out my yoga mat has gifted me, what my yoga practice has opened my heart space to. One gift is authentically becoming aware of what my mind is saying (and how) and returning to my heart when there is not a connection. I know by my energy which voice I'm listening to. Here's the truth as I feel it: when my energy speaks of love and connection for all, it is my heart speaking (feeling), and others are listening to or hearing from that energy.

So roll out your mat and begin listening through breath awareness, heart listening. Be present in the nothingness where the soft, subtle voice of energy is speaking from your heart. Now feel, listen, and become free! Just be. And all is well once again.

What You See in Me, I Can See (Feel) in You

February 24, 2020

I taught the tribe, our office family, yoga. They will always be my family even though we sold the practice in 2015.

Another favorite saying: "Your vibe attracts your tribe."

My life has truly lived up to that statement: I believe our energy does attract in our lives certain people, situations, blessings, and drama—although we at times will not fully understand until much later why some of the drama was delivered or dropped into our space. So be careful of judgment, because, at times, seemingly negative things you feel you've attracted may turn out to be rainbows in the near (or later) future.

Life is about energy. I'm hoping you will read different entries about energy. Though some of them won't create satori moments, there will be that one (or more) that will. What does your energy communicate? I am surrounded by a tribe of people who I feel amplify my time here on earth. When I am ready to leave, I can look back with gratitude and feel I made a difference. Isn't that what our time playing here through life is truly about?

There are definitely days, times, and moments where I feel disappointed with my output (choice) of energy—times when my emotions lead me to a choice that I later wish I could rewind, replay, even reproduce and direct, reworking that part of my play. These are times when I realize that if I'd been more aware, I would have chosen a more loving scene to begin with.

Another journal moment: Here is where journaling is truly a blessing. I recommend taking three or four minutes before and closing your eyes, just breathing. Alternatively, you might practice, as I have, looking at yourself in the mirror, looking deep in your eyes, while breathing. Try this before or after journaling. Do not look away.

If it is a person you're journaling about, afterward (this is what I prefer, because you may find that if you reread the journal, your energy becomes more loving), perhaps ask that person to sit while you look into each other's eyes. I used this at untrainings—"time-out" at the office. Please take the time-out, become still, and write your thoughts. It's amazing how often you will rewind by reading past journals and see, through satori moments, how that was not your inner I, your inner self, but rather a choice that is in the past. You now have the freedom to choose differently.

These are the times I have come to believe do in turn bring rainbows— rainbow bridges to miracles that allow us to look within and make decisions that lead our vision, our future, into a higher dimension. A lighter feel. Free!

We always had fun at the office. Not all of the tribe members are in this picture, but most were there from ten to twenty-five years. I miss and love them all so much—forever my chosen family.

So what I choose to do from that space is whatever I am able (and yes, we can listen to our hearts and feel our emotions), to make it right with my self, conscience.

Use the miracles of those replay clips to choose differently—if not now, then the next rerun—and often you'll seeing a change in energy or vibes almost immediately. Do what it takes to change the flow of energy! It begins and ends with your choice. Choose freely, noncontrolling, and then allow it to be.

When Naomi walked into our practice to interview with me, she was just twenty-one. She is now fifty in biological numbers, though forever

young, ageless, in spiritual energy. Ironically, the preceding picture is from her twenty-first anniversary as a member of our tribe! I loved and looked forward to celebrating each tribe member's anniversary of years spent in our practice as part of our family. Yes, our *family*!

I can only pray that other owners begin to think of the people who support and give service to their businesses as not just employees. That they begin to view everyone holding hands in a circle, not positioned on a ladder, and that there's a oneness, a connection. Then perhaps it would extend out even farther, to streets, towns, cities, states, and countries! It is contagious. I have experienced it, witnessed it, time and again. Yes, throughout the world. Please don't allow your mind to block this heart's thought or energy. It is possible! Believe it into being, beginning in family and work environments. Join hands! Eliminate the ladder climbing.

Dr. Ratra (center) was one of the angels who came to work (play) at our office while Darrell was going through his journey. It was as if everything was just perfect in its imperfection. And we would continually choose to know that as truth.

Naomi was not the first choice, but I'm so thankful the vibe, the energy, was playing regardless. I am very blessed that our first choice accepted another position.

Our journey, our tribe, expanded—and what a ride! We both remember that day, etched in love and appreciation for the events that took place. The next twenty-five years, Naomi was a part of my tribe and I a part of hers!

So here is an example where I might have been frustrated by the fact that the first applicant chose differently, but I already knew that it was meant to be. How many times (journal time!) have you (or has your life) taken a different turn and at first you feared it was the wrong one? Now, looking back, you understand.

I often say that when we look back, we can recount so many times when our hearts were full of tears and sadness, fear and doubt, but the journey continued and the rainbow and the walk across the bridge into the hidden miracles kept opening, birthing new chapters of love and kindness, growing, flowing into more-profound depths! Isn't that what life is all about? I believe; won't you?

It continued into the new business we started: Smilin' Rylan Kids Yoga. So often, the little yogis were the teachers and we the students. We all experienced how the energy would change as we as a tribe would walk along downtown Hanford, spreading smiles and love as the little yogis would place kindness rocks around. Or visit a senior living community and practice yoga with the residents (on the front page of the Hanford newspaper). Good news does rock! Or chalking up sidewalks for people going through hard times. Endless possibilities for acts of kindness.

Just watch as the little yogis' practicing yoga (both on and off the mat) changes the vibes and brings, in each moment, more calmness, love, and kindness into the world. These vibes change one moment at a time, transforming the future.

To me, life is a lot like owning your own business. Anybody who has owned a business knows what I'm talking about when I say it's a journey! You learn a lot (a lot about yourself). That it is essential to have patience, a sort of stoicism. Faith became one of my mantras.

You'll be presented with opportunities and situations in which you'll have the choice to either give up or nurture the ability to go within and accept that it's all about you. Breathe, make the decision to ride the waves of life, and make the choices needed to continue the adventure of your story—or not. Remember, though, that just as you are not your business, your labels are also part of your play on earth. You are not your doingness. You are your inner self, the I-ness that is unchangeable.

Your vibrations attract just what you are, or your energy is, giving out and communicating. I came to understand that I was receiving what I needed to grow or choose not to. When I say *grow*, I mean continuing to go within and uncover what that moments are there presenting to me. I remember several satori moments that jolted me into the light—where I knew, felt, it was an opening, a choice I could make.

Journal time/meditation: What do you desire your life's business to be, tell, and feel? Your story? Your book of life? What is your story? What is it attracting?

The tears, frustration, and doubts never outweighed the joy I believed was yet to come—the excitement, fun, and laughter that we all experienced on a daily basis in our office, our practice! Yes, call it our daytime practice of life.

It extended to everyone who touched our office. Our tribe not only included us, our office family, but extended with open arms to our family of patients, the distributors from labs, pharmaceuticals reps, and every company tied to our practice. They were all part of our tribe!

The love was felt. And yes, the rumors are true! We danced, sang, did yoga in the welcome room, served coffee and muffins, and did the laughing meditation (the patients really thought we went nuts)! We shared acts of kindness to all the arms of our office, our business; homemade gifts, painted rocks, hugs, and words of appreciation were the language of our office, helping us express gratitude for all. So blessed.

Of course, when you go against the mainstream, you have to be self-full. We were criticized often through our thirty-plus years. And at times, I would begin to listen to these so-called successful businesspeople. In many people's eyes, they were consulting me: "Joni, you are the owner (well, Dr. Kirby and me), and your employees work for you. They are your employees, not your family. They will take advantage." This is one I often heard. And I would reply, "Some family members take advantage, and I still choose to love them."

I felt, and still do, that if the business/family/tribe is not a place where everyone can come and feel surrounded by family, love, caring, and kindness, then I don't want to own a business. I'll just go get a job with benefits.

It really doesn't matter what product or service is provided—each of us is our own company, our business. It's our energy, our vibes. Whether with family or business, what vibes are you attracting? What are your intentions in every decision you make? Your life's message? Another great journal prompt, beginning your meditation.

What Hat Do You Put On First Thing, before Your Feet Touch the Earth?

Love and Faith were wonderful fur employees at Dr. Kirby's office, now iCare of Hanford.

My morning begins somewhere between three and four o'clock—usually four. Most often, my first inner dialogue is "Thank you for this day," and I smile. I usually have at least Love (one of my fur babies) with me in bed, but during the winter, often both Love and Faith are cuddling. If they aren't, once I start my meditation music, they will be close by, and it is not unusual for them to end up on their backs, all four legs wide open and surrendering to the peace.

Well, it was several years back when, finding myself in the same dreaded morning routine, I was blessed to get so uncomfortable with my day's opening moments that I found myself being led toward the perfect books and mentors. They seemed to arrive at just the perfect time.

I made a choice back then—and it's been probably ten or more years—that I was not going to get out of bed and set foot on the floor until I felt a connection, a sense of

Singing our morning song to Grayson before he sets foot on the earth.

peace, an alignment of knowingness, a knowingness that all is well, and that my day was going to be beautiful.

My beautiful daughter has carried on the morning shine. Rylan and Grayson are also blessed with the passed-down singing—"Today is Monday! Today is Monday! Is everybody happy? Well, I should say yes!"—as Mommy is getting them up for the beautiful day awaiting them.

A normal place to find Jmom and Rylan, singing, reading, and laughing a lot. For years, I have been sharing, during my untrainings, the challenge I

 went through (for a very long time) that led to this beautiful awakening, this satori moment. It was not easy for me to change my paradigm back then. I had a tape-recorded script that seemed to play every morning, a constant dialogue in my mind: "You have got to go back to sleep; it's too early. You need more sleep. Oh my goodness, this is Monday. Yikes! I feel a little sick. Joni, you have to go back to sleep." And on and on. The truth is that when my husband was first diagnosed in 2006, staying in bed felt safer.

It was, at the time, an unwelcome miracle in disguise for so many reasons, turning my life upside down and sideways. All of a sudden, I had enormous responsibility on my shoulders, especially taking over running the practice while helping my bestie, Darrell.

Sometimes (when cell phones became a bigger part of my life), I would even reach for my phone, and that would make it worse. It's amazing how we get used to routines and don't even realize the rut we have chosen to make our normal. We become comfortable with being uncomfortable.

Blessings, satori moments, led me to the openings, allowing those thoughts to be washed away, and the deeper desire to fall into a meditative state of bliss would slowly but surely replace the old script. Now it is just part of my life. I feel I was gifted with this awakening, this blessing of understanding that my day begins early in the morning and sets the stage. I (yes, me, my self, and I) set the stage for the opening, the first act, of my day. And it becomes beautifully scripted.

I feel that once I was on the path of excavating my stuff, and actually enjoying the rediscovering of who I am, time just began to seem so magical and unreal. Yes, I have challenges and at times feel overwhelmed, but I soon remember they are giving me exactly what I need in this moment of time: space to be who I really am.

We have it within ourselves to be open to see (feel) the blessings, ready and willing to allow the perfect answers to our hearts' calling. Children, especially now, would be blessed during these times to experience more stillness, fewer phones and games (which I enjoy playing too), more times of calmness, and more family time in nature. There truly are so many calming ways to spend some of our time and reconnect within. And it's a gift we can give that keeps on giving as children grown up. That is my belief.

I see and feel firsthand what a difference it makes when they are offered more space for silence and stillness. They welcome the times to just be, truly.

As always, in all ways, we would be doing a beautiful act of kindness to ask our inner selves what our actions are speaking. Our words may encourage times of stillness and silence yet are not heard because of the loudness of our actions. The actions we rehearse time and again take over.

Teach children to be—to become still and breathe. They will teach you that the ability is in fact innate in them. Continue to encourage and celebrate them unwrapping and bringing this into the moment.

I can't imagine going back. Are there some mornings where, because of circumstances or my own choice, my morning ritual is altered? *Yes*, of course there are such times, like when I'm spending precious time with my grandson and my beautiful daughter and son-in-law. This is such a part of me. Often taking a walk or even just stepping into the backyard, I am floating in the moment. Peaceful silence is enveloping me, and I am once again delivered to the now, feeling the amazement of life—my life. I call it my meditative state.

I am now often able to be in a room full of people and find those moments—moments when there is no time, only space to be. It's hard for me to find the words to make sense of my experiences for others without sounding as if I am flying high on something. Actually, I am—we call it life.

I love to share about it. It's one of my favorite things to talk about—well, besides the beauty of love, and kids, and life, and friends. And there's chosen family and of course family. Well, let's just say that everything is better when we can share our treasures of life.

So perhaps tomorrow morning, early, begin to rewrite or simply rearrange your script, your regular, usual play of morning. Rewrite the script, and put the music on that speaks to your inner self. (You know, the one that feels warm and full of love.) Wait until you feel excited (and peaceful—yes, you can have both) before your feet hit the earth, before your first step out of bed. Please remember it takes time to change scripts and routines, but for me, it has all been worth the patience. Every moment is a treasure, one you will definitely share with others. Happy first step into morning.

You are loved.

Who Am I?

September 14, 2019

Rylan knew he had something called *cancer*. His parents told him up front when he was very young that he had cancer but that he was not cancer. They told him of the treatments and side effects. And even though there were some activities Rylan could not do because of the cancer—"normal" ones that kids his age could participate in—it did not define who he was. His family treated him as the amazing young man he was! Life was filled with all kinds of adventures!

Ask yourself who really knows what the next moment holds. Life, flight—everything is just perfect in its imperfection. Why would we spend so much of our time, our moments that comprise a lifetime, in fear of what we call *death*? Where do we come up with all the fear-filled stories?

When do we as adults start using our stories, stored in the subconscious, to label, identify, justify, and even judge who we think we are? "This is just the way I am" and similar scripts continue. How about this one—have you used it or heard someone say it about a family member? "My mom is like that, and her mom …" It truly takes our willingness to become still, breathe, even meditate to use our awareness before we habitually open our stories and continue returning to the same scripting, the narrative journeys

71

to nowhere. So why not? Begin a beautiful practice, meditate, breathe in stillness, and start to rescript your story. No, it isn't easy, but the little yogis show so beautifully that when you become open, it becomes more natural, bringing stillness and allowing space and, from that space, opening up the possibility of choosing differently.

Rewriting our stories requires courage, challenging us to move into being uncomfortable. When we feel stuck, we are in a pattern of thinking we simply are this way because of this or that—"It's my parents' fault," "It's my ex-husband's fault," and the list and blaming goes on.

We add another chapter to our already-exhausting story. At first, our emotions will want to lead us back to what is familiar, regardless of whether that familiar or "comfortable" is leading to destruction or unhappiness—attached to the response that allows our familiar story to ring true, to at least our ears. As miserable as that story is.

This past week, I did an untraining at an office, five hours of reaching deep within. It continues to remind me (shock me, at times), even more deeply, how often the preceding paradigm comes up. We are miserably but comfortably, familiarly unhappy. Whoa—tongue twister. We're even anxious because of the way we perceive life's challenges and our responses to those challenges. Unfortunately, so often, the fear of choosing a different response brings a resistance to change—a change that brings the unknown, uncomfortable choice difficult for so many, yet a change that, with time, could lead to so much more awareness, which leads to so much more peace and joy, exposing all the residue of the past moments and allowing all emotions to flow without labeling

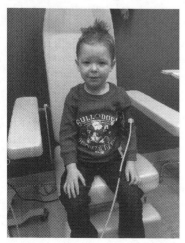

them good or bad. They just are here now, and we can experience the feelings and release them. They don't have to become a permanent part of our stories of why we're unhappy. With the passing of newfound moments created and grounded in love, we begin to find a decision to love that is not only nurturing our selves but reaching out to others.

Rylan did not have a story he connected to that was anything less than Super Rylan. He was and is an old soul.

The truth is that change is challenging. It is not easy once we've developed our habits and implanted them so deeply in our brains, making them our chosen stories. We wrote them and published them in our minds, but our hearts speak entirely different outlines and themes.

I have witnessed that for many adults, when there is a breakthrough, tears often begin beautifully flowing, opening up space for a real desire for change, releasing (often temporarily, at first) the desire to hang on. Then the work (play) really begins. It is so easy for us to resort back to comfortable choices even when those choices have caused heartache. It really takes both *R* and *Y*: "Remember Who You Are" and "You Are Energy."

And we continue on our adventure with the little yogis with different and fun pathways for them to relearn—to remember that being who they are is perfect and that we know who we are when we feel good (the feelings of love, peace, and joy) about our choices. Our conscious recalls subconscious, consciously. What is comfortable is not always what brings us back to who we really are, but the journey back can be so exciting when we choose to embrace the question, Who am I?

I Love to Share with Others Spirituality, Not So Much Religion

August 26, 2021

Those of you who know me know that one of my favorite (well, actually, my favorite) topics to talk about is spirituality. Not religion. I have the most loving spiritual friends from all different religions, yet we are all the same in our belief of love.

And no, yoga is not a religion! I have had people ask me whether I was all sorts of religions (labels). That is one of the most inspirational things about yoga; it deepens the core (not only of the body) beliefs of most religions. There are many different places of worship I can go and feel the spirit. Where there are two or more coming to gather, together there is the opening to feel the presence or energy of spirit. For me, praying can be expressed many ways, nowhere, anywhere, especially through singing! Tears flowing with so much grace—love me some "Amazing Grace."

"Peace begins with me." Stop what you are doing, become still, and sit in silence. (Even if it's on the front porch with Love and Faith looking on in peace.)

I have heard so many share, as I have, that yoga deepens our faith, as our spirituality is at one with who we really are, welcoming the I and watching as it begins lighting up the heart's space.

74

My experience was, for the first few months (even after that off and on), the ego would sneak in and take over quite often while I was practicing on my mat. With patience and stillness, and by nurturing my awareness, understanding the practice, and turning within, I soon began understanding that—if we are willing and commit to practice—yoga brings us to a place where faith deepens and opens the ability for satori moments. This allows our personalities to begin falling away and our deeper selves (the I) to become more present. I am free once again, so beautifully free to be, now, at least for this moment in time.

As I reflect, I realize that early on in my yoga journey, I cared more about the poses being perfect and about the workout, getting a good sweat going. Little by little (safety was definitely important), it became about my presence, the oneness I felt with my self, the stillness. When the poses became more difficult, I discovered how I became more present, my breath softly moving me through my moments in patience, calmness allowing awareness to guide my beingness into the now. With time, I began returning to the knowing of my self. Now the spirituality is the main part of yoga for me. Early on my transformation back to my self, I began my mantra "Yoga is life, and life is yoga."

It's powerful how my flow of moments was becoming similar on and off the mat. Many satori moments later, little by little, the ego faded to the background more often, and through poses and breathing in stillness and meditation, I began to rediscover even deeper who I really am. Not the person but my self, the unchanging I. I allowed my self to gently, with time and patience, detach and cut the strings of importance to the material world—at least far more of the time—enjoying *things* yet becoming aware of the difference of nonattachment.

Rylan naturally practiced yoga, on and off the mat.

Ending in Savasana (corpse pose), from my years of meditation, I fell right into the deep gratitude of the end of practice (life), so filled with peace, a knowingness to release both on and off the mat. I am so grateful that I discover and rediscover my self so often. I feel such a oneness, a wholeness, moving through poses (life) while meditating in the stillness within.

Of course, it is a daily practice, a moment-to-moment decision, both on and off the mat. It's such a blessing, and I thank Darrell's doctor silently in my prayers for recommending this practice to help him, hoping it would be a means for him to be still and focus on his self. You all know the story, and it continues, the story of presence delivering the gift of love and faith.

Think of all the blessings, the different gifts that we receive, when we live deeply from within, carrying it all outward to others. Where there is communication through love and our conversations are given life, the energy is felt—and wow, how powerfully beautiful the now is and our lives become.

Energy speaks so much louder than words. And different words can carry the same meanings, or different meanings, depending on people's experiences and intentions. Energy carries intentions. But love is all—I truly believe that. It just is so *present*, real or not. I feel that when our moments are void of love, we are not really living.

I enjoy hearing the stories behind other people's beliefs. What inspired them? Spirituality? It saddens my heart when hate is born from fear of perceived differences. Differences can and often are blessings. Why is that difficult for some to take to heart?

So often when there are differences, the overarching message is the same (hopefully)—that we are here to "love one another, as I have loved you." "Do unto others as you would have others do unto you." The words may be different, and of course, there is always a percentage of people who are extreme—at times moving toward violence, with words and their meanings becoming twisted, leading people deeper into fear, anger, and even hate.

I do believe that love is present in their hearts. There have just been so many layers and layers of anger and fear, awaiting an awakening. "Forgive them, for they know not what they do"—and remember that "peace [as well as forgiveness] begins with me."

Why are so many of us looking, insisting, to be right? Desiring to find or make others wrong? Sacrificing what we have in common to find a difference? Often, it is a word (or a difference in definition of the word) or simply an alternative way of celebrating our faith. We must remember and be open to differences, as they can be refreshing.

I often share with friends the question I ask my self when I'm feeling lost: What would Jesus do? I walk with Him, talk with Him, laugh with Him, and cry with Him.

When I am with my best friend (my self, I), I hear Him and see Him in my mind's eye—actually see Him (and feel His presence) walking side by side with me.

When I share my experiences with people of different religious backgrounds, with friends, I most often have tears welling in my eyes. It is so beautiful and is often the same as when they share their experiences of faith and worship. Regardless of the man-made building we may choose to worship in, our sharing of faith, the deeper presence, is the same. We're much more similar than we are different. We share that the difference is how we go about our worship, the words we give to the practices of faith. We choose to celebrate and love the differences. Shared times wrapped in loving to gather together. Amen.

There are possibly different roads, different journeys, to the same destinations. I often talk to Jesus and ask how He feels about people actually killing one another over where they go to worship, people killing in His name, in words or action, and friends fighting and at times no longer friends because of the differences. I feel such sadness, until His love envelopes me, diminishing any fear or doubt. My disappointment lessens, my anger dissolves, and once again, I am reminded that with love all things are possible. Peace returns.

In my heart space, He reminds me again and again to love God with all my heart, love others as I love my self, and believe—know—all is well.

Our beautiful practice in Hanford was our life, and there were no barriers of division. When we walked out of our home on Encore and into our home on Myrtle Street, and everywhere in between, it was home, and we were home. Of course, I often feel that no matter where I am, I am home. When we become so at home with ourselves, wherever our bodies are, we are in Spirit; we are at home. We worship filled with love and gratitude.

Through all the years, we served our family of patients—all from different religions, backgrounds, and nationalities, yet all entered through our front door as members of our office family, visiting our home office to have their vision checked. We would often say that it was just the cover for us to serve in love. That was our mission.

We came to gather together to celebrate human kindness—so powerfully beautiful, so freeing—and we had so much fun! We all have a choice

 regarding with whom and where to share spirituality, and hopefully we feel open to live it daily, leaving religion as a name on a building. When we welcome faith and our oneness climbs into the front seat, religion moves to the back, opening up space for the celebration of our diversity.

We so enjoyed—yes, loved—our time spent at the home office.

I would still consistently have people ask me, "What religion is your practice?" The first couple of times, I would be speechless. Then I began to answer, with no judging on my part, "My religion is love. In this practice, we celebrate love and kindness." Sometimes I would explain it as a religion of spirituality.

My experience has been that with the most loving, caring, helpful, godly people I am around, I am often unaware of the buildings they choose to worship in—the physical dwellings they go to on Sundays or any day of the week. They are filled with God's love regardless of day or time or location. It's so apparent, and they walk in faith regardless of the buildings or locations in which they are present.

Many years ago, I would often be asked at times some pretty bold questions. I will share one that was asked that left me asking WWJD. I would walk with Him and talk with Him and get pissed off with Him.

I would really have to breathe deeply when I was asked what faith Rylan's family was. What brings people to believe they are doing God's will by questioning the religion or church? It was usually followed with "What church do they go to?" This was when Rylan was living by loving through cancer, and times were challenging, to say the least. At times, I felt more for his loved ones than for Rylan himself, as that little hero was fearless! I truly felt God's presence all the time, even when I was not with Rylan—a circle of faith beyond measure!

Some would be pretty bold in their view of Rylan's healing, or lack of healing, expressing their belief of the conditions that held the chance of a miracle healing his body. Yes, a couple of people made their judgment calls with such authority. I knew and still know in my heart that such people truly feel they are doing God's work. So I say a silent prayer both for my patience and for them.

I would often ask for prayers for all who were suffering, including all those who were present. I meant it with total love and faith. Those who offered prayers were (and are) a blessing, sending prayers of peace for all, all the while knowing there is in fact a heavenly plan. We may not see the miracles for a while, but I can testify that they are there waiting and so beautifully orchestrated.

It was amazing when 2020 hit and we could no longer physically go to a place of worship. I continued to be present in my church every day. For years I've attended, sometimes several times a day, often within my inner house of dwelling (at least once a day through internet, with music moving me moment to moment and my singing along, as I do so often).

When my ego throws me into judgment with anything but a loving heart, I feel yucky, and I don't enjoy that feeling, a flu-like illness. It's a definite sign I'm on the wrong path and I've lost my self, disconnected from my spirit within. I quickly go within to reflect, and I am reconnected—I return.

Tears Flow Often When I Feel, Am Present to, the Miracles of Life—God's Tapestry of Life

One of my favorite (first-thing-before-stepping-out-of-bed) songs captures the pines as a place, a church, to go to and celebrate in prayer of gratitude. I often step outside on my porch and look out to the beauty of nature, not holding back tears as they flow but inviting them. The song plays in the background. The I is present and at one with all. I am in heaven.

Some of the words of the song (and mine): "Gloria in excelsis Deo ... But here in my heart I allow, welcome the wafer and wine that is right now, and I join the choir singing of this baptismal creek of rocks that can sing the divine that speaks a secret language beyond sound, in praise of hallowed ground ..." Of course, I am known to make up my own verses. This morning, my neighbor caught me and smiled—happens often. So as I continue singing, I leave you in harmony with your life, where perhaps you're singing, contemplating where your next place of worship will be, right in this moment.

This is my always church. Every moment I'm praising, singing, and filled with so much appreciation for my life and yours!

Love the Moment, Live the Moment, Learn from the Moment, and Laugh Often

Laughter is contagious. Love to catch it, but choose to be the carrier.

WE *LOVED* TO LAUGH. I MISS HIS PHYSICAL FORM, BUT HIS ENERGY IS NEAR.

Add an Extra *L*: Love, Live, Learn, and Laugh in Each Moment

November 10, 2019

Rylan's brother, Grayson, playing with his Jmom. We are so sure Rylan is with us.

And in my opinion, laughter is the best medicine! Last week's blog was missing its caboose. We begin each Smilin' Rylan Kids Yoga class with meditation, followed by the laughing meditation. Just watch and see whether you can resist laughing, because laughter is contagious and truly the best medicine.

Please take the time to view and enjoy the related videos on our Smilin' Rylan Kids Yoga website.

I love to laugh. Everyone should lighten up and love, live, learn, and laugh a hell of a lot and then more! Warning: watch out for the benefits that will follow, as the caboose will bring treasures.

We began an untraining with everyone watching a video from laughing meditation. You should have seen their faces at first. It was hilarious. Then, as an office family, we started doing it daily.

We would choose a time, and one of us would say (bringing an arm up and slapping it on one knee), "Take a deep breath," and the entire staff would laugh in response! It was terrific to watch the patients in our welcome room, eyes open, without taking much time joining in—well, most of them. Of course, our family of patients grew to know we were out of the box. For heaven's sake, we did a *flash mob* in our office.

How wonderful it would be if all families made it a daily habit, of course always in all ways remembering that laughing at the expense of others isn't funny, choosing humor by laughing with and not at people.

Laughter is contagious, and so are smiles. Have you noticed that when someone smiles at you, you can't help but feel a smile coming not only to your lips, your face, but to your heart? Well, when you're feeling down, find friends to laugh with. I know it helps with a sense of well-being.

So start hanging out with people who love to laugh. Laughter helps with stress. I enjoy watching company be so comfortable that one of my friends begins to share clean jokes. Naomi's husband is great at this. It has been proven that when you laugh, blood flow increases and endorphins are released, helping you feel more relaxed not only physically but emotionally.

Laughter boosts immunity. One study at the Indiana State University School of Nursing found that joyful laughter may increase levels of natural killer cells, a type of white blood cell that attacks cancer cells. Incredible and true.

How about we allow laughter to open our hearts, acknowledging mistakes without becoming angry or frustrated? Laughing at mistakes allows us to recognize that making errors is a part of being human! I used to always say that there are no real mistakes, just *miss takes* that give us the gift of retaking moments a little differently.

Laughter is a natural alternative medicine for depression. Being unhappy may possibly turn into a sort of habit the mind has recorded, becoming a pattern or mindset if you don't bring awareness to the moment. Become the witness to the situation rather than being a victim.

Even forced laughter releases a cocktail of hormones and dopamine that can help improve your mood. This not only has been researched and found true; I can attest to its validity many times over.

Laughter helps pain and discomfort fade into the background. It's not that we won't experience the pain, but we are able to handle the pain much better.

So take a deep breath as you reach an arm to the sky, and as it comes to slap your knee, start the laughter going. Oh yeah, it's so much fun the more you practice it. Make it a weekly event in your home with the family, or, better yet, practice it before dinner every night. Just feel the difference in the energy throughout the evening, especially if you've had a rough day. Just do it and enjoy the benefits of stepping out of the box of life. And, of course, laugh a lot.

Stella and Maximus sharing an inside job while in tree pose.

Be Calm: Enjoy Being Home and Wash Your Hands

March 20, 2020

When the facts are clear, our choices become obvious, or they should. This is something that I (and my family) have been conscious of for years. As I was in the hospital so many times with both Smilin Rylan' and Doc Kirby, as well as my dad, doctors and nurses hammered it in. So I just became used to its importance. We would count to thirty and stay *calm*!

So stay calm, meditate, and find the joy, the peace in silence. Choose to be kind, and please take a breath and don't worry about the TP. Rylan didn't, haha!

(April 2022 note: For those of you who weren't present (or aware) during the time when toilet paper–finding missions often failed because of the COVID outbreak, people really started to stockpile, and to this day, I don't fully understand why. Actually, I thought it was humorous at the time, even when I was using tissues and at times paper towels (ouch), but always found TP someplace or asked the neighbors when

Found this picture and had to share!

85

desperate. What was hard to watch was how many suffered the loss of loved ones and had their lives turned upside down. Here what we initially thought was a very temporary flu turned into months. So my heart goes out to all who experienced or are still experiencing loss.)

There's nothing we can do to fight against the facts. While you're at home, as I have done, treat time like you're on vacation. I feel like I am at the best hotel! I get to take my fur babies, and I have packed everything to come with me. (And I didn't need a bunch of luggage!) There's always a rainbow after the storm, somewhere, and oftentimes patience is truly a gift, a virtue.

Play games and make up your own. Play Simon Says with yoga poses.

And, of course, laugh with your family! Even during challenges, it is much better on your mind, body, and spirit when you try to find something to be grateful for and always look for an opening to laugh and become lighthearted.

Get on FaceTime with family and friends. Keep in contact with those you love and care about, which you can choose to extend outward to those in need who perhaps you physically do not know, remembering that spiritually we are all one.

May we all take time to reach out perhaps a little extra at this time. How about healing a relationship you have lost because of pettiness (which is even more obvious during this time)? Even if you search your soul and still feel it was the other person's fault, who really cares in the end whose fault it was? Really. Count your blessings and remember contact doesn't have to be in person—be creative. I am sending loving energy from my heart space to yours.

Remain Unattached, Fully Alive, Free to Be Here Now

September 4, 2020

Darrell, Satori, and me in Cambria for a short vacation.

Satori awakening breaking through another aha moment: I must meet the challenge of going even deeper into the reservoir of acceptance and diving into an even clearer depth (view) of my inner self, my soul, fully rediscovering that I did in fact, and I do in fact, hang on to life — be it a memory, a thought, a person, or, yes, a thing—more than I believed.

Awesome! This means more chains to release, more space to open up and receive—space to live my next moments and not my past. That's my recent challenge.

My loving family and friends remind me it has been only two months since Darrell took flight. I am aware that I miss him, and I allow the emotions to come up and move to a recent gratitude thought. Darrell and I would talk about this, more in our younger years, if one of us were to leave before the other. I will say that it's rougher than I thought—really not something you think about.

Is it wrong to hang on to a good memory? Who's to say it's wrong or right? There is not, or shouldn't be, any black or white but rather blite (what you have found is right for you). What I have uncovered from my life's journey is this: When I am hanging on to even a good memory from the past, it will keep me from fully enjoying the present moment, perhaps leading me

87

to judge or compare. Compare what? Compare *what was* with the actual *what is* that we're living right now.

Do we hang on to good, even not-so-good, memories in order to protect ourselves from the uncertainty of the future? This is one of the types of questions I ask myself through meditation. My recent life-changing experience has brought me to dig even deeper (excavating time) and once again (and again) reconnect with who I am. Truly, I am going back, which is always an adventure in trusting, accepting, and trusting again. Period.

The period does not diminish the beautiful entity written of the present, now past. It offers the possibility of a newfound truth, reminding me that for now it is my belief of life but that knowing it doesn't mean an end to a newfound sentence or paragraph to the story. It's a story that never ends; it's written page by page, word by word, to be read by my heart—messages cherished for future reflection yet nonattached so that I can continue fully living.

I am not my memories of the past. I am not the me in my future imagination. I am here in this moment, fully alive and present. When I make the decision to be present in the now, I am free, already home, alive to just be. I do believe in visualization and imagination of future moments, but not at the expense of missing living fully now.

As I begin a new chapter of my life, I will title it "Letting Go Again"—letting go of not only memories, so I can experience this moment fresh, but also the accumulation of things. Many years of happiness, my happiness, our happiness. These, too, shall pass, as hard as we may try to hold on. I want to be and therefore do the best with the time I have here.

I found that I was more attached to things—my home, my yard, my neighbors and friends—and as I said, there's no right or wrong. But how do people move into the next moment carrying over their shoulders heavy garbage baggage but also wonderful luggage (Neiman Marcus) and have the strength to begin and welcome their new journeys?

How do we step into our new journeys, even new days, new moments, reaching back into our bags and pulling out memories, people, things, and items that weigh us down (and I have found the happiness can be the heaviest) and remain fully in the moment, the now, the only real life to live and truly experience?

Breathe. This doesn't mean I don't keep the preciousness of the memory. I am just more aware, and I do the best I can from where I am and let it go. I ask, "Am I living the present moment, or am I going back and comparing the past beautiful memories to the present moment?" And if the latter, then guess what the present moment is? Gone. In the past. This is one thing I really try to communicate with the little yogis: you can't fully be in more than one time zone.

How am I truly, fully, alive? Fully living now while remaining in a wonderful past memory? How am I able to be me now when, quite humorously, I have one foot in the now and one foot in the past?

OK. Let's stop here, take a deep breath in, release any uncomfortable feelings, and enjoy the exploration. It's a trip, so as if on a trip, enjoy the exploration and discoveries. It's so much fun as we are reawakening to life, unpacking and traveling light so we can truly, fully, live in the moment and be freely, heartfully, present.

Let's take a new trip in each moment of this Labor Day weekend, moment by moment, breath by breath, and explore. Happy discoveries!

Fall Away from Thinking, and Feel Soulfully: Release and Feel with the Intelligence of a Child

April 30, 2021

I continue to love, live, and learn through the gift of children. Tamsin's beautiful mother messaged me a video of Tamsin teaching yoga to her teddy. (YouTube: "Smilin Rylan Kids Yoga - Yoga with My Teddy," https://www.youtube.com/watch?v=6aWaygP9LTc.)

It brought those fluttering, warming, loving butterflies to my heart and also my gut (the center of our will and our power to be who we really are).

It reflects a knowing that there is nothing to judge, no one to blame—"I am free to be no one but me," a child of God.

Lily and Stella making a picture frame of love for a Valentine's gift.

Living and breathing like children takes us falling away from the repetitive thinking we often innocently slip into. We begin falling back, back into a child's knowing of unknowing, and life becomes much more real—a dance of truly letting loose, rocking out, and living the moment of now, being free to just be!

When I teach yoga, it gives me so much hope and reassurance to witness the connection and openness of parents such as Tamsin's who demonstrate a beautiful presence—one of guiding instead of dictating. While they always have their children's safety at the forefront, they don't allow it to steal their children's authenticity, or their children's freedom to be who they truly are.

We were and forever will be Smilin' Rylan Kids Yoga. Love truly is *all*—just feel it here. Cheri and her grandson Landyn. He truly lit up our yoga class!

Parents who allow their children to simply be are encouraging them to maintain their wonder through exploration of self as well as others, which is such a gift. As for children, it is natural, or just is, and life becomes (or remains) a mystical journey, not their parents', grandparents', or others' scripts. They write their own scripts as they move from moment to moment continuing to live out their true selves.

Again, I feel I should emphasize that parents should of course keep safety at center yet encourage exploration without fueling children's dependence on labeled answers to their discoveries—their inner travels—with their discovering (or uncovering) being their own breakthrough of new life. It's often a newness of simplicity in the midst of (at times) the overly complex, serious world of adults.

When we're teaching children the meaning of *namaste*—actually, they could teach us—we become still, with our hands in prayer at our hearts. We together say, "Namaste," extending it from our hearts to all others.

Here is one of my own definitions for *namaste* (and children live the message): the love and light in me acknowledge and celebrate the love and light in you, and together we shine, bringing this world that much closer to a oneness of love and therefore peace.

Can you feel the loving energy through the picture?

They are able to take time and celebrate love. It *beams*.

You can feel the smiles as they celebrate oneness. Kindness radiates through their physical bodies, and energy is felt in the room!

Journal or meditation: When was the last time you looked at someone and wholeheartedly saw, felt, the goodness in that person reflecting from the goodness in you? This question serves (yes, serves) to make you hesitate, or nudges you, a soft voice whispering to the deepest part of your spirit, your soul, and presenting you with the choice to go deeper within and reflect.

Therein lies your blessing, one of many that can serve to return you—time to live, love, learn, and laugh a bit at yourself. Dig deep and celebrate the freedom to be you, giving others the space to do it as well.

Because you know what will come next? "What you see in me, I can see in you" rings true, and peace flows.

So, this week, as I quiet my loving angel writers from above and begin to close this magical experience of being their hands (loving it), may we once again take a cleansing breath as we begin again in this lifetime moment, bringing smiles from our hearts to our lips and sharing them brightly, no words needed. Love from here to you all!

Look Above, Below, Past, and Forward, but Be within Now

February 26, 2021

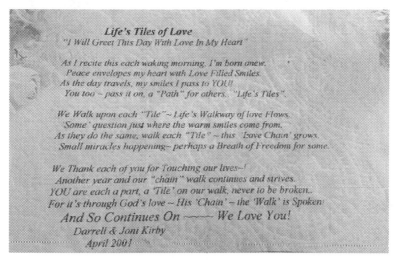

I have written more than two hundred poems, usually for family and friends, often dropping by their homes to deliver them, along with treats, and run (not to be seen). So much fun!

I look past, and I'm reminded how much time I worked toward my parents' hopefully being proud of me. As a little girl, all the way to graduation, and actually until my late twenties, I sought their approval. Of course, not until I started my excavation back to my self would you or anyone else be able to tell me, "Joni, you are losing precious time with your self trying to earn love."

Journal or meditation: Are you still living for the approval of others—family, friends, or acquaintances on Facebook, Twitter, or other social media? Perhaps the first step is to step outside yourself and be honest, and sometimes that takes the time. We tend to tell our selves excuses. That of course requires strengthening our awareness muscles.

Begin approving of your self. Stop feeling or being a victim and searching outside to fill you up. You truly hold the key—or, better yet, the tools to begin the excavating. Failing to take this step will eventually lead to disappointment, frustration, and even anger associated with the fear that you are not enough, without your ever tapping into the deep, not-yet-realized knowingness that you are. When you try and fail to meet others' expectations and approval, it often causes even more feelings of inadequacy, of not living up to what you feel others want of you. Then the cycle begins, more often than not the blame game.

For me, my inner uncovering of self was characterized by the love and patience I gave my self. I feel that is so very important. Yes, it was and still is at times very challenging, but that's where I would acknowledge all the satori moments presented to me, I believe, from my self. I began communicating from my heart. So often people don't spend time relearning the importance of sharing from within and demonstrating courage balanced with consideration when communicating. It's such a valuable paradigm for nurturing healthy relationships.

Journey back to your self and rediscover who you are and always have been. There's no need for outside approval. It can be and is nice to hear, but you are unattached to it.

I learned how important it is to be gentle and spend time with me. Journaling daily since my twenties has helped me gain time and space in rediscovering my self, and it continues to be a part of my life. I enjoy the exploration and the treasures I discover, or uncover.

If we aren't careful, we tend to turn to external events, people, and projects to bring (fill us up with) happiness. Yes, I love massages, chocolate, mani-pedis, and new clothes, but if you're leaning on those things for happiness, remember they're fleeting. Exterior pleasures are fun and exciting, but if that's where you go to feel good, it will eventually leave an emptiness, until you're planning the next event that you feel will bring you pleasure and fill up the inner void. So we begin a cycle of achieving pleasure, leading at times to addiction, when all the while it's right there waiting inside of us.

When we can *feel* love, contentment, and fulfillment just by being with our selves in the moment, nothing can replace it. We are able to give with no strings attached. Here's the thing: it takes becoming very brave and willing to point the finger back to you. You have a desire to go within and begin the excavation back to your inner self. That finger is pointing with and in the love that is, was, and will always be waiting within.

So, with patient awareness and so much uncovering as well as releasing, I was able and open to see how I was looking desperately to earn love, approval, and brownie points. I wanted so badly for my parents to be proud of me, and I still remember how my emotional need to earn left my inner self so unhappy. Another later-in-life rainbow or miracle? You bet! Because I experienced these unhealthy expectations and emotions, I was a better mom and actually all-around person. My parents were unaware of my inner insecurity. They were busy in their lives, with four kids, work, and on and on, as the story goes. Communication, not dictatorship, is crucial. I am speaking of communication that is well balanced in courage and consideration, with awareness driving in the front seat.

I did in fact make it to the top ten of my graduating class, and—wouldn't you know?—I didn't walk the line. I didn't even attend the graduation ceremony. All the years I spent thinking I would earn my parents' love and approval through my grades. I truly believed making good grades and being at the top of my class was the way to their hearts. I wish I would have listened to my heart's space back then, but there was a gift awaiting. And I don't regret one bit!

My parents didn't try to talk me into either decision—whether to go and be part of graduation. I remember that brought me even more sadness and disappointment.

I go into the past to revisit, to remind myself, how fleeting accomplishments can be. They are wonderful and do serve a purpose, but they don't fill us up. I don't go back in the past to find regret; I go back to remind myself how I felt, and I use it as a gift for now and the future.

I was trying to hurt my parents by not going to the graduation, and really what I was doing was hurting myself, of course. What a *be-you-to-full* miracle—the rainbows of awareness that grow out of hurts and, if we allow them to, will guide us on our continued journeys to be.

This picture—of a mended heart, stitched up—was hung in my yoga room in Hanford for years, reminding me and others to heal and allow our hearts to fill our spaces and to forgive not only ourselves but others.

Once we work through some deep self-discovery, we can in no way continue to feel blame. It was I who needed to learn to forgive, and through forgiveness, freedom waits to open the magic of each moment.

I realized that no matter how many phone calls I made or how many attempts I made to bring merit for Joni, whom I had labeled "the third daughter," earning my parents' love was not the answer. I eventually learned I was perfect being me. Feeling we need to aspire to something besides who we really are is a facade, a temporary fix—fleeting.

I believe that parents do the best they can through the paradigms they are looking through. I have had many try to argue that point with me, but what makes you feel better? Does it make you feel justified to find ways your parents failed you? I stopped that anger/fear mist, and at times when it tries to sneak back in, I'm not comfortable with the feeling it brings, the emotions left.

Understanding the fear mist and choosing otherwise is a much more love-filled choice. Everything becomes clear and beautiful once again. You will often hear me say that I started telling my daughter Krisi that, when it comes to her parenting, I'm in support of however she chooses to diverge from how I chose to raise her. She is incredible, and why would we not as parents want our children to change what didn't work for them so that future generations also have a choice?

By looking within, I was set free to return to truly loving myself, again and again. I looked up to feel so much reassurance about looking forward as I continued being within each moment. At times I look below, grounding myself, as I travel in this incredible human body and navigate this journey, choosing to take care of it and use it wisely.

I was ready to be there 100 percent for my dad and mom when my dad was diagnosed in 2008 with lung cancer. This is going to sound crazy, but I have some of the most wonderful memories of that time. My dad became stripped of everything he knew to be, he was humbled, and I was humbled!

I was able to be with him—at times it was just him and me—and with tears, he did his best to apologize, and I could feel his love. This was a gift he gave to himself, but I received it with open arms.

I didn't dread driving them to Fresno for chemo. My mom and I would go to breakfast, talk, and at times cry. We were discovering things about each other we'd never had time to talk about before. At times like these, often we become less guarded, we begin to let go of our outer labels some, and the closeness truly guides us through these challenges of life.

My dad shared more openly with me those last few months than he (or we) did all the years prior. While he was hooked up and receiving chemo, the stories he told—I truly feel the last months of his life I was able to get to know my dad, and I am forever filled with gratitude.

I was the last family member with my dad the night he took flight. In fact, I was giving permission for him to fly, sharing with him that during Darrell's own appointment the following morning, the oncologist would be giving him news I'd already received: the cancer was back. It's so true how cancer can bring so many beautiful miracles, often hidden, at times wrapped up times very tightly, until much later. Unless we dig deep within, we have no idea how to allow the butterfly to break free and take flight. And the rainbow appears—miracles begin to spring from what at the time we felt was tragic.

May we look above for the strength that comes from within; below for our faith, our foundation, the grounding as we walk through life; to the past for remembering our gifts received through experiences; to the future for our vision; and within for the love we have for ourselves as it blossoms and expands out, unbiased, to people, nature, and all creation, all the while discovering, receiving, and creating heaven on earth.

"Peace Begins with Me"

April 7, 2020

Yes, peace truly does begin within me. The little yogis are so open to remembering that simple yet challenging fact. Watch as they practice what could easily be forgotten as time moves them through their little lives in the blink of an eye: "Smilin Rylan Kids Yoga Peace Begins with Me," https://www.youtube.com/shorts/h_aNBtfIRzo. They use their fingers to create a meditative movement, taking them into peace. Of course, this comes after their jumping around, practicing monkey mind, which we as adults can really relate to.

Why is it, then, that we tend to look outside ourselves for that peace we all say we want—for the perfect mate, the perfect someone to *make us* happy—and never quite reach the peace of knowing it is right within ourselves?

There is nothing outside me that will provide a lasting peace that I don't already have within my inner self in this moment of now. Yes, at any time, the question is, Where is my attention?

There is nowhere to go. I am perfectly where I'm supposed to be: home. And that statement is literally true for all of us right now. What I am talking about is the peace within that brings us home, with nothing more to search for.

No Facebook entry to attach my moments to, nowhere to go, no one to be, just me with my self. And, as I say often to people who start their sentences with "just me," I drop the *just* and say, "I am with my self." All the while I am perfectly at rest with my own presence, my innermost feeling of

98

peace. Then, and only then, am I able to find my place right here with me, in this beautiful moment of now, at one in this present peace-begins-with-me moment.

Circle of love: Smilin' Rylan kids went to the Remington, bringing peace and joy to the seniors. It was beautiful. It was in the Hanford Sentinel.

So let's all as families gather together in the now, with no place to go, no place to be, only becoming present as families, practicing the meditation portion along with children.

Repeat, growing quieter each time, "Peace begins with me," and feel the nothingness (*no-thing-ness*), the nowness of peace. Enjoy your time becoming silent and still, and *breathe*!

The Lightness: The Joy and Peace of Letting Go

April 9, 2021

I enjoy being in my new little home filled with Love and Faith, my fur babies.

My chosen family is such a gift, and I celebrate the moments I'm with them accordingly. We spend time together, not watching TV or looking at our computers or iPhones (well, Maximus sometimes). We value our time together as if every visit is our last. I ask myself that question often: What if this were my last moment to live here? I return to the presence of now and celebrate!

I love my life, I loved my past life, I love the present, and I am always aware of whether I'm too attached to any of those time zones of life. I feel my emotions. Sometimes I have a good, long cry over missing someone (Darrell, especially, these past months) and take a deep breath in. Sometimes I take several. And then several more. I allow the energy to move through me, understanding that stuck energy comes out in not-such-pleasant ways.

Take a breath, go within, and ask your self how often—this is where you have to get real—you are actually living in the moment, how often you are present in the moment, and how well you are able to leave the past, remembering it yet releasing attachment. How about thinking a lot about the future? Addressing such questions takes awareness, courage, and practice. Practice? Yes, practice being present.

I am extremely blessed—I refuse to call it luck—blessed that, for the most part, I am able to live in my moments and live them fully. When I am asked how I have been able to aspire to this place in my life, a place where I feel the peace more often, a nonphysical place where I am actually living the moment at any location, what's my reply?

There are so many different lifetime satori moments I attribute to guiding me, delivering me—at times by giving me a swift kick in the butt. Of course, you have already read about my experiences and practices, and I enjoy presenting them in different ways. I know through all the years, many would (and continue to) express to me that satori moments hit them at different times. Sometimes they'd heard several analogies and, for whatever reason, that particular example or explanation was just perfect for their present awakenings and many to follow.

Untrainings are often about journaling. I love giving and receiving the energy of love.

Journaling (for years), meditating, mirror and laughing meditation, yoga, nature walks, writing appreciation, painting and delivering kindness rocks, baking, "The Work" (Byron Katie), music

Now, versus how I was years ago, when I am distracted and not present, I am much more able and open to catch the moment's lack of realness and return sooner into the present moment of now. I feel each is in fact my lifetime to be lived fully, to be as alive as possible, unhurried.

A class full of amazing Smilin' Rylan yogis—and seldom did I have to ask them to be present on their lifetime mats. They were like sponges.

During this beautiful time of year, I reflect often as I walk the beach, open to rediscovering yet another rebirth, uncovering any blocks that seem to keep me from lightness as I track my footprints in the sand. I am brave enough to call myself on any hidden baggage (really getting good at that) I have not unpacked (or have perhaps repacked) and to allow myself to let it go or at least start the unpacking. I avoid simply rinsing it just enough to put it back as clean—it still stinks!

Leaving more space, I plan on being in this lifetime for several more years. So I'll keep on unpacking, rejoicing, and having fun.

Baggage, of course, could be material things that we hang on to that take away our joy of the moment, replacing it with a constant fear of either losing those things or not being able to keep up with the Joneses.

It truly takes courage to look in the mirror, looking deep into your eyes, and ask yourself, your soul, the question, Who am I?

I was definitely in a happy place as I guided the group through untrainings.

While presenting some of the untrainings, I would ask individuals to stand in front of the mirror and focus on their pupils for a length of time, looking and feeling deeply.

After they spent a couple of minutes just looking into their own eyes (which I would recommend to everyone—it's amazing how difficult it is to just look into your eyes and find your self in the mirror), I would then suggest that people talk out loud to their selves. Although silence is wonderful—and I do feel silence is even more transforming than words—I will share that, personally, talking to my self out loud at first helped my mind better relax (become calm) and not be as apt to get distracted or jump on the crazy train of drama. I now go to silence and easily fall back in love once again, with my self welcoming me back. And once again, all is well, and all is one.

A more troublesome type of baggage—one that can steal our moments from us, literally rob us of living the moment—comprises not so much the material things but rather the emotional items we've packed, such as memories (that are no longer real) from our past that do not serve our souls. Those can become the heaviest baggage to carry. They rob us of the preciousness of life, and oftentimes we don't even notice. We can take steps to lighten our loads and play as we unpack.

Here we go, another Friday, ushering in the weekend. May we all begin in the present moment now. Make a commitment to practices that nurture silence and heighten awareness. These are gifts you give yourself! I love gifts, both giving and receiving, but of all the gifts I have received, these are by far the most lasting and precious of all. These gifts never become tiring to unwrap and enjoy.

Dance More, Laugh More, Love More, Let Go, and Live More

March 5, 2021

Have you ever noticed that you can feel down and out, even stuck, in the mist of fear, or paralyzed in PMS (poor-me-syndrome) quicksand, but you can let go and play when a child runs into your arms? Perhaps you even dance and all of a sudden nothing matters but that moment. The joy of laughter, the joy of dancing, the joy of becoming (going back to being) a child.

It was truly amazing: after several busy days, since I hadn't been in my new little home for very long, I welcomed and felt very blessed to spend a beautiful afternoon with friends Christy, Alysia, and the beautiful little Alyvia. I was once again taken into the moment.

While we were dancing, Alyvia made a comment to me in her soft, sweet voice: "Wow, you are pretty. Pretty eyes." That literally stopped me in my dance step. I was taken aback. I was feeling sweaty and naturally smelly from totally rocking out. We had been dancing up a storm! Not that I was thinking anything, but I definitely wasn't feeling particularly pretty. She wasn't seeing the outer-body presence.

But rather, she felt the light in my eyes, the happiness, love, and laughter as we danced together. Not my exterior—not my sweaty smell or garlic breath. "Wow, you are pretty." It was one of those memories that you're so thankful someone caught on tape. So not only do I have the gift of being able to rewind the tape in my awareness memory, but I now have an actual caught-on-tape video.

I have often shared the analogy I used since my daughter (Krisi) was a little girl. I still do share it often with others. Here it is: We all have our own video players constantly filming our moments. We must ask the question (which turns on awareness), Am I going to feel good, or is a retake an option I will make as I rewind my day before laying my head on my pillow for the night?

For me, laying my head down on my pillow, I would rather have the film of myself dancing through each moment as if Alyvia were right there in a blink of a moment's taping, delivering the joyfulness we have available in life. Yes, of course, this isn't always the dance we would prefer, and at those times we must call forth our own Alyvias from within our souls. Yes, grab your partner of choice and feel the freedom to live as if this truly were the last dance of this physical life.

I have learned and continue to experience that when I have a chance to dance with life instead of sitting it out, I never regret my end-of-the-day video review. Of course, I also enjoy time journaling my day with the gratefulness of choices made from love instead of (what at times seems the easiest) fear-based thoughts and actions. I not only dance myself to sleep, but I feel I am flying high in the knowingness that I have lived the day fully with no regrets.

If I'm journaling on the past day, rewinding my video-awareness tape, and I find it doesn't leave me feeling at peace, I rejoice in that also.

I rejoice knowing my internal landscape has become that much lusher and more heightened for next time. Prepared, I will choose to grab a dance partner (often my self) and dance my heart out as a situation or a choice comes my way and I reflect on my replay—one that I know at the end of the day will fill my heart with all those fluttering butterflies, reminding me how special my time here is. And I once again celebrate!

Here we go (come) again. Another week ends, and the weekend's dance floor is ready, awaiting your moves. Get out there and shake a leg. Pick your partner or simply dance with your self. Take a breath, moving into each dance move with the rhythm of love. Enjoy as you create your own beat to the music of life and rock out. Watch how love moves, creating magical songs—songs written within your soul. Dance your heart out. I dare you.

Another Satori Moment Brings Me Back to Life in the Moment of Now!

June 4, 2021

Once again, another satori moment. Feeling blessed, extremely blessed, as each day I begin with a walk on the beach—or, I should say, playtime on the beach—with Love and Faith.

From what I hear from the locals, it's unusual that the dolphins were coming so close to the shore and jumping out of the water. They seemed to be showing off.

That morning, there was no one there except for a couple and me (and of course Love and Faith). Truly it was magical. I was in awe of God's creation, but I'm in awe many moments of the day, especially when I'm in nature or around children and of course fur babies.

There is a deep knowing in my heart, in my spirit, especially when I'm connected and aligned within my soul. It's a knowing that we miss out on in life when we're searching for something more than, or different from, what our present moment is offering us right before our hearts' or our minds' eyes.

Each satori moment offers a deeper knowingness of life's miracles, life's gifts. This most recent one was not long after I moved to Cambria from Hanford in December.

Wow. It was like I was coming home to the ocean—the ocean is what I grew up with as my backyard—and because I am on my last chapters of this physical life, I found myself searching the ocean for the magic, forgetting, not remembering, that it is right before my eyes, my heart, within each moment that I am open to and present in.

My satori moment was a reminder that the magic is in each moment. That the main thing is to keep the main thing the main thing. Ready? And the main thing is that it is, was, and will always be within; the magic comes from within.

Searching for that spout from a whale or a glimpse of dolphins or otters—yes, looking without for the next best thing to come into my view—all the while, I was missing the magic of each moment right before my eyes. We miss the specialness of the now when we look for something in our minds' eyes that we feel is the trophy moment, which is in fact within our hearts.

Of course, I'm just another crazy person to so many, and I don't hold back my heart's voice. On occasion, someone I'm walking with or sharing time with will stop and begin searching, straining to catch a picture-perfect scene of ocean life on the horizon, missing the blessings of the moment. The present is a gift right in the moment—it could be as beautiful as somebody walking by with a loving smile and sparkle in their eyes.

We (my chosen family) celebrated our birthdays together as well as the differences on the outside—age; gender; hair, eye, and skin color; size; and so forth—all the while remembering we are all the same in our hearts.

Humans are a beautiful species, creation, and individuals come in all ages, sizes, and colors, each unique yet the same, in my eyes. We are missing the beauty of the human creation if we find only differences (and fail to honor the wonders of uniqueness) without the belief and knowingness that we are all the same in our hearts.

Perhaps we miss a single wildflower deciding to take root, peeking through the carpet of ground cover. Sometimes I feel as if I'm looking at a painted portrait—it just seems so perfect in all its imperfections (weeds, to some) and so beautifully colored. I'm reminded that nature offers us beautiful differences, as well as opportunities every day to see the canvas in which each moment itself becomes the painter, the artist.

When I am not seeking something but rather taking in the moment, I catch the spout from the whale, the dolphins playing in the ocean, the otters on their backs, the perfect flower as it touches my soul, and the smile from a stranger (now an acquaintance), and I am grateful for it all.

So as another week comes to an end, preparing the canvas for the weekend, I celebrate my neighbors here getting used to my singing, living the moment through a dance movement, or raising my arms to the creator giving thanks, as my past but never-forgotten neighbors in Hanford had become accustomed to (I hope). Take a leap of faith and sing your heart's story of appreciation as you create your work of art and begin your painting of glimpses into the wonders of your play of life.

Love to everyone, every moment, everywhere, in what we call *time*.

Be a Superhero

July 22, 2019

When Rylan was a little hero, barely a year old, we started playing superhero. He loved the idea of saving people. I would fly and stay several days at a time with my superhero—what a blessing! We'd wake to a new adventure as the sun introduced the new day, and Rylan would eagerly begin the day's adventure, experiencing each moment and then surrendering to secret garden as the sun traveled and darkness arrived.

Rylan's secret garden always had the same theme: he was a superhero, in a different adventure each night. At bedtime, he would jump into bed anticipating the magical journey about to begin. With his Jmom as the storyteller, Rylan knew the story would be wonderful!

The story always began the same way: "Once upon a time, there was a boy named Rylan. At night, he fell into a deep slumber, surrendering to deep sleep. An angel would appear and gently touch his forehead …" Using my fingers as a magical wand, I would softly tap three times, and Rylan would become Superman Rylan, his first love of the characters he would become. Early on, the story would not have a villain. Instead, one or more of his family members would be in trouble (Mom and Dad as well as his Vovo, aunt Mar, and grandfather). He particularly loved when his fur baby, Chanel, needed his superpowers.

Darrell's T-shirt reads "My Grandson Is My Hero."

But soon heroes would change. As he became older, Spider-Man Rylan was a favorite of his. He loved that he could "shoot webs"! I started including a villain who would kidnap his Vovo (or any family member I would include), and Smilin' Rylan would save the day! My beautiful fur baby Satori often was his partner. He loved Satori and once told his mom that Satori had saved him. She, too, was an earthly angel.

We can all choose to save the day! We are superheroes. At times, we may lose our way and forget who we really are, but the inner hero never leaves—it's just pushed to the background.

During that lapse of consciousness, we may choose and possibly feel more comfortable being the victim. At times, we may even play the role of villain, perhaps speaking an unkind word, passing judgment, having a heartless thought, gossiping—all poison to the soul.

Satori and Rylan had a deep connection. He often included Satori in his adventures.

This week, the little yogis will be learning (relearning) more about awareness, which they already are aware of. We are going to share examples. They love to share their stories, and we welcome tales of carrying out acts of kindness and helping others—being heroes. We encourage the little yogis not to back down in sharing their acts of heroism! How important it is to keep and unwrap this gift we are born with, not allowing it be pushed out of sight to lie unused and gather dust. Just watch a baby … so aware.

What happens as we grow? I explained to my daughter when she was young, as well as to my grandchildren (blood and by choice), that awareness is like using a video camera in every moment. Imagine stepping outside ourselves and watching as if each night before sleep we will rewind the tape of the day and watch what we gave and what we received. I know, for myself, I have wished I could erase and take two, or rerecord, on some of my days. But I believe it feels so much better to be a light in the world than to sit and complain in the darkness.

Love is truly all around us, every day, everywhere. Be as a child, an infant, and heighten your awareness. Your light will shine: You'll notice the beauty in a baby's smile. When you meet the gaze of a stranger as you pass each other, there will be love. It is our awareness and being in the moment that brings the light of love present! It's the warmth that floods our hearts. It's presence, it's joy, it's peace, and it's love.

Children know this—until life happens and amnesia sets in. But we can open our hearts and reawaken once again that feeling of being a superhero, and we can live through our light, spreading kindness. Just imagine.

*Rylan's daddy and Chanel, Jmom, and Rylan
playing Super Fur Baby and Rylan.*

Live as If This Is Your Last Visit, and Live the Light of Life through Love

July 27, 2019

One of my visits to see and be with Rylan in person was extra special (even though each hello and goodbye was filled with tears of love and foreverness).

When Rylan and I were together, we definitely lived in our conscious state of being. As we explain to our little yogis during discussions about what "living in the moment" truly means, self-awareness is the first of four gifts they are born with. They really receive it openly and seem to understand this more than many adults do.

As we begin to unwrap the second gift, the inner stillness voice (consciousness), we will be exploring how we play life using our four gifts, unaware of a beginning or end to each gift's giving but enjoying the magical experiences that early life opens us to.

As life unfolds, for most of us, we tend to forget about these priceless gifts. It's as if we wrap them back up and forget about these gifts of peace and the joy they bring to our lives, woven in as they become part of each moment.

Rather, we choose to live very few of our moments. Most moments we spend living a past, therefore rerun, future movie composed and even directed in our subconscious. We're unaware of the replay every morning as we step out of bed. It's what we know, what we become comfortable with.

I have read that about 97 percent of our lives we live in our unconscious, or subconscious. For most of us, as we grow up, we live only 3 to 4 percent of our time awakened, living consciously.

It's the difference between entering a room in darkness and choosing to stumble around and turning a light on and truly seeing what is present—except instead of an actual room, it's our souls, our hearts' minds, that bring light to the moment through conscious awareness. Free to be present and truly alive, even for a moment in time, experience consciously within the voice of stillness.

There is a difference between being positive and being proactive. Yes, being "positive" has become a label that is not very positive. You have probably heard often—and possibly have said it yourself—that positive people aren't looking at reality. We all have probably heard that judgment or have been accused of being positive and unrealistic, even "not truthful," which is definitely not a compliment.

So what's the difference? Proactive people do face reality, in the heart's mind of understanding there is a choice—a choice of how we are going to respond to any situation. Yes, we all have a choice. Even if you have told yourself you don't, you do! Be *response-able*, or choose to be reactive! Be responsible for your actions. Isn't that what we as parents do our best to teach our children?

Proactive people use their awareness and conscious voice of stillness to drop into the space between what happens and their responses to it. They do in fact face reality with the light on, not in darkness!

Unfortunately, some who live most of their time in darkness love to label proactive people as positive. They are just simply forgetting they, too, can turn the light on. It takes courage, but that's where true peace and happiness reside. It may be painful in the beginning, but eventually it will bring a sense of peace, turning the painful times into a knowing that you had a choice, and then the pain subsides. Perhaps the pain won't subside all the time, but you'll feel aligned with who you really are, and that's what all of us want regardless of whether we know it at this present moment, taking responsibility in that space, in a grounded realness: the space place.

Rylan loved to hug and carry out acts of kindness in so many ways! He would get just as excited to spread his acts of kindness as he was to receive them.

This week at Smilin' Rylan's Kids Yoga, we are spreading acts of giving kindness to those in need, those who are homeless, with no judgments or assumptions about how they may have gotten into the situation. One very special young man brought up that his parents said they are lazy and should work. It was so obvious this little yogi did not agree but was simply repeating what was being scripted to him.

Kindness comes with no judgment, no strings. Plant the seeds, as the song says, and let it go—some will die, and some will live. Plant them anyways! Kindness planted will grow, and we may never know how it grows, but we plant it anyway! So throw some seeds; plant your kindness! Live in the now, and live in the light!

Naomi and I started Smilin' Rylan Kids Yoga in honor of my grandson Rylan. During one of the playshops, we practiced a yoga routine to the version of "Love Train" featuring Jason Mraz. We presented it in the beautiful area of downtown Hanford. It was a huge success. Continue reading and opening your heart space. Life is so amazing.

Throw Your Hearts Up, and Let Your Love Spread through the World

November 18, 2019

Hearing the words of "Being Kind" would touch your heart deeply! We are dedicated to bringing the entire meaning and experience of yoga to the Smilin' Rylan yogis in as many ways as we can, and that suggests no end to the experiencing!

"Well, my heart starts sinkin', and I'm thinkin', *What's the reason why we're holding back from being kind? What's the disease?* But then I sense *we are fine.* It'll all happen one small act at a time."

"Feeling grateful today. Never thought this day would come where I would feel it and say that each and every one of us has paved the way doing good and now we're all just moving up. When I'm kind to you, you pay it forward. This is how we build *trust.*"

Then the chorus, which the kiddos belt out: "Throw your hearts up. Let it fly high. Let your love for all the world spread through the skies. Let it drop down. Let it all go, spreading kindness to every single living soul. Can you see *your* love for me shining through? 'Cause what you see in me, I can see in you, and soon enough, you and me—we'll be out of time, and kindness will be all we can leave behind."

We are throwing our hearts up, allowing our love to spread over the sky. I just noticed my husband, Darrell, is watching (to the left, hands in pockets). I miss his physical form, but I'm so glad and blessed he is no longer suffering.

So open your hearts up and let them fly free. Let your love for all the world spread through the sky, spreading kindness to every single living soul!

And, on that note, what if we had thanksgiving every day—if every day we celebrated thankfulness? Just Imagine!

Thanksgiving Every Day, with Everyone Present

November 24, 2019

What if we had thanksgiving every day? If every day we celebrated thankfulness? If every day everyone gathered as a family, actually sitting together at a table, sharing a meal together, perhaps sharing words of gratitude around the table? Have we lost that special time with family?

What if we perhaps shared how wonderful it is to be unique, accepting and embracing one another's uniqueness?

Just maybe the once-a-year Thanksgiving would become more ordinary, yet somehow more powerful, possibly minimizing or keeping at bay some of the anxiety that family gatherings can cause. Perhaps by coming together more often with the soul-filled desire to welcome everyone's uniqueness and love one another as we have been told to do since we were very small, we could all put into motion that simple but at times challenging act of love. So call up those family members and get together this weekend.

It seems we hear more and more people talking about dreading Thanksgiving or other holidays. Often family coming together opens the opportunity for hot spots inside all of us to activate, for our buttons to be pushed. Just maybe we could all work through it a lot quicker if every day we simply gathered with family under the same roof. OK, OK, I know that's a little much. How about once a month, maybe?

Gather together celebrating differences while being present—having awareness presence in the moment. I just wonder, *What if we put it in law?* I'm just kidding.

We all have heard it said that we at times treat Facebook friends better than we do our families or our closest friends and loved ones. For the likes? We're teaching to our little ones with our actions, our habits, and then using our words to tell them to get off their own gadgets.

What if we started confronting that habit within ourselves, paying attention and putting down our phones so that we can be truly present in not only word but deed? Present with the ones we say we love and care about the most? I really believe everyone would benefit, and life would become a journey of love, spreading like a love wildfire, moment to moment.

So here's to thanksgiving every day.

Sometimes You Make Your Dream Vacation the Now and It's Magical

January 29, 2021

A magical trip around the hospital halls can become an adventure or can turn Rylan's Make-A-Wish dream vacation to Disney World into a reality. What is your dream moment? Are you willing to explore? Imagine?

If you remember from either my untrainings or a past entry, one of the four gifts we are blessed to be born with is the gift of using our imagination for inspiration, in spirit. It's a gift that often seems to be left untouched, unopened. What happens to that gift as the days, months, and years go by?

I don't accept (humbly) people describing me as someone who "dances to her own beat"—I also like to include that I move to my own dance of life. I believe in choosing my dance, and the frequent unwrapping of my four gifts guides me as I continue on my make-a-wish in each moment. I choose to wish and to choose to have it come true: my choice to live fully my dance of life, speaking through energy that is open to all, all the time. You dance, too, to your own music and beat of life! Yes! Honestly, together is better.

There truly is nowhere to go. I am already present, already home, in this moment. I choose to be home and free. When I allow my me to deviate from what I know to be real, I feel the disconnect, and I don't like the feeling that follows.

Secret garden—time to find the space of peace and stillness. We grown-ups would eventually find so much more happiness (from within) if we would return to the habit of meditation! Savasana is a time to be at peace with one's self.

Now is the perfect time to become still and silent and feel your I (gift of awareness) becoming present as you unwrap and consider, Where did we lose the ability to welcome with wonder and enthusiasm each moment we are blessed with? The magical experience of the now?

We can take a simple walk down the street, and it becomes an adventure of wholeness, newness, as we look through our eyes—the projector—and we become directors. Each of us, then, is the main character. Life becomes an adventure, a journey, as we have the choice of love or fear in any moment.

As I have shared before, Krisi and I have often talked about making our own movie of the day, though it could also be a movie of the moment. I would say to her, "OK. Let's make a movie. You're the main character, and I'm the cocharacter. Let's make a good, funny scene!"

Sometimes, in stressful situations, we would come up with just feeling like we have control of the next moment, of ourselves. How do we write our screenplays in such a way that we remain present in the moment of now? What will be our gifts to ourselves as well as others?

Rylan and I had many adventures, and we still do. You see, Rylan is still with me. We still—well, I guess I should say *I* still—use our gift of inspiration of imagination. I am so inspired to keep my imagination alive as I continue to explore this magnificent

Krisi and me at one of her photo days for dance.

existence we call life. I just happen to have a body, and he has his beautiful spirit, energy of lightness, and love.

Rylan loves to play with me, most often through butterflies, but as another of my new favorite songs says, "as a moth is to light"—I sing about my love for him in the way that a moth loves to fly toward the light at night. Well, today, to pick up my mail, as usual, I pulled up alongside the mailboxes. Love and Faith waited for me in the back seat with the windows down. The two of them looked human watching every step of my journey to unlock the

119

box, as, during this daily routine, I often return with a treasure; their treats come from that magical gray box.

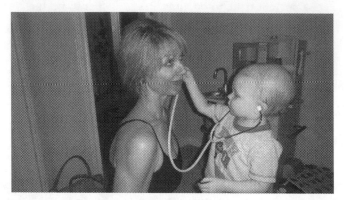

We loved to use our imagination, an inspiration for Rylan to become the doctor for a change. That crazy patient needs some meds.

Today as I approached, there was a moth on *my* mailbox. It was not frightened by my hand welcoming it to take flight. "Fly, my love." It flew right into my shoulder doggie bag, snuggling down into the darkness, waiting for a light. These normal communications happen often. You have to believe, to have faith and be aligned in love.

I knew it was Rylan playing with me. Some would say I imagined it, I know, yet it still brings those warm, fluttering butterflies throughout my body, reminding me to never give up on spreading light into a world that at times seems in the dark. There is always light, and as a moth is drawn to light in the darkness, we, too, can be a light for others, for ourselves. We are reminded that we, too, will be guided toward the light even at some very low, dark times in our lives. We just need to be willing to stop and feel that which is still, light, and set free.

Let's begin with the end of the week and decide on creating your weekend movie, inspired by your light, imagination (camera), and action, now screenshots imbued with love and so much fun.

Please take time and visit "Smilin Rylan Kids Yoga - Rylan at UCSF" on YouTube: https://www.youtube.com/watch?v=EvXOZQtPhv8. It will make you smile and be in the moment of now.

All Is Well: All Are One

Loving Mothers of All Life's Play,
Physical and/or Spiritual

May 7, 2021

Two loves of my life: my daughter, Krisi, and Smilin' Rylan.

Mom, Christy, and Wyland. Love, love, love Wyland, an angel now.

WHEN I'M PLAYING ALONG THIS JOURNEY OF LIFE, MY HEART OPENS (extra) with so much compassion and love on days like Mother's Day, especially for those who've lost mothers.

I also have so much love for those who've lost children, such as my sweet friend who lost both of her sons less than a year apart.

Those of us who know the feeling of losing a grandchild, including chosen grandchildren, are reminded of how truly precious life is. Every moment counts. Where is your attention most moments? Is it time for a wake-up call?

I hesitate using the word *lost*; they're never really lost from us, from our hearts. I know, for myself, when I become very still, bringing awareness to my breath, remaining centered and quieting my

Brian (oldest) and Mom (my dear friend Reba). Brian is now a heavenly angel.

Greg, Reba's youngest son, is missed dearly.

thoughts, those I have lost physically find a way to communicate. I can feel energetically, vibrationally—perhaps a sign, a feeling, just comes to me.

Rylan and my beautiful daughter. "Red Baby" went

everywhere Rylan went. I would include him in his hero adventures at night. He was with Rylan in his last resting place in the physical. I wonder whether Red Baby is an angel too.

All of a sudden, a butterfly will pass (Rylan's message) skimming my presence yet touching my soul deeply. A penny, feather, or numbers will pop up from Darrell. It's magical and yet expected, not surprising. There is a knowing, not a question.

There are times I will ask for a sign. While walking on the beach with my girls, I asked Darrell what sign he would bring me. The answer kept popping into my mind: heart-shaped rocks. I didn't want to hear that answer, doubting there were any rocks I would recognize as hearts. Boy, was I wrong! To this day, I will come upon one right before my next step on the beach! I add another to my collection of many heart-shaped love rocks. Another satori moment: when you ask, be open to the subtle answer, and *believe* when it is sent to you!

*We all are one. May we gather in love and
light with prayers of oneness.*

Wyland was taken from the physical world through a very selfish act, but as I have felt from his energy, he is having a blast! I was in a yoga class the evening after he took flight, and during Savasana, I had a vision, a dream so real—yes, it was so very real: Wyland and Rylan were playing Frisbee with Satori. I left during my deep meditation into a movie room of laughter. After a challenging lifetime on my mat, I was ready for corpse pose, and it was magically joy filled. I was crying with loving tears as Naomi and I left the class. Just beautiful! I shared with Christy through a text as Naomi was driving us home from yoga. I love that friend so much!

Christy has received signs from Wyland. Can you imagine the two, Rylan and Wyland, just a couple of months apart in human years? Here comes those swarming, fluttering butterflies throughout my heart as I think about them.

When I was a child (well, up to twelve or thirteen years old, to be honest), my baby dolls magically came to life at night, and often during the day, too, becoming my children. Sometimes that included my stuffed animals. I would visualize having a house full of children.

When I became pregnant with Krisi, a crisis turned blessing, my first and only pregnancy, it was hard for me to believe I'd thought about not having the greatest gift I've received in this life.

I love being a mother. As I have shared often, I believe a houseful of children playing is a blessing. Well, that was not going to be in my life's play, at least with lots of biological children. I have many blessings of chosen children and grandchildren, and my home has often been an arena of *craaaazy* fun times.

Yes (at least for me), you start believing that there is a larger, even-more-beautiful plan playing out. I will say with so much gratitude that I see it and feel it. I received it back then but, it often went unnoticed. I live it right now.

I pray that each one of us throughout the year takes the time and reaches into the hearts of those who are hurting, perhaps saddened and grieving, over what they believed their lives were going to be.

I wanted four or five children running around my home. There are couples for whom having just one child would bring an overwhelming feeling of gratitude. And maybe that hasn't played out in the scripting of their lives (yet), but perhaps their knowing someone cares will soften their sadness even for just the moment of now. I know I say this often, but we are all one. Take a moment and feel the connectivity. It's beautiful.

I recall one time when I thought I was pregnant, but once again, no. While working at the pregnancy center, I remember judging young, beautiful children of God who came in frightened, fearful of being pregnant, wholeheartedly feeling like they didn't have a choice because of their situations. Boy, I would judge, but I would camouflage it with "I'm doing this for their own good." Yep, I was judge, jury, and sentencer.

I won't go through all the different scripting that was in my vocabulary and my heart at that time. Well, actually, it was in my mind. I feel sometimes that we judge other people when there's so much hurt (and consequently anger) inside of us. I call them hot spots, sad spots that grow within our hearts, taking up space otherwise reserved for our love toward one another. Many try to mask the anger, hurt, and fear by standing righteously and declaring judgment. I didn't last long there; I am so grateful I had many a satori moment! Amen!

Just where do we get what is rightful judgment? As I wanted more children, those coming into the clinic were desperately trying to solve their crisis, heartbreak, or what many of them felt was their very survival, and I justified my judgment by labeling it "loving." Hmm ... *Really?*

Wow, what a satori moment I had back then. It's amazing now to think that person was really me. It was more than thirty years ago. I saw so many, talked to so many, who would come back just to visit and say that having an abortion had led them to their awakening. (They perhaps wouldn't call it that, but I did.) They opened up in a much more loving and peace-filled way toward life and the sacredness of life.

Ironically, events twisted, and it was like God spoke into my heart, and once again, one of my favorite stories: if you have never sinned, be the first to throw your judgment (stone). Those "mothers" need our love, not our judgment.

I don't know about you, but call it sin, misjudgment, naive, or whatever assumption we feel we're entitled to make about others, labeling them, we never know what their decisions will bring in this world as they play out. I've just seen it happen so many times.

A convict, a child of God, ends up being one of the miraculous blessings in this world. Sometimes such people's decisions bring them to their satori moments of awakening and they serve others with so much love and compassion that some of us can't even begin to find in our hearts. I believe with all my heart there are miracles in times of judgment, if only we would step back, become silent, and believe—another satori moment being born.

Take your time throughout the year to send a card or give a hug to someone whose heart you know breaks, perhaps someone who has lost a child during pregnancy, or who chose an abortion and carries lingering guilt. Send your love to these people and help them believe they are loved, just as they are, nothing more!

Many of us have a friend whose child was tragically taken from him or her. My dear longtime friend Susan lost her son Zack. He was an absolutely awesome little boy who grew into a fun, awesome daddy. His first day at a new job, sitting in a work truck, he lost his life during a random shooting spree. He was such a kind spirit. He loved Rylan, and I have kept a text from him from the time when Rylan was in the hospital (which was often). I adored Zack, and I love his family so very much.

Another example we often neglect to acknowledge— well, you know we are all very busy. We would all confirm that. Perhaps in our lives, for just a moment, we should just imagine and empathize with the tragedy of carrying a child and not bringing that child home.

For those who have lost their mothers, send love and a hug, card, phone call, or prayer. I am blessed that I still have mine. And yes, I lost my dad, my husband, my grandchild, and many friends and their children. I will say that when you experience loss, your heart opens and deepens, and everyone becomes your father, mother, daughter, son, grandchild, or sister. You get my message here: we are all one family.

For those who are hurting for whatever reason, may we all take a breath, go to our hearts, and allow our minds to soften, slowly, deeply breathing and finding that space in our hearts. If we reach out to people, they will bless us. The most amazing gifts we can open are our hearts. The gift of simply opening our hearts and giving, feeling the blessings just flow from every direction. The best gift is a silent prayer sent with the energy of love.

So, as beautiful as Mother's Day is, my daughter celebrates me every day of the year, and I do my best to call and celebrate my mom daily. With that being said, I think it's important for all of us to remember there are so many people hurting. We say we are our brother's keepers—well, let's truly keep the love moving and enveloping all!

Take time this weekend to do your loving part to ease someone's sadness, even if only for a moment. Remember: this moment is all we have. We have actually every day of the year to wrap our hearts around someone's hurt and sadness and celebrate the oneness we are called to show and be. l celebrate *we*. We are in fact one.

Be a Super Person at Any Age—
We All Have the Love to Fly

March 18, 2021

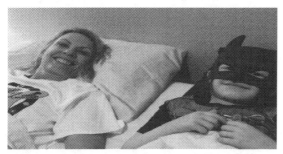

Rylan and Jmom sharing superhero bedtime stories.

I would like to begin by saying that I had a conversation with a beautiful soul, and she told me that after reading one of my blogs, she felt her forgiveness meant she "should" call a certain person back into her life.

I replied that that is a decision I feel only the one forgiving can honestly answer.

Of course, we then live with the consequences of that decision. As I have talked about in the past, I truly go deep within my soul and ask the question, What decision am I going to feel more at peace with? What choice do I feel is going to serve my soul, my self, in a loving way? I seek a choice that will fill my heart with love and joy so that my energy will then serve all I come into contact with.

When we choose to forgive (it begins first and foremost within the me), it doesn't mean we simply give a free revolving pass to someone to be in our lives. I do hope you choose to be with your self as your first pick. Forgive yourself, and it becomes so much easier to extend forgiveness to others.

We choose who we want to spend our moments with. And yes, even on holidays. If I choose to surround myself with someone or a group, I decide I'm going to live each moment with love and nonjudgment. Of course, do I fail at times? You betcha I do, and I often say to myself as I become lighthearted, "Joni, pick up your big-girl panties," and I do my best to forgive myself so I can ask for forgiveness from others.

That goes for making a phone call, answering the door, or stopping to talk with someone in a grocery store. It is our choice. When we make that decision, we make a decision to open our hearts and once again be present and aware from within, allowing acceptance of the now. On the next occasion, we may choose to choose differently.

I know this may sound crazy to some, but it actually ends up bringing so much more joy, freedom, and fun play into our lives. Or at least it did and does for me. I am always simply offering what I choose, and for me, it is so much better than those times I choose the alternative. There are definitely times when we do wish we chose differently. So next time?

If I decide to make or answer a phone call, answer my door, or stop to talk to someone, for the most part, I have asked myself, "What are my intentions?" I then choose to make a decision, a choice, knowing it is wrapped in my energy! I don't call or talk with someone and after the fact blame the interaction on somebody else—no, I made my choice of action.

So it goes: I choose to talk to the other person, and if I hang up feeling any residue of anger, sadness, or fear, I do my best to work through it as quickly as possible. If not, as I have shared in the past, I feel as if quicksand is pulling me deeper into muck and stink! Yuckiness.

We are all meant to be super persons. By that, I mean we make a difference in this world every moment we are alive here in the physical.

I understand if that doesn't make sense, so take a breath and become still. Allow the words (and their meanings) to marinate within your heart's space or mind. It truly is about the energy, our energy. What does your energy speak of you? Love, I am sure.

Even when I'm being with myself (don't say "by myself") at home or on a walk, it doesn't matter where, because energy extends outward. At the end of the day, the energy we have lived and shared continues on and accumulates into truly making a difference. In this world, it is all about what our energy is creating and leaving behind. No words to explain.

I believe every one of us is called to be a super person. I am not referring to a supermodel, or being super wealthy, super strong, or any outer-body characteristic. I'm talking about being super present, super kind, and super love—a super person to truly save the world.

The weekend arrives, being delivered by the days of the week coming to an end. Or are they at an end? If you really believe that every moment is life in the now, and the now is what is real (or is it? it's over in a moment), then why not put your super person's soul-filled self on a ride to continual love and kindness? Now it's a continual week that never ends, and every day is a weekend.

Of Course Smilin' Rylan Would Choose April Fools' Day to Take Flight

April 1, 2021

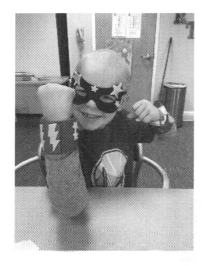

Happy birth-to-flight day, my sweet super person. I will never forget the day you chose to leave us physically, from the moment I woke up in Cayucos; to your mom and I talking on the phone, sharing April Fools' jokes; to the phone call I received from your mom just a couple of hours later.

I'm shocked and unbelievably heartbroken, but Grandfather and I knew you let go and showed everyone how beautifully Smilin' you would take your flight.

Rylan wanted to make sure his last moments would be remembered as part of a day on which we all choose to laugh a little more, joke a little more, and just plain have fun a lot more—something

that Rylan did freely and that continues on as his legacy.

Krisi and I talk a lot about Rylan getting a kick out of his little brother's endless energy and lack of fear. We are sure he is part of the instigating, egging on Grayson as he climbs the barstools, falls, and gets right back to climbing, adding another bruise. What a fun brother you are.

It's going to be interesting on April 1, today, how much more Grayson ventures into uncharted territory. Mom's just waiting for the next fall—some tears and a lot of yelling. Rylan, your brother has some vocal cords. Tears don't last long (just like with his older brother), and then he is right back to it.

My spiritual, intuitive, and very dear friend Barbara shared with me before Grayson came into this play of life, "Grayson will be powerful, and it will be important for those guiding him to be patient and allow him to use his powers." Boy, she was right on! This was a few months before his physical birth!

I believe that on both our day of birth and the day we take flight into the nonphysical a celebration is felt in the heavens. Yes, both are a celebration of new birth, and as we celebrate birth and flight days in honor of our loved ones, we present the gift of appreciation, for the days they have been our gifts and the awareness of their energy in our moments now, sharing our physical lives with us. Just because your loved ones have lost the vehicles (physical bodies) doesn't mean they're not here present with you.

Hospital room becomes a basketball court.

Rylan, you have been a gift to so many, living in every moment of every day, though perhaps not always *Smilin'* Rylan, as there were times—one in particular comes to mind—when I was visiting you at UC San Francisco children's hospital and you, for example, refused to have

Jmom did score once (maybe!).

your blood pressure taken. In this case, you were too busy; we were playing basketball, you and I.

Nurse Kelli was so amazing, understanding, and patient. She came back a little later, and you were ready, with no pressure, just having creamed your Jmom in basketball. You scored twenty more points in no time. I seem to remember I did get a basket, though.

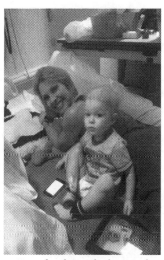

Early on, when you were a toddler, came the blood work, the poking of your arms, fingers, and spine, but as soon as it was over, you were down running around, dancing to the Wiggles, ready to have fun forgetting the past and arriving to the moment. You were a present of presence in each moment. You truly were! Just think if we all played out our moments as if we were gifts to others, not to mention to ourselves. Wow, what a beautiful inspiration to visualize and feel in our hearts.

When we are present in the moment, we truly are gifts to others.

Rylan, your mom and I talk at least once a day. We believe we choose our presence (or not) in each moment. When we are present, acceptance becomes doable,

Loved to lie in the hospital bed with Rylan.

even in the most challenging situations. There's a knowing that all shall be well. It's not about positive thinking but more about having faith in the adventure we all are experiencing. When we are excepting the moment and not resisting, it opens us and others to much more peace, and once that moment is over, get your dancing shoes on and bust a move.

Happy April Fools' Day. May we all remember to laugh a little more, joke (awareness of kindness) a little more, and practice our dance moves no matter where we are, welcoming our inner spirits to rock out.

So much love is flowing to you—and there's no April fool in that message.

Synergy Can Bring Kind Energy—
Let's All Be a Part and Start

November 20, 2020

Officer Anderson doing tree pose with the little yogis—makes my heart smile!

The amazing officer came to pick up what the little yogis had collected for the homeless.

No longer do I use the word *fight* in relation to any cause. Instead, I replace it with *a willingness to love*, or a willingness to work together for a cause that is greater than any one person's imagination could possibly have hoped for. It reflects an awareness that what we fight against (resist) tends to grow (persist).

We must ask ourselves, "Are we moving toward love or toward fear?" I choose love. Love changes things. Throughout my beautiful life, there have so many times when I felt I was "right" and it had to be my way. I reflect back and acknowledge that, deep down, I knew. How? By the way I felt. My I, who I really am, felt and knew that I didn't want to go down that road, but my pride, my ego, was driving my mind, and so often my words and actions were in the back seat, just going along for the ride.

The little yogis enjoyed spending time lovingly with the "mature residents" of the Remington in Hanford, California.

Now, having said that, I became motivated at times to dig deep within, and I was able to truly get to know (remember) who I really am. Yes, miracles in disguise. I often hear (and begin to sing) the words from one of my favorite songs: "Long time after we are gone, the fruits of our tree will carry on."

Relationships can be such blessings, as well as treasure maps. I believe that one special reason for having a closeness with someone is that it teaches us, shows us—if we are willing to listen, feel, and see—who we really are. We must ask ourselves, "Who am I? Are these thoughts, words, and actions who I really am?"

We rediscover and begin to find the relationships with our selves, and then all relationships become treasures of experiences, leading to journeys of discoveries—journeys filled with exploration and love as our tools, with patience and love for ourselves and others.

It can truly guide us to the real answer to the question, Who am I? Of course, this happens only when we can grow from the digging, excavating, all the s—— (walls) we have built up inside, layers of what may feel like protection but in truth only hinders us from truly experiencing life and each moment.

And yes, this doesn't just happen overnight. It's a moment-to-moment hike up hills and often steep mountains. At times, we'll lose our footing, tumble down, and get mired in muddy struggles. But for me, now more often than not, a breath unveils breath, and I take in the scenery, noticing a beautiful valley, sounds of a creek speaking softly, rivers of peace flowing freely, becoming part of the beauty and mystery of the hike of life. I'm free to experience the landscape (lifescape) of this play of life with joy.

Together we become a light for the world when the world seems so dark. I enjoy how the kids love to talk about *namaste* and what it means. I have taught them a version that radiates my heart's message, and we say it together: "The light in me sees and connects with the light in you, and together we shine that much brighter."

Namaste.

133

I will end this week's entry here because I love to write (and could go on and on).

As we journey to another end of week and head into the weekend, we are reminded that our journeys with ourselves are most important. Take the time with your self, and become silent and in that space: peace of mind! Enjoy! Rejoice in the fact that life is precious. Live it fully.

Another April Fools', We Celebrate Smilin' Rylan—His Physical Form Is Gone, but Smiles Continue

March 31, 2020

As we continue on this journey, all of us together as one, I'd like to call on all Smilin' Rylan yogis past, present, and future to smile brightly and perhaps do yoga and dance (Rylan loved both) tomorrow, April 1—if possible, around noon, but time is irrelevant. Especially at this time, when we're locked down but not locked out.

With the coronavirus, I believe all of us across the entire world are going through a time of a kind of death. It's a time of grieving—grieving the loss of what we felt were our lives. We're dealing with the passing of what we felt

We loved to cuddle before bedtime, and of course there was much fun and laughter.

The cutest of the cutest of the cutest. Well, everyone is—I'm really not partial.

comfortable with. And with no choice in the matter, we must let go of normal as we knew normal to be, the one we came to be familiar with in our day-to-day, and allow the releasing. Most of us are resisting quite a bit.

This time is birthing a cycle, a new cycle we must go through, all of us to varying degrees. As for me, as much as possible, I choose to stay in a gratitude mindset, which guides me and moves me through times of denial, uncertainty, and, quite frankly, pissosity (my made-up word, translated from *anger*). I'm feeling frustrated but doing my best

135

to move through these periods of grief as healthily as possible, remembering it is normal (healthy) to open, feel, and release fear and denial and then feel free to choose to return to the moment of now, where all is well. Yes, in this moment, all is well.

This is perhaps a time inviting us to be open to strip away anything from our pasts or the present that we can now acknowledge does not serve who our souls are calling us to return to. We must be open to the possibilities of a new normal—one that now consists of deeper longings for togetherness, gratitude for one another, and a greater intensity of love and sincere compassion for others. Do these sound like miracles, rainbows, appearing? I believe.

We may fall down, but we don't let go of the faith we have. We breathe in and breathe out; we are together as one. We move together, and we are connected. Allow the hope of knowing to be your light and guide you through this—a light shining ahead, bringing the newness, a rebirth for what I've always believed was just underneath the knowingness of what my soul was calling my life to become, to return to.

It's a cleaning-out of stuff, clearing the haze of our daily busyness, looking to the horizon as if a new sunrise was our first light, opportunity, to

rise up. A rebirthing from the freshness after a rainstorm.

Sometimes as days turn to weeks, weeks to months, months to years, we become numb to the accumulation of stuff within and

without. We're not even aware we're blocking what our souls are calling us to be. Perhaps with some new breakthroughs resurrecting us, we may become clearer and lighter as we release so we can receive. Receive? you ask. Yes: a new beginning.

Rylan loved music. Here he is at my house when he was about one; I got to babysit him while his parents went on a minivacation. I will never allow those memories to be lost!

And they'll never fade, but I also won't allow them to rob me of my present moment of now.

A few years later, while Rylan was in remission, we would be blessed to have him visit here again at our home. There was no doubt he had a mission in life—a mission that I feel many of us discover during the grieving of the deaths of our past lives. May we be reborn to the beauty of life, the beauty of loving one another.

Pete Lives the Adage "If You Love What You Do, You Will Never Work a Day in Your Life"

September 5, 2021

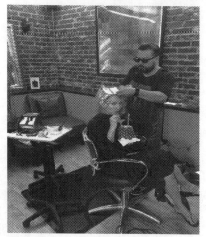

Pete spoiling me.

Those who have been blessed to have Pete in their lives know that he lives each moment loving what he does. It doesn't matter if he's walking down the street, enjoying time at home or in church, or serving those of us who go to him for his talent for hair—which he uses as a cover-up for just plain loving to serve.

I met Pete more than thirty years ago. First time I went in to have my hair done, I felt like I was at a composed comedy show and the side benefit was that my hair looked great when I left.

I still remember my first visit—or should I say my first experience with interactive theater. Lucio and Pete played many comedy skits as I was the character in the hot seat, as well as part of the active audience, and I laughed so hard. I am sure many of you had and still have the same experience of entertainment and so much joy. Laughter truly is one of God's gifts, always available to us.

I wanted to begin this week's entry with Pete as the main character, so to speak. The opening act. And I know many of you are continuing prayers for his healing and for all his family. Let's get Pete back onstage, out of the hospital, where the virus took him to be for now. He's perhaps helping many of us look within and set aside our complaints as we move back in the audience, where we'll be clapping for Pete's performance of healing and his returning to the stage as our prayers are answered.

Pete and I laugh, cry, but I feel he would agree that our favorite headliner we'd end up talking about is our spirituality. As I often say, it's my favorite topic. We share books we have read, spiritual teachers we listen to, and our love for one another that extends to all.

Pete truly lives "If you love what you do, you will never work a day in your life." He never worked a day in his life. I love him dearly, I miss him, and I pray every day as I pass his home here in Cambria.

At times, we may feel that this world carries so much grief and sadness, especially this past year or so, bringing most of us to our knees, asking for God to guide us back home to our inner love and faith, delivering us to peace, calmness, and the belief that, with faith, all shall be well and this, too, shall pass. We choose to see the blessings. Sometimes we have to look with our hearts wide open.

This brings me to a thought: People often ask me, "Doesn't it drive you crazy not to be working?" First, often I will reply, smiling within, that I haven't worked for thirty or more years. But many don't realize I just came from a full-time loving job involving my best friend and husband taking flight. I never separated work from play. At present, I am enjoying my writing, hoping to finish my book October 31 (not set in stone).

I do understand where they are pulling that energy of thoughts from, yet it saddens my heart, because I also understand that sometimes people need work and busyness to feel accomplished in their lives. Often, they derive their self-worth from what they do instead of who they are minus the labels they wear. I have watched loved ones lose their identities when they no longer have their job titles, and some inevitably become sick.

I have shared this before, but I'm going to share again at this curve, this point. Please be aware of the judgment that may start surfacing. When I tell the story, it's so amazing to see people look at me, and at times, you can feel the energy of disbelief. They start giving me excuses and justifications for my choices, I believe, to make themselves feel more comfortable. I do my best to put them at ease, to reassure them that it was all in the larger vision and I was prime to be broken open. And what a blessing awaiting when I finally did.

During my late teens and early twenties, I played a victim, and I played it very well. Going from two quick marriages to two divorces, jumping from job to job, and blaming outside factors as the cause. The challenges (blessings) were giving me the opportunity to awaken—if I so desired—to look within and begin. Some of the first satori explosions, changes to my paradigms, were immediate. I call them the miracles, the rainbows I talk about. They were and to this day are miracles.

Still (and, yes, stillness), the change of my life took patience and a whole lot of forgiveness—of others as well as myself (for my part in all my story, my dramas—yes, a lot of *mys*).

Everything comes back to us, and the contrast we lived can and often does bring us to our knees, guiding us into alignment (or not). For me, it was about looking into my personality and celebrating as I saw that everything lay within me.

Once I started healing, unpacking, and excavating, I began to follow my heart. I became passionate about returning to who I really am. I enjoyed returning, and I would go within my heart space, discovering and reconnecting as I began not feeling that I was at a job, or working. It was not about money or power. For me, it became all about service—the loving service from my heart space of I, the inner self.

I started feeling and believing in myself, not looking for a relationship to complete me. I worked at (and enjoyed) being complete and self-full so as to become selfless. I desired to bring my whole self to my marriage, work (play), and life!

This was our mission at our home as well as our practice (home practice): I believe many can relate when I say that, oftentimes, as you raise a family, and it continues after your family is grown and out of the house, there are times when you choose to put love and faith smack in the middle of chaos. In the moment, allow the communication to be courageous enough yet delivered in consideration so as to release tension, therefore welcoming, allowing, the opening to dissolve the craziness and carrying everyone into a decision to love. It's about finding that space in the uncomfortableness as it turns into a knowingness and a mutual decision to choose actions of peace for all.

And, once again, we are called to serve in love. This is the first entry that is published at the beginning of the week, and as the week flows into the weekend, may we continue prayers and acts of kindness for Pete and his family.

I am sending love and prayers to all, taking time out to stand still as I move into the space between my thoughts and celebrate love, service, and Pete.

Love Heals All, Bringing to Life Blessings from Tragedy

August 12, 2021

When we give, we actually receive—what I feel is a greater gift. Yes, I understand so many of our human brothers and sisters are going through tragedies and difficult times. So I would like to encourage those of you who are always looking for a satori moment to allow this to marinate on your soul and take the time to read on.

I have a feeling many of you feel as I do. These past couple of years have seemed at times like a science fiction movie. If someone had told me this would happen, that a virus would spread throughout the world and kill more innocent people than any war has, I wouldn't have believed them. So many of our brothers and sisters are out of work, more homeless. On top of that: the realization that climate change is real. We are having to look in the mirror to confront how we treat not only all living beings but also our beautiful world.

I always felt that we can't continue to abuse Mother Earth. For me, it is so sad to still hear people say climate change is false. But as always, if I am part of the solution by my giving of whatever means in love, then I don't necessarily worry or get too focused on the negatives. I use my awareness to carry out an act of love and give. We are all one, and in this moment, all is well.

I, too, become overwhelmed at times, and I often share that the little voice inside me enjoys to hound me, accusing me that I should do more, give more, be there more, and on and on, exhausting me at times when I allow it to continue—that voice (I call my *nagging twerp*) that can hound me unless I return.

The ego (*edging God out*)—the ego twerp never quite satisfied with my self—loves to judge. I believe we are not meant to give in to this judgment under any type of stress or with negative energy.

If it doesn't radiate in your heart's space, if it isn't done in love, it just may not feel right (perhaps timing etc.). Bless the individuals and keep them in your prayers.

By using your awareness (quieting the twerp), either change how you are looking at the situation or choose not to judge in any direction.

When you make your decision, say a prayer of peace and strength, giving energy of loving prayers of peace. There's a gift! Amen. Please choose not to give if there is judgment or criticism attached.

I feel and know in my heart, my deepest self, that at times I not only allow my mind to scold me to do more but also am very aware if my ego mind attempts to compare tragedies of any type, somehow judging what is more "deserving" of the donation or time or judging in an unloving way how it was or is being handled. As if we know what really is going on during that difficult time. As the saying suggests, walking just a day in someone else's shoes will bring you (hopefully) to your knees, humbled.

Using these words to describe it is hard—even the words bring yucky energy—but I can tell you that, these last years, I have heard and witnessed many times judgments about who is entitled and who isn't. I've heard people give reasons why or, again, made judgments about how people "should have" handled their situations.

Why not choose instead a choice of action—to give or not—either choice made with no judgment? And if we are all honest, we recognize that voice. The ego twerp loves to give its two cents. Next time, laugh at it, and let it fall into the background. There is no right or wrong choice if and when that choice is made in love.

Everything goes back to where we came from, and if we're honest, we can hear the calling. May we follow the love of that calling—the calling to look after and care for one another, especially during times like these last few years.

I choose to believe most feel as I do. When I am giving, I am receiving tenfold. If any of us at all has faith ("the size of a mustard seed"), we believe in that. We feel that truth. We live that truth.

The blessings we receive in return fill our hearts with a magical spiritual presence. No words can explain or come close to describing the joy, the warmth, left in place of the giving.

Truly, in the end, we are already where we're supposed to be, we're already free, and we're already home, right where we are. And what we can do right now is let go and allow our hearts' space (our selves) to choose to kick that twerp into the back seat—better yet, the trunk.

At this time, it may be a prayer of healing. It may be a dollar-amount donation. And when it's done in love, the act is the giving. It's the intention, the energy of love, the blessing.

Thank you. And thank you ahead of time for allowing your heart's space to speak softly and, instead of brushing it aside, bringing it to life. Follow that voice of self.

Together, we are all so much better, blessed as we bless others.

Friendship, Where Love and Kindness Set Us Free to Sail through Life as One

October 2, 2020

Wouldn't it be wonderful if friendship and family merged as one? I find it unfortunate that we often separate those two words, their meanings. When asked, "Is that a family member or a friend?" we are so used to choosing one. Wouldn't it be nice if all flowed together, intertwined in love? Friends were family, and family friends, as one?

Obviously, even family members aren't always friends. Friendship is like a ship out in sea. We are all aboard, in it together. If not, the ship may go down, possibly sinking. I believe that friendship is a bond—one we choose to nurture. We are aware and know that, no matter what, we are there for and with one another. There is no judgment, no score keeping. Our vision is smooth sailing as we join together; even during heavy rainstorms, we know, have faith, that we will survive.

The friendship stays afloat even through challenges. Get those storm jackets on and paddles in hand for the times that call for it, as together we await the sun's rays, welcoming the rainbow of assurance that, as long as we are together, we will make it through to the amazing miracles before us.

At times, a family friendship cannot even leave the dock, as it's tied and held in place, bound by old patterns, old maps. Instead of sailing, navigating by the compass, we must follow the heart's compass toward peace, kindness, and joy.

I have to giggle because now it's very funny to me (back then it was very hurtful and heartbreaking): Once, I was accused of not calling a family member often enough by phone, and in my trying to defend myself, I only made it worse. The family friendship truly went off course before even launching. Soon that storm passed, but as always, it erupted someplace else, becoming a cyclone of judgment, score keeping, division, and accusations, soon becoming a huge unconscious, unloving parting. The hurricane destroyed the friendship. It literally sank.

When you have smooth sailing, it is beautifully maintained by chosen family members who navigate through their hearts, nurturing life's journey as an adventure. The friendship weathers through the sea of life regardless of the forecast, be the waters, or present moments, calm or not so calm. For the most part, there are no instances of seasickness or times during which anyone feels the need to jump overboard or abandon ship.

I am one of those who doesn't give up easily, but truly there is a time where and when you do release it and give it to God, trusting that perhaps one day, hopefully sooner rather than later, the family friendship will have its holes patched, be repaired (be characterized by forgiveness), and take sail. Have faith that, next time, everyone will grab a life jacket and hang on for dear family. Amen.

What can be such a beautiful miracle is our growing in belief, beginning new from everything every moment we experience, deciding it is worth the times of struggles.

It truly is our choice in every moment to use and nurture (and at times unwrap again) our four birth gifts—self-awareness, inspiration to imagine, conscious voice of stillness, and free will to be—as well as our vision to see clearer in the future. We must be open to seeing it from another's point of view. Our futures and everyone we come into contact with (and even people we don't come into contact with) can become the rainbow of renewed commitment to change. It's less about teaching with our words and more about our actions, intentions, and energy.

Choose to be the kind of friend you desire for your self. I am talking here about your self, the inner I of who you really are, not your conditioned personality. Take the time to nurture through kindness, being present for your family, friends, and so forth. Choose to be family and choose to be friends: chosen family. Then set sail on the journey of no return.

With adventures that bring warmth, even through the storms, you feel a combined commitment—yes, a warmth. You feel radiant and alive. There's a mutual knowing that the time spent is a vacation of memories called life, in which you enjoy smooth sailing and experience times that are a bit turbulent. It's all part of the journey we call life.

Different Is Only Dangerous When We Forget in Our Hearts We Are All the Same

January 15, 2021

Amen, and if the statement in the title finds your mind a little unsettled, if you've perhaps done some questioning or judging recently, push pause, take a few moments of silence (yes, off Facebook, Twitter, and other distractions), and allow awareness to become present.

When I am in that place of judgment or misunderstanding (remember that when we get into the place of fear, we lose the space of freedom to be love), my mind definitely takes over, and I start bringing up reasons to justify my indifference—pissosity— regarding someone or something outside myself.

These are times I choose to be gentle with myself and hold myself as if holding a very delicate young child in my arms (easy? well, no, but with time, you do become more patient and less judgmental

Grayson loves for Mom to play with pictures (scary but not real).

of your me, the personality), and then I breathe in gratitude for the moment.

Our embrace was so magical.

Perhaps you find that you tend to gravitate toward others—those you feel will stand beside your judgment and even fuel it. And, yes, at times, it can be healing and important to be able to voice your feelings, but share and then blow it off, as I do, as if it's a mist that's clouding up my true vision of what is. And for my self, what is, is a life, an amazing gift—a gift so precious that losing moments in fear

146

(anger, blame, jealousy, judgment, etc.) is a place I no longer feel welcome. I have become a stranger to it and elect not to accept the invite.

So, once again, I want it to say, "Once upon a time"—it would be like *Groundhog Day*. I would allow myself to continue to replay the same environment, group, person, events, and activities, and I would blame them for my own choices and experience. I wouldn't even realize my mind would go to auto replay, my *Groundhog Day*, morning, noon, and during sleep.

I love this analogy (yes, I use it a lot): the snakebite is not what will kill us. It's the running away in fear and allowing the poison to flow through our bodies. It's the poison inside us, if and when we allow it to stay.

I am firm in my belief that we choose who we surround ourselves with. Of course, there are times we feel we have no choice—or do we?—like when going into a grocery store, retail store, or any other public place. Although I also do believe, to some extent, that we attract certain energy toward ourselves.

So often in my life, I have experienced times during which I questioned why I brought that energy into my life. It would soon become apparent, and I would understand. The rainbow would appear, the miracle of a life's gift would slowly unwrap, allowing time to settle back into the now.

Once again, as always, the week ends, and the weekend begins. May we all choose to believe, perhaps even light a candle, and remember the world is filled with love.

Love Is Friendship on Fire: First Person Is with Self

August 20, 2021

Give your self a big hug. Be your own self's best friend. Love your self unconditionally, and you will become self-full to love others unconditionally. It makes sense but isn't so easy—I know. I'm still learning, accepting with no resistance.

Hugs and namaste. Be you. Hug your best friend, you, often.

If we don't have our own selves wrapped around our hearts and souls daily, the bodies, the personalities, will soon and frequently burn out. Depression will leave our selves to watch from the background, the heart space softly, intuitively, nudging us.

We forget who we really are. The miracle, rainbow, and blessing to always remember? We can return again in any moment.

How can we be our own best friends, filled with love that flows out to others, when we have such demanding lives? At times, it feels like there aren't enough hours in the day. We feel we're torn in so many directions.

I would like to suggest (actually, we all already know this) that all of us ultimately choose how we spend each of our moments. Yet we don't have to become anyone. We're already home, with our best friends, at any given moment. Feeling the inner happiness? Good! You have a wonderful bestie!

Stop here. Begin releasing any urgent feelings in any direction. Feel as you breathe in, and slowly, in awareness, feel as you release the breath. Keep the awareness

Naomi hugging in love for her self. Here's one from me.

on your breath for several minutes. So simple yet so tough—and oh so beautiful! I love to be now. You can keep your eyes open, or you can close them.

Our real selves don't operate with any urgency; they wait patiently and love our own best friends, always present in the softness of the heart space, regretting and demanding nothing. The real self comes from a knowingness—is everythingness yet nothingness. It's always present, calmly awaiting, observing as the awareness.

We need no fancy workout system, prescription, machine, book, outline, online class, or to-do list on how to make our lives stress-free. Each of us already has it right within, already patiently watching and waiting, right here in the now, the present moment of now.

I know this sounds cliché—I get it—but I'm here to say that there's no special potion. It really is about finding space to just be with your best friend, flowing together within, feeling what is still and free, and loving your best friend, taking the time with your self completely.

Alyvia truly loves her self, and I love her so much. Hugs, Alyvia.

Just who are you speaking of? you may ask. Take a breath. It's the one who remains when you, the person, the body, dies. It's so natural yet so mysterious. Yes, an oxymoron. Time for space: pause, breathe, and feel the breath. Amen.

Once again, you've heard me say that I have nothing against massages, facials, and fun times like going to wine tastings, hanging with friends, dancing, and singing. I love it all—all the doingness of life. At this moment, that's not exactly what I'm talking about. Hopefully when we experience those fun times, there's not one ounce of guilt or feeling as if we should be doing something else with or for someone else.

Enjoy those nows with your best friend, your self, surrounded by people you enjoy being with. Again, that's one of the main reasons I fell in love with yoga practice right away. There was no place to go and no one to be but me. When I'm on my mat, I'm with my best friend yet surrounded by others, often unaware of who they are but

Big hugs—I can feel their love.

nevertheless feeling the energy in the room. It doesn't matter where, who, when, or what you're doing. All is all right, and we find our way back home.

I love the untrainings, both the giving and the receiving, and I have presented for all the years. I self-fully have had, I believe, the most satori awakenings. You can have yours also.

During the untrainings, when we would begin talking, sharing, about different proactive practices to nurture ourselves and return to the present moment, what would consistently pop up? Schedules and time.

"But you don't understand my life." We begin giving explanations for why our lives are unusually hard while others have much easier schedules. We all can relate to having those thoughts and feelings. Just think of all the time we've spent justifying, comparing, and thinking and talking about it.

First things first. Begin by becoming aware. Take a moment and give your self a hug.

One of the most challenging acts of love for our selves is to be honest within. Which version of you is repeating the dead-end scripting? Is it your repetitive, judgmental mind or the soft heart-space voice? Which voice (awareness) are you allowing to steer your friendship? Allow your feelings to be your compass, and ask if you're you experiencing smooth sailing or cyclones or turbulent waves.

The you in the background, your best friend, is watching and listening so calm and patiently, waiting for you to return in love. Allow that you to steer. I believe that if we're all honest, we know it's that soft voice urging us to do or not to do. Can you feel whether the intentions are wrapped in love? Or fear? Is the friendship sailing calmly, and is all well?

If not, decide to choose differently for the sake of not only you and your best friend but all others who feel and experience your energy as you sail alongside them. If we are not aware of the forecast, we can become seasick enough that eventually we turn the controls over and possibly aren't even aware of the soft voice as it takes center front, now the captain of the friendship. And you are one in beingness.

Before we go any further, and so you can unclench your jaw, know that it's less about totally changing what you're doing and more about the energy you're being as you're doing. In the past, sometimes an analogy would help my mind wrap around a thought (nudge) and welcome another satori moment of awakening.

Yes, we have children, grandchildren, jobs, daily activities, responsibilities, and so on. Just another suggestion: begin by changing those daily scheduled activities into *love* chores.

Many people I talk to do that; they begin to choose to enjoy reviewing homework with the children at night, fixing dinner, cleaning up, running errands, and the like. But for many of us, we return to negative energy while performing some of our daily chores, often not feeling like our own besties, with our ships off course, often fueled with resentment and frustration, perhaps sinking. We begin drowning in our own choices of direction, with no life preserver left to rescue us, not even a floaty.

What if we changed our choices of energy? It takes time, but making dinner can be fun if you include the family on certain nights. Start to use your awareness and become inspired to imagine turning chores into love chores—and have some fun.

When my daughter was very young, I started having her fix dinner with me. I got her an apron, kids' recipe books, and

It feels so warm and loving
to love your self.

all the cool accessories. On certain nights and at weekend breakfasts, she became our cook and server. She enjoyed it! We appreciated her service of love.

What do you have to lose? Begin putting your inspiration and imagination to work (or play), rather than having the mind and body work so hard. Bring your imagination alive and make homework fun. Can you imagine becoming inspired in so many creative ways? There are so many new adventures and locations for you to venture on your fun, loving friendship.

Beautiful Alysia—her love shines.

Of course, it depends on the child and circumstances. Customize it. How about making cleaning fun? I have come to enjoy cleaning—well, most of it. It now becomes less about what the activity is and more about energy, the fuel of your beingness. The waves become calmer, the sailing smoother.

It is not about trying to control but rather about accepting, becoming more and more aware and understanding that resisting, fighting against, only brings negativity. You know, the yucky, mucky feelings. Quicksand. Title waves of emotions that can make life's sailing a forecast of hurricanes. Help!

What I know to be true is that it takes so much more energy from our inner spaces when we are resisting what is, and we're often not enjoying it. Do the best you can. It's all right. Be your own advocate and best friend. Love yourself wholeheartedly and let go of anything that is not serving you. Take a breath and feel your feelings. Now release any disappointments, your expectations. Set yourself free.

Remember—I have shared before, and believe this with my entire self and live it (well, at times)—as you wake in the morning, before your first step out of your cozy bed, ask, "What energy am I bringing to my day and therefore to others?"

I can only share what I have practiced for years, birthing so many days of gratitude. Even when the outside world looks as if it isn't cooperating, it is. Each morning, I meditate or pray thirty to sixty minutes. It's always different. I follow it with spiritual music, and when I feel full of loving energy, so filled with gratitude for my life, I step onto the floor. I don't need an alarm. I have an inner compass that wakes my self around a quarter after three. I have to admit that when it went from four o'clock to three fifteen, I fought it at first, but that's the time I am meant to shine and begin my awakened state, at least for now.

Of course, at this point, you may be thinking, *How can I do that? I have children. I have a job …* And the list of why "I can't" goes on.

Time for a hug: During a Zoom class with Smilin' Rylan little yogis, we still would spread "air hugs." Now you take the time to hug your self.

No argument from me: It's not easy, especially when you begin, but what's the alternative? You are going to get out of bed, hopefully, so why not begin something that's for you and your inner self to do together? It's choosing and getting into a habit, so to speak, especially if you're in the habit of waking up and groaning, resisting stepping out of bed and into your day. Excuses to stay in bed win, until you're rushing to get all of you together and your possible addiction to adrenaline takes over once again.

After a while, it's not easy to choose not to. You just may find your self and discover how much you enjoy spending some one-on-one time together, first thing. It will never be the same. Through the years, with marriage, the business, and my dad, husband, and grandson dealing with cancer, I still found time with my best friend.

I used to have to set my alarm. Of course, individuals' time will be their own, so make it your own special time. I know the excuses are going to appear and speak loudly. Don't fight it; just make your choice. I promise that, little by little, you return to you—it becomes you.

From the first step, you carry the experience through your day. Yes, you get thrown off course in moments, with certain emotions, but you have a place to return. You are alive, and you are lightening your load as you let go of the past, living the moment, in the moment. Just keep being your best friend on fire for love.

It's your life, schedule, and priorities. When it's quiet, meditate or pray, do some yoga (or tell your family it's your time to do some yoga together), or go on a walk in nature. Learn to be silent with yourself.

Trey used to come to our untrainings on Wednesday mornings. Time is amazingly unreal.

The treasure is unending. Choose your practice and learn to say no with the intention of love.

Smooth sailing!

We Are All One: What You See in Me, I Can See in You

December 11, 2020

Happy birthday, Kristin. I truly pray that everyone feels as blessed as I am. At times, it's refreshing bringing awareness once again and becoming appreciative of our families, not allowing ourselves to become complacent with the specialness of having close ones close in heart.

Be grateful for family and/or chosen family. You can truly see one another in one another. Even though I continue to see the good in everyone, at times, if I'm being totally honest, it's a struggle. It may take some time to move into the gratefulness. I often reply to people when they say loving, beautiful, things to me, "What you see in me, I can see in you." I feel it, I know it, and I believe it with the deepest part of my spirit.

Marianne Williamson, one of my favorite spiritual teachers, says it so beautifully: Regarding the spiritual purpose of love and relationships, there is no greater intimacy between two people than the shared belief that they are each other. This doesn't have to be a romantic relationship. As Williamson says, "Relationships are laboratories of the spirit. They are hospitals of the soul. They are the places where the wounds that we hold will be brought up because that's the only way they can be healed."

Oh my—so beautifully said. Our relationships with one another and ourselves make it a safe place to be. When two gather, or are mixed together, it's like an amazing recipe of love. What a gift we have to give to one another, to ourselves. Savor that thought. What a wonderful taste!

I also believe with all my heart that there is so much more to life than the deeds we all do, the things we have, what our bodies can do, and what the mind's ego can imagine—just so much more. And when we do find the courage to strip away all our labels, our to-do lists, welcoming the time and space to become still, even in the turbulent times that surround our outer bodies, awareness becomes present, and there is fearlessness as we again unwrap and rediscover who we really are. Willingly we live there, at least for a while in time.

Understand that labels are not bad; only when we become so attached to them, when we identify ourselves as *being* those labels, those roles, do we lose our true inner selves. We become so attached to the deeds, as well as the approval of others, that we no longer know our selves.

Here is a perfect time, in the imperfection of time, to remember we are free to realize there's no place to go, nowhere to be, except right here with our selves. We can choose to surround our selves with others who together provide the space for all to be safe and heal hand in hand, step-by-step, heart to heart. Altogether. Amen.

"Heart Seeing" Brings Magic That Can Transform a Flower into a Jumping Dolphin

October 14, 2021

Seeing with our hearts can bring magic, from a beautiful flower to a jumping dolphin. Yes, but we must see through our faith—remain open to believing—and not allow our mind chatter to lead.

Of course, a flower is beautiful, but when a bloom can transform into a dolphin jumping out from a cluster of leaves, it becomes magical.

Now, think about it: When we see only through our minds—or actually listen from the mind and not from the awareness of the heart space—what other magical life moments, miracles, do we miss? How often has this approach caused us to miss truly beautiful moments, possibly miracles yet to be seen?

I believe that by choosing to see only with our minds, at times, we give rise to hurt, maybe anger. If we'd be open to believing a different perceptive, an alternative view or paradigm, we'd just possibly find a blessing lurking beneath the judgment.

Miscommunication can be a gift if we allow it to be, giving it room to transform. We may just discover things about the giver or the receiver or both.

The beginning of the dolphin mystery: We all begin new (as a new baby, new parent, new student, new spouse, new employee, etc.). Perhaps it

would be refreshing to begin again often, choosing to begin from a still mind connected with a full heart, and rebirth often. Imagine just what may appear.

When my new loving neighbor, Mary, gave me a starter from the plant she enjoyed, wanting to share its magic with me, it took a few months for it to feel open to bloom in its new surroundings. When I sent Mary a picture of the first flower, she replied, "Oh, so you're having dolphins appearing on your plant now." I had to do a double take and let go of (the mind's perception of) the flower, and through my heart, the dolphin immediately jumped out.

Following my belief of that first sighting, it wasn't long before several dolphins joined the pod. I have talked to my plants for years—I truly believe that they are as alive as we are and that they feel our energy. It is just so magical and miraculous.

I know a couple of people who can't see the dolphin in spite of the flower. I feel that one person in particular does see it but just wants to stand firm in the literal truth.

"It's a flower, Joni." Well, how about both? Is it possible to see both? I believe it is. Looking through a different lens—why is it so hard for many of us to do? To possibly experience a different way of perceiving? We must understand that no two people experience reality in the exact same way.

Now, of course you know I'm going to elaborate on this, using it as a metaphor. It's like someone who has lost or never embraced the belief of angels. Where's the proof? they ask.

Well, we know yesterday happened (or did it?), yet we don't really have any proof. We can argue how individuals experienced their "yesterday," and—*poof*—it's over. Going, going … it's gone, no longer (or never really was?) real. It's like a dream we've just awakened from. Two or more people could experience the same day together yet describe reality differently than their friends.

Hopefully we remember beautiful dreams and not too many nightmares, just as, in this moment, we can awaken and possibly see the blessing in the nightmare if we choose to find the opening, the rainbow after the storm. Such is the handiwork of God, laced in miracles.

Hopefully that brings us to be more open to other realities. Perhaps in certain ways we interrupt things. We may even choose to argue or find a reason to be suspicious, to judge someone's belief or paradigm.

I know that years ago I was more stubborn in what I believed to be right: "the literal truth." Now I find so much gray—so much! I often see the dolphin in the flower a lot sooner. I see blite, where truth, rightness, finds oneness and black and white release a need to fight. We are in fact all together as one.

Unfortunately, when we get so caught up in the busyness of the day-to-day to-do list, patterns, and beliefs, often handed down generations, our vision can become myopic and often blurred. Our ears and eyes close, and our mouths tend to be overworked. I'm sure you've heard this powerful statement: we cannot change what we are not aware of.

Perhaps if we take a breath, choose to be in silence, walk in nature, and become aware, possibly, just possibly, we can be open to another's beliefs and point of view and see, feel, the similarities instead of the differences.

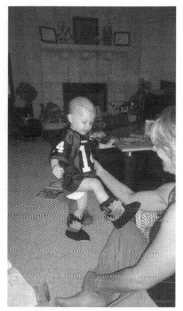

So often I see and hear about people who get stuck on what is different, and in all actuality, if you pull yourself back and open your heart space, you can see all the similarities, and the differences can become the bridge to a higher possibility, where all feel at home.

I am convinced that if we want to make a change, it will take our going within and feeling from the heart's space instead of thinking from the rigid mind's scripts, written and copyrighted many years ago. We must make a change *now*.

Rylan thought Jmom was perfect in all her imperfections.

Watch how differences give birth to change—a change that becomes the miracle, the blessing. It may take some time to be seen. We can begin by being more open to synergizing; it's not my way or your way but together a higher, better way.

When we begin to awaken and our awareness is heightened, we find we often choose our responses differently—we perhaps aren't *reactive* as often. We begin to choose space between what happens (or we perceive has happened) and how we choose to respond. There's the blessing. We begin to truly live. And so a wonderful journal opportunity: What does it mean to you to truly begin living? Take a few moments and allow the question to penetrate your soul. Are you really truly living? Or are you just existing day to day, at times moment to moment?

We learn we can choose to stop the patterns and begin again. Yay! We can consider that, for example, a particular situation or way of life that we were choosing to see in a certain manner could be seen through an entirely different lens.

So often, our words may be different and we stand so firm in what we say (ego) that we lose sight of the blooming of the dolphin. Words often can be misleading. Our interpretation just may become a possible blite area now. Blite brings light!

Blite: we are open to feel, to see, what is not seen with the mind's eyes. The mystery is felt as a subtle knowingness—for me, the warmth of the swarming butterflies sending love from my heart center to every part of my body. Where there are no words that can possibly explain, there is a presence of home, a feeling that I am free and all is well.

Blite opens the reflection of light, and we are able to become the best we are to be in this moment. Open—where the bridge, the rainbow bridge, carries us to become one on the other side. It's just perfect, in my book, when we can celebrate the love as we come to gather together, perhaps not perfect but perfect in our imperfection.

All is well right where we are. We will find our way and now, once again, rest in the lap of God.

5

Nothing Can Still Your Joy

It takes courage to be happy, but it is possible. There is always a light waiting to lead you out of darkness.

It Takes Courage to Be Happy

March 10, 2020

RYLAN AND I ALWAYS HAD SO much fun, and we still do. We loved to laugh—really laugh! As if nobody were watching or listening, even in the hospital surroundings, we found the happiness from within and the joy! Yes, it came from within; the environment didn't matter. I believe it was all the loving

In remission: time to gather with others and play tackle football, together again as we play this love—yes, love.

energy coming from Rylan and me (though we all have it within). Happiness isn't always presented as laughter and high energy—no, often it's a deeper joy, a joy of peace, silence, and stillness, untouched by what or how the mind thinks we should be or act. It just is.

I desire here to emphasize that outside people and/or situations seem to bring us happiness but that it is in fact only fleeting, temporary. True, lasting happiness comes from our inner selves, not external factors like people, situations, and objects.

Some people may not understand this, but most of the time, I'm happy. Let's not get caught up in the descriptors and their different meanings—though I do feel the better-reaching word here may be *joy*. I just can't imagine anything but a happy, joy-filled life.

I am forever filled with gratitude and appreciation for this moment and

each moment of my life. I can't put a finger on what activated this intense knowing, but it's where I want to be. When a temporary storm presents itself, I choose to hope through faith and love that the rainbow is waiting through the challenge and will appear with the brilliance of color and light once again.

Yes, yes, and yes, I do have moments in which I feel sadness, deep sadness, stemming from fear. The feelings come, the thoughts return, and at times, I

feel like they won't find the space to leave, that I won't be able to return to my heart's space of the now, where all is well. And the exterior may in fact not look as if all is well, but the knowing I am connected to *is*, and I flow into it as a river flows back to the sea.

During those times, my stillness and breath guide my inner satori moment once again. I'm left knowing that happiness truly comes from inside, and I am reminded just how true that statement is—that it takes courage to be happy. It takes courage to acknowledge and express when not-so-happy times are on the horizon.

Yoga gifted me space, though not at first. I soon realized—well, maybe not so soon—that yoga is not about fixing myself or others. I went to yoga initially to encourage my husband to feel better, primarily physically but also mentally. But practicing more yoga on (and off) the mat, I had another avenue to excavate, or could peel back even more layers of my onion of life.

I love that my yoga experience continues to bring forth many (onion) tears, some accompanying or delivering sadness, many of gratitude—and all satori moments. Through cleansing breaths of awareness, they continue to bring deep, deep joy, and I am abundantly joy filled

With each layer peeled back, the flowing tears cleanse the lens of life. Moments become magnificently clear. Sometimes an onion layer opens a floodgate of tears, and I allow them to flow. It's OK—in fact, it's to be celebrated. I continue to this day getting so excited about my yoga life both on and off the mat. There's a knowingness that it's OK for me to be happy, joyful, even when others feel I am "out of [my] mind." I actually consider that a compliment now.

We may even feel that being happy is selfish and that if we show our happiness, others will not accept us. In those times, I find it healing to remember that happiness doesn't come by the approval of others or by good deeds. For me, happiness is a feeling (actually *the* presence in my heart) that is not dependent on any label.

When you are totally being you and connected, you have discovered the authentic joy of happiness, and you may find yourself with your self quite often. Celebrate time with presence.

Perhaps, though, it becomes challenging for others to be surrounded with your joy-filled energy. You may feel *their* energy—be aware. This may bring up emotions and thoughts. When you're feeling energy of others toward you, is it possible you're labeling them, projecting your own judgments or feelings? Once again, it goes back to our knowing that we have no one to be, just our selves. There's no one to impress, so nothing is going to dim our light.

Do you find that you're feeling judged often? We can make a decision and drop the labeled feelings (both sides of the coin, self and others) and now feel the emotion. Emotions take longer to work through, but it is possible to change our mindsets. That's all about the excavating I love to share. Where does it come from? Where did I pick up that overused labeled emotion?

What *thoughts* are marinating in those emotions? When I'm struggling and unable to return to my peace of happiness (again, I know that's a word with old baggage, so how about *joy*?), I most likely will excuse myself, spend some time with self—no labeling of judgment toward others—release, and just be.

Why must we feel we need to judge in order to justify a decision to change our surroundings, our environments? Here's an option: simply (well, maybe it's not so simple) move through and go with the energy that serves your soul. Is it your ego or your inner I, your self and spirit? I believe that if it's your innermost self, you will move into energy that is just perfect in the moment.

We all are responsible for the energy we bring, with no strings tied to outside surroundings. We can't remain stuck in our minds of judgment about situations and people that we can't control. How about going within to a possible choice to influence the situation—or not? Then let it go, allowing the energy to move through the mist, evaporating into the now past.

Yoga opens opportunities to guide me further to understanding that it all begins with me and will end with me. It is all about me. When I can release any judgment I have toward others, the feeling, the emotion, behind the labeled judgment, then my life becomes freer, opening up space for happiness, joyfulness. When this happens, it brings me into the present wholeheartedly for others, with no judgment and no attachment to the outcome. I acknowledge it is truly about me unconsciously looking for reasons to be offended by others. Celebrate such uncovering! Continue the excavation! And celebrate the lightness—release even more!

So it does take courage to be happy. May we each decide to be filled with gratitude and appreciation for our lives and celebrate the opportunity to love ourselves so that we are filled with kindness toward others. I am worth it! You are worth it! We *all* are worth it. Amen!

Don't Worry; Be Happy

September 9, 2019

Yes, the positive saying "Don't worry; be happy" can be overstated, especially for those of us who have, at times, felt defeated, tired, or depressed.

How can anyone expect us to be happy when we don't feel happy—when, at times, we are deeply sad?

I have argued those exact facts many times. Maybe life slowly taught me, in a very patient, loving way, that when I choose to fill my thoughts (perhaps with happy memories), taking a walk in nature (or in my backyard) and opening my heart's mind to all the wonders

Boy, do I miss these little Smilin' Rylan yogis! They bring such love and light!

and miracles that surround me, I seem to move into consciousness, and happy inner feelings bring the blessings in just being. The trees, hummingbirds, flowers, the sky, and clouds pull awareness into my heart's mind, and there the fluttering butterflies, warm and subtle, take flight.

Even when my heart was broken, there was always a light I could feel, find, to guide

me through my darkness. At times, my mind would take me on an adventure, a crazy detour train ride. It would do its darndest to talk me out of the light (choice), leaving me searching blindly in the dark for hope. I would choose to blame, adopting a victim mindset.

Through all my chapters of life, having written on my heart a reminder, I find a glimpse of peace, joy, and, yes, happiness. I know for my self that when I do make the decision to breathe, become still, acknowledge how I'm feeling, and step off the wild train, I will once again see (feel) clearly.

This week, the little yogis will be practicing postures and meditation and, during the funshop portion, talking about the choices we make and how they influence our lives as well as others'.

Greet the Familiar with Openness, Newness, and Presence

June 2, 2020

The words I began to write have gained a deeper meaning these past days. Thích Nhất Hạnh talks about breath and peace in each moment, about always keeping a beginner's mind to remember, return, to your deepest desire.

My desire for the past several years has been to live each moment as if it were my last, loving, appreciating, and accepting each moment as much as possible without resistance. Yes, of course it hasn't been perfect, but I have loved my life. The good, the bad, the indifferent—they are all a part of the whole, and I believe each holds gifts within. We only need to be open to them and unwrap.

As I'm writing this, my life, my familiar life, has turned upside down, and an intense moment-to-moment life has taken center stage. When

things happen that demand immediate attention, it seems as if life stands still; everything appears so much more precious and fleeting. Once again, I savor the pure essence of now, remembering through my breath that this moment is precious and a lifetime in itself.

I hug my daughter so much when we are physically present. And when we aren't, we talk at least once a day on the phone. Hug your loved ones often!

As I talked to my beautiful daughter, Krisi, this morning, we were reminiscing about how important it is to make good memories and not allow them to continue to bring sadness in the present moment. Yes, feel the emotion, and do your best to use the awareness when you become stuck comparing or wishing to go back to that good or perfect moment.

It's a gift I'd like to give to so many people, and I've said for many years: Experience each moment as if it's a lifetime, and enjoy it—live it fully. But then release it and move with open awareness to the next lifetime moment, then the next.

With the COVID lockdown and Darrell at postacute, I haven't touched his physical form since May 19. I miss him and love him.

These past few days (especially), there were times I might have honored that belief even more. It's amazing how life will bring another miracle to remind us to live in the present moment. There are no reruns. I don't believe in regrets; I believe you  live your life so you have no regrets—that no matter what is happening, in the moment, you welcome it and wrap it with love. What I have been struggling with these last few days is wishing I could go back to some of the beautiful memories, and as I remind myself (or as awareness reminds me), this is the next moment. This is life. What am I choosing to be present to? How will I live this moment? Love or fear? I choose love, many times taking the train ride for a bit and arriving back through conscious awareness, and know that all is well.

May we all choose to live in the next moment of what we have come to know as time.

Nonjudgment, Acceptance, Courage, Forgiveness, and Loving What Is

May 26, 2020

At the time of my writing this entry, Darrell has been in the hospital for a week. He is not doing well. His mind is not here in the now, instead continuing to be tortured in a dark place as his body is further breaking down. I pray he allows his inner self to be front and center. I hope he finds his way to the front of the train and turns it around, releasing from the constant fear that is crashing into continued doubt and anger.

As we are all called to accept a "new normal," may our presence also find and be filled with an even brighter light of inner peace, unclouded by things and doingness—simply (yet with some challenge) becoming brighter, lighter, and more joy filled in our moment-to-moment lives. Yes, it takes a lot of awareness. Be gentle with yourself and others; we truly are all in this together!

How about using this time to accelerate the unwrapping and embracing of gifts of the moment? I have been called to an even deeper searching within my soul. At times, moments are earthshaking, eventful lifetimes of releasing; surrendering to acceptance as well as forgiveness and, yes, love; and welcoming and not resisting the flow of grace.

I'm meeting the deeper surrendering of the condition, situation, without my expectations interfering, and opening to the knowing of blessings yet to come. My mantra lately is "Allow it to be," which opens up for self-awareness, reminding us of what our truth is. It's believing that all we truly have is in this moment, and it is already the past, so allowing nothing to steal our joy. It's about feeling the happiness! We must breathe and look around with eyes of newness, witnessing what is right before us, and within us, as we become filled with appreciation of the knowingness that this, too, shall pass.

I find duplicity when my thoughts become the judge and jury. I feel I am not my self, and wonder why I am deceiving my self, with thoughts that "life shouldn't be like this" and "we planned well, and this isn't what we worked so hard for and visualized our future would be." I am not my self when I'm resisting and struggling against what is, wondering what happened to the life we had and thinking, feeling, that our moments should be like they used to

169

be. These thoughts spiral us down a deep unending hole of resisting what is. It's the perfect time to take to heart, breathe, and release.

When I'm not able to feel my breath, find the breath of life, when my mind is taking off without my spirit and the dialogue is all about fear, it's at that sacred moment that I have the opportunity to deepen into an even greater realness of who I am. I know, am so familiar with, this moment—a gift to go deeper, to stop what I'm doing so that I can quiet the chatter and busyness and just *be*.

I believe and have a knowingness that when I can look back at a time that was very hard to live through and see, live the miracle, the rainbow of blessings, I have now reached into the wisdom of my I-ness, my self, who I really am. Yep, the fluttering butterflies begin again, gentle and warm.

Just a few days ago, I talked to a beautiful hero on the front line. She told me that sometimes she just rolls out her mat and lays on it (as I often do) and becomes present with her breath. This was one of the loving reasons Naomi and I started doing Zoom yoga at no charge for others: to be there and care as so many are doing for all of us!

Naomi and me doing yoga, breathing in the gift of knowing others will enjoy the replay, hopefully feeling playful and free. Giving the parents of our little yogis (at no charge) the opportunity to practice yoga with us too. The energy of love circulates! Can you feel the love?

I understand some people like to have their special areas where they go to become present. Candles, kneeling area—it doesn't matter the space, as long as it's a spot you go to discover how to carry the present inner peace as you venture from that sacred place of solitude into life, your every moment life. You can drop into that space, be taken back home into the awareness, and once again become one with the moment, celebrating life in so much gratitude and appreciation.

When I struggle with my thoughts darkening my moments (even if it's just a glimpse of spiraling down to craziness), when my heart is no longer consciously filtering my thoughts, I have become disconnected. I will definitely roll out my yoga mat. It doesn't take my self long—the I will let go and allow the moment to guide me. I will end on my back, surrendering into Savasana. My heart becomes my messenger. Yes, call it *meditation, praying, beingness* … they are all words. Just *be*!

Who Are You Now? Not Referring to Your Past or Future—Could There Be More?

February 5, 2021

We come into this life with ourselves and will leave with ourselves. I believe my husband, Darrell—Doc, Dr. Kirby, Dad, Grandfather, the titles and labels go on—especially during those final days, unwrapped and rediscovered who he really was.

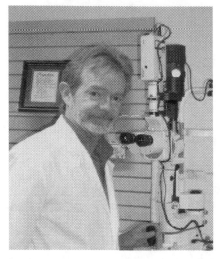

The journey was rough and comprised many years of built-up resentment, thirteen years' worth of feeling God had let him down. Forgotten about him. There was blame thrown in so many directions. As his spouse and best friend, I found it troubling at times to watch, to remain being present yet remember not to allow myself to fall into his quicksand of no return (well, I did often, and then I returned more aware).

He was stripped of every role, every materialistic label/title, and able to be with his self more, opening space and ultimately welcoming peace to fill the moments during his last few days of physical life before he took flight. He was so present and peace filled. You could feel it in the air; you could sense he was in the space. He was returning to the love affair of the self with himself.

Through Darrell's fight with prostate cancer, which spanned many years, and especially looking back now, you see how (little by little) he was stripped away of everything he'd thought his self to be.

We would often talk about it through the years, but I would feel and experience through his energy how he continued to hang on tightly to those labels: his titles, schooling, degrees, and IQ. I also saw how that tormented him. It would break my heart that he identified who he was using those exterior labels. And they were slowly failing him.

His fight (which was killing him quickly) with cancer came from his fight to hang on to what and who he believed his self to be. That facade would gradually fade into mist in the background, giving way to who he really was, now front and center.

If I could have given him anything through all the years, I would have given him the space where he could feel safe, where conscious love could hold him in the warmth of grace. I tormented myself at times wishing and praying for him to surrender to peace, the peace of awareness. But he was to find it in His time, God's time, and it was perfect, as I look back, in the imperfection of it all. Perfect.

When Darrell finally found peace of surrendering, dropping the anger at what cancer could, would, strip him of (all the roles and labels), the light of his soul would ultimately bring him peacefully home. I could feel, witness, the moments he became free, his fight to the flight of freedom. So there may be moments we feel are torments of hell but are actually pieces of heaven just awaiting the breakthrough, the rainbow, the miracle.

I feel Darrell now more often than I felt him during the fight—his lengthy struggles, battles into an adventure, metamorphosis, and breaking free to the ultimate *flight*.

It was when Darrell let go of these titles, who he'd thought he was (and quite honestly who I at times had thought he was), that the light shone and he began to feel free to be who he really was. And he was at peace—yes, happy.

I love to share that I am so blessed that, through his loving care and dedication, Dr. Sorensen, along with his wonderful nurse, Pam, as well as all his family of assistants, brought Darrell home so he could spend the last few days with me. Darrell was so touched that, finally, what he wanted was being heard loud and clear.

Darrell was surrounded by chosen family, who celebrated him and his life and let him go into his flight of peacefulness. This impacted everyone present. I was able to see and feel firsthand who he (and all of us) really was and is. I hadn't felt that for many years. Yes, stripped bare of all labels, he shone. It was, is, and will forever be magical and breathtakingly beautiful.

You could say I was in a dream state, he was in a dream state, and we were all in a dream state. We were all present, living in the moment. I have to wonder, *Were we in a dream state, or …*

Do we live in a dream? Are we walking moment to moment in a labeled, titled exterior, focused on and carrying possessions we've accumulated through our choices in life?

If so, it's time for us to wake up. Perhaps we are so conditioned to be what we have collected from physical birth onward and don't give it a second thought. The accumulation of roles we were (and are) expected to play—we accepted and may even feel that we *are* those labels and roles. I have a feeling that many of us would rather not be rehearsing them over and over, yet we feel trapped. Perhaps there's something deeper we have yet to discover. Possibly that something is to begin excavating and return much more often to who we really are. Yes, it takes a lot of love and patience, but it's worth every release, every bag we choose to drop, so that we can once again feel the freedom.

Ask yourself whether you're measuring success by the things you have, the deeds you do, or the relationships in your life. Are they really who you are? Temporary, in every case. It's amazing how we try to justify or live up to some title or label. It can be so very stressful and fleeting—here today, gone tomorrow.

Where do we—you and I—focus our attention each moment? As I've mentioned many times, I've had several satori moments that have guided me to move through some thick s—— (*stuff*)! My life definitely smells better, and I'm still excavating and enjoying the journey.

When Rylan was around, Darrell often would let go, release, and surrender to the fun of now. You could feel the joy they had together.

Well, you know what? I don't know about you, but I vote for living each moment in a dream state of reality. And through that reality of awareness, I choose to be open to the surrounding realness so as to feel the realness surrounding me. Each moment waits to be noticed and must be lived fully, uncluttered by so many layers of roles, goals, and labels. Now acknowledge the power of letting go and embrace it wholeheartedly.

Forecast Ahead Is Calm: Cambria Beach Walks / Friendship Knows No Distance

December 18, 2020

Remember past entries about the friendship? It's a relationship in which all choose to stay on board, even through turbulent times, perhaps when tidal waves are in the forecast. There is a safe harbor where our vessels of emotions find shelter, especially from rough waters and tough times. Two or more individuals gather together, confident there will be no jumping ship. Amid rough seas in these friendships, we find security, comfort, and times of refuge until we are back, connected to self. So get your sea legs ready and enjoy this amazing journey we call life.

Forever friends: Leaine (Cyndi's daughter—and mine too), Krisi, me, and Cyndi (my chosen sister of forty-five years).

The friendship will not go under, and if it ever starts sinking, everyone on board feels, is, the oneness, and the friendship stays afloat. My beautiful daughter and I have this conversation so often: life is so short (or is it?). Choose wisely who is going to be in your space, and then, after making the decision, look within your self and find the joy in the moment. Live it fully, because once again, it really doesn't ultimately depend on others or outside happenings and conditions. Nope, it's not about them; it's about you. And it's about me. And it truly is liberating, so freeing!

Forever my chosen family: Darrell; Maximus,
on my lap; Naomi; and Victor.

What are your choices? Who do you choose to spend time with? Where do you choose to spend your time? Are you proactively nurturing relationships, serving, unconditionally depositing into others' emotional bank accounts?

Or are you choosing to unconsciously spend time being in unimportant moments—moments that seem to lead often to a crisis? Do you spend much of your time scooping out water from your ship just to stay afloat, while your so-called shipmates sit back and criticize? And perhaps you mirror back to them. In these moments, we may forget that our minds are habits. Unless we step consciously into the next moment, we are living from scripted, rehearsed plays of life. Friendships characterized by these moments and dynamics spend most of the time in turbulent waters.

When we have nurtured and spent time in the heart's space, uncovering or discovering happiness within, smooth sailing is in the forecast. The outside surroundings can be turbulent or calm; they don't even affect us. Well, I can't say they don't ever affect us, but again, it's like those sudden waves (sometimes tidal waves)—the forecast isn't showing calm, clear weather for a while, but we don't choose to jump overboard, giving up to outside weather. We make our own inner sunshine, shining brightly in love. The sunshine is always in the sky above as well as within. The weather doesn't affect or change that.

Chemo and all the medication Rylan was on didn't slow him down or keep him from wanting to save the world. I know he had an innate knowing that all is well.

The deepest part of us—call it soul, Spirit, the I (self) of who we really are— knows that all things, all matter, will pass, dissolve, leaving that which never dies, and all truly is well. Our lives open up with the most brilliant rainbows and reassure us once again with calm sailing, sunshine, and happiness!

Naomi and I have been through a cyclone of weather conditions these past few days, and our relationship is weathering the storm. At this writing, I'm still waiting for the rainbow (I see it peeking through).

I know it's coming! I feel its presence before my vision recognizes it.

I honestly don't think anybody would believe what these last couple of days on board our friendship have been like, with Naomi navigating the journey to help me (and my self, I) move. When I am with I, my self, no amount of bad weather can take me under and leave me helpless in ego-based confusion. I feel the togetherness, and there's a peace.

When chosen family members are on board with you, any given moment becomes an adventure of love. There truly is nothing that's impossible; there is the knowingness that this storm will pass. The beautiful bow from the rain will tie all the blessings together and become present, always right there yet soon to appear for us to feel, to see. Yes, the rainbow of light—feel the warmth and the beauty.

Chosen family members are most often very proactive and look back when the waters become a little less rough with hearts full of understanding and so much giggling (anybody who knows Naomi and me knows that to be true). Another memory is left as a map to return to if need be. Well, we made it through that storm, and the rainbow was that much brighter—worth a little seasickness and a little upset.

These memories remind us that everything is truly a gift, and when so many people are going through challenging times, as we are now, we must look for all the gifts, the blessings, that we have, never forgetting that we are connected at the seams. And yet, in truth, there are no seams; we are one.

Yes, I understand. From time to time, life can become very challenging, but what's the alternative?

For my self, I will choose to see the blessings and the love and to witness love in smiles, or in the sparkle in a person's eye when she looks at me, I look at her, and she knows once again that I see her! Namaste, and I truly love you all!

"Twinkle, Twinkle, Little Star": We Are All Stars—Shine On!

January 8, 2021

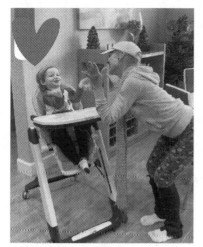

Grayson and Jmom doing "Twinkle, Twinkle, Little Star" with the Wiggles.

Do you ever wonder why certain songs attract little ones? Grayson, my sweetheart, can be crying and upset, and all we have to do is start singing "Twinkle, Twinkle, Little Star," and he becomes a light for all present.

Isn't that also true for us? Is it for you? Don't we lose our shine at times and forget that we are here to twinkle, be brilliant lights, shining stars, in this world?

Yes, there are definitely reasons why (especially now, with the stay-at-home mandate) we may find it especially hard—perhaps a good phrase would be *difficult to grasp*. We may find it challenging to feel our light within. We can definitely find room (there goes our space) for reasons to latch on to, to justify our unhappiness, all stemming from fear.

When I feel unhappy or stressed (fearful), I really become as aware as possible so I can focus my attention and energy (where my attention goes, my energy flows) on one of millions of blessings that surround me.

I first make sure I'm present in the breath of now. At times, I will close my eyes and breathe in, and as I breathe out, slowly releasing, I'll open my eyes as if I'm seeing this moment as a newborn baby would—full of adventure, with little (actually no) expectations (well, except perhaps a diaper change or bottle), in awe of the present scene before me—and I (my self) just am.

Of course, hindsight is always the best lesson, the most obvious myopic vision. At times, when I feel my vision is blurred, as if I've lost my inner self's shine completely, I return to the knowing that I can't control the outside environment. I may be able to influence it at times, but I can always find the space to remember the mind is not good or bad; it just is. The mind harbors thoughts, habits of thoughts. I return to becoming aware of the movie playing.

I *enjoy* becoming humbled; I love to share it with somebody (safe friendship mate) so that I can acknowledge my lack of presence and, with no judgment, using my awareness, choose to embrace and learn so as to return, allowing the memory to fade to the past and move on. I see it as it is—who I am not—and take steps that I now feel would be a gift to myself as well as others. I am once again back in alignment with who I am: I-ness, my self.

My mission is not to beat the me up when or if it takes longer to clean my lens to clear my vision. Remembering once I am clear again, I let it go. I let the baggage slide off my shoulder, and I feel light once more. I arrive in the moment free to be.

This is another perfect opportunity to do some journaling! You can truly use it to wipe away onto paper any leftover residue! When we choose to move on, forgive ourselves, we find space in the moment—freedom. That freedom allows space for others to do the same. Have you ever noticed that people who are really hard on themselves are hard on other people? Why?

So as the end of the week becomes the weekend, may we love ourselves, forgiving and enjoying the mistakes, as we move on and shine bright as twinkling little stars.

What Is My Fruit Bearing in Each Moment?
Breathe, Feel, Love, and Release

August 6, 2021

Take a moment and breathe. Feel the emotions from your heart. What is the energy taking up residence in your presence of the now speaking, saying, perhaps loudly (not so much what is happening but rather the energy left in its trail)?

When you are open to truly be the moment, in each moment, handling what is presented in love, knowing this is temporary—there's the fruit. Perhaps it doesn't crop up in this moment, but it will be coming, as it's developing the perfect ripeness for your life's harvest. Have faith in this moment that all is just perfect. The present exterior may be imperfect, but it will fade. Believe. Yes, it truly takes love and faith.

There's the harvest, the energy that's left. Acknowledge that and the fruit given as well as received. We perceive experiences differently depending on the lenses we look through. We all have our own perceptions. In some cases, the smell from past dirty laundry we have yet to clean, the stinky stuff we're still carrying around as luggage or baggage, can leave us exhausted and reactive at times. They can fog up the lenses we use to view the moment, distorting the beauty all around us and obscuring the blessings to be found, leaving our fruit appearing less than inviting.

The reason I named my miracle fur babies Love and Faith.

And we allow the smelly past items left within to inform our view of the moment. And that is not necessarily bad. It may seem like it at the time. It may feel as if our cocoons are smothering our souls, often leaving us feeling miserable. Yet sometimes we become so miserable that it moves us to begin (again) our excavating. The fruit just may be a perfect harvest—just may be salvageable when we begin clearing out the stink from within. So it is a blessing. We may just not be ready to recognize it. But it's there.

I look back now and see that the times I was in my deepest dirty-laundry drama (drowning) were part of the metamorphosis, the coming satori moment of awakening. They were just awaiting my decision to go deep within and rediscover (again) who I really am. Those moments quite honestly have been some of the most beautiful satori moments in my life. The key word in this is *honesty*. It's about being honest with myself, digging deep as I open to what is waiting to be uncovered and released.

I'm hoping I received a satori moment after all that crying.

Seeing through a particular lens is not the problem unless your vision is so blurry that you can't see the light—the light that protects our long-term vision from distortions. In these cases, fear becomes the focus instead of love. We are definitely out of focus when we continue to feel stuck in the muck. Ask the question, How do I feel?

I believe that a wonderful first step—and I know I share this often—is to begin bringing awareness to the acceptance that your happiness does not depend on someone or something separate from you. You are your happiness (or not).

Of course, it doesn't mean you don't have boundaries that you choose to place in your life and live by. I like to share that it's not about me demanding someone know my boundaries but about me living my boundaries and sharing with those who have a desire to be in my life. Of course, it is with nonjudgment, love, and acceptance that we release those who don't.

I have found that when you are surrounded with friends who desire to be part of one another's moments, things simply are. If you're living your boundaries, they speak loudly without the need of enforcement (in *most* cases, I should add). I have never been a big believer of tough love; the word alone doesn't serve who I know my self to be.

When I'm living my life with love and respect for my self, I am then free and therefore, at least presently, whole for others. I'm not expecting others to constantly pick up my pieces and put them back together. How can they? They are looking through their own lenses, distorted or clear.

At times, our lives may feel as though they're in perfect focus. Then there are times our lives may feel out of focus. We may not be clear on the view we are receiving, perceiving. But, once again, all is well, and we are open to refocus. We are aware it will pass and the fruit will ripen.

Life eventually falls into place. We are where we're meant to be. I feel and know that. Even suffering can be accepted and embraced as an adventure of understanding what the suffering is gifting us. Once again, what is the alternative? My experience has been that when I resist it, it will grow and continue robbing me of the preciousness of life. I am in no way saying I look forward to times that bring hardship—no, quite the opposite. If it is out of my hands, so to speak, embracing a situation is an option of least resistance. My experience has been to embrace and step away from it as much as possible, to view it as if I'm watching a movie.

There are times I don't give up very easily, willingly. I tend to keep on within an adventure, an experience that I feel deeply about, and at times, I allow my boundaries to ease up some. More times than not, it births exactly what I know to be my life, in my life; I am filled with gratitude.

There are of course times, perhaps people, often in the family, I don't want to give up on and I relentlessly keep trying. Obviously, they don't want me (or what they feel when they're with me) in their lives, and I have to remind myself that they have chosen their boundaries and I need to respect them and let it go, allowing the waves to carry it back to the ocean of life.

Honestly, it's usually the best road to go down. There seems to be a lot less hidden drama, fewer replays and falls in deep pits of stuff. It's a tough decision, though, as family can be hard to give up on. At times, letting go is holding on, remembering that no one, nothing, can steal my joy.

So it's not bad to see (perceive) things in a different light—as long as it's through light. Not darkness, distorted from past fears and doubts. Seeing things differently can bring a deeper since of a newness toward forward thinking, being. Better yet, no thinking, just whole beingness.

"If we are all the same, only one is needed." I remember I heard that years ago and it ignited another huge satori moment: Joni, quit trying to change others!

I have loved to dance all my life and couldn't quite understand why not everyone liked doing it, or practicing yoga. I sing even if others flinch and hold their ears. Be open to express your energy, your fruit. Well, sometimes it may not bring the best harvest, Joni!

Here's a related example from my marriage: Darrell was a night owl, and I'm an early bird. I stopped trying years ago to change him. He was a little less willing to see my love of the early mornings and early evenings in meditation.

Yet we loved each other regardless, and it didn't divide us in arguments. It tried, but with love, everything is possible. He enjoyed watching sports, and I grew to get excited too. I never nagged him about that. When I did make comments, he simply ignored them anyway. He knew I wouldn't continue on. I respected his love of sports. I would bake and practice yoga, what I felt joyful spending my moments doing, being grounded in love.

Yes, we are truly all the same inside. I do believe our personalities truly want to be heard and loved and desire to be respected.

The challenge is when there are two (or more) groups (or individuals) and, whatever the dividing factor, those on one or both sides demand everyone else go all the way into their homes, dwellings, wherever their hearts live—when they ask others to adopt their shared paradigm, the lens they're looking through.

Of course, I am strong in the belief that intentions fuel the action. So I am in no way an advocate of being open to beliefs that have intentions married in fear. Now, with my having said that, again, often several roads lead to the same destination. Why not share the journey? The scenery and adventure just may be even more beautiful when two (or more) maps are traveled, explored, discovered, and enjoyed together. On all ends, you can't go wrong if your intentions are wrapped in love.

Take a breath, leaving the ego behind and instead heart listening. Can you imagine the new world birthing—the one in which we all begin listening from the heart's space? I believe it's happening. More are seeing the world through hope and faith, in knowing and believing, and coming to gather together because of the truth that we are humankind, and all of us kind humans. Feel it and believe it.

Far more of us believe that we as humankind, being kind humans, are beginning to shine wholeheartedly our light as one voice coming together, advocating, speaking in actions of love. (We just don't make as much noise and drama as the alternative.)

When we care for one another, beginning and continuing every moment by falling back in love with self, the fruit begins to bear the loving harvest of humankind. We must celebrate differences with the knowing that, deep within, we are all the same. Differences bring space for birthing future hope of those differences, new awakenings—anything becomes possible.

Rylan loved to be Batman. He lived to help rescue people.

Rylan lived love. That little boy (old soul) did not know fear! Through his short life were lessons of love! He loves his Jmom, and I love him to the moon and back. He was so quick to go up to people and hug them. When I went for his first day of preschool, he was everyone's friend. We all watched in awe. The little ones were drawn to him, and the adults wanted to be around him.

I have found that I have so much more energy (and so much more fun) when I, too, am like Rylan: *present*, enjoying serving the ones I love, as well as those passing by. When everyone is part of the family, the

Maximus and me (in loving memory of Rylan).

energy just grows in love—not to mention that choices made from fear are exhausting. I am spent of energy before the choice is even put into action.

I often use the analogy of the planting of a seed. We are given the opportunity to plant, spread, water, fertilize, care, and nurture. We must take the time, moments, to pull the weeds (fear) that will otherwise strangle and destroy the harvest. We must allow the love to spread like a wildfire, igniting acts of kindness and leaving the harvest plentiful. We need to continue to evolve, grow, and spread love to everyone, a harvest of kindness where the fruit is love.

Batman got rid of the bad guys, but what if we all understood that there are times when, deep inside, we're the villains (weeds of fear)? Hopefully more often there are times when we're the superheroes of our lives, spreading through energy to touch others' hearts. We then have compassion for the villains who help make life a play of miracles and rainbows.

The weeds may creep up in the cracks of our lives when we are not aware. We all want to believe our world, our lives, will become better. The challenge is that when we are not present, not aware, we can become lost. We tend to look outside to fill our hearts, hoping that's where our happiness, peace, and joy begin and will fulfill us.

At first it may seem to fulfil us, but it's fleeting. When it leaves us empty, we often become upset, moving into blaming, reaching for other ways to meet our need for happiness, but with the same outcome. It will eventually return back to a vacant space, still in search of something else to help fill it up.

Hence life becomes another cycle of disappointments. Consider these questions (you can uncover the answers simply by listening to your heart): What am I reaching for, and what is causing me to make the same choices? Why am I continuing to reach outside my self for answers and temporary relief, hoping to fill the empty space just for the momentary fix? If you're searching for the feeling, I will say it again: it doesn't last.

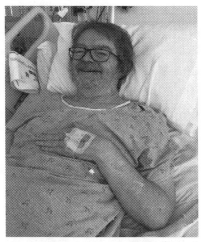

I remember this hospital visit (one of many). I loved to make him laugh. I was probably singing or dancing.

As I've talked to different people throughout the years, and going through this myself, oftentimes I hear, see, and feel that there's a false belief that a person, thing, or event will bring love and happiness. What materializes most often is only a temporary fix, a very brief period, and then we're back to feeling void of peace, happiness, and fulfillment. We're *reaching* once again.

We all have encountered people who demand we feel exactly how they feel. There's almost a feeling of pressure for us to see how things need to change in their way and only their way. Boundaries—at times, they're blessings. To my heart, my soul, I ask the question, what are my intentions? And are my intentions coming from a heart of fear, or is my heart filled with love for all involved?

To bring a future of togetherness, we need to strive for not my way, not your way, but a higher, better way—one that moves future moments into peace, with our gentleness regarding differences nurturing a higher way to acceptance. We must truly go through the labor and know we are birthing as one a new, kinder world—a happier, gentler world.

Perhaps this is a good place to pause your thoughts and either journal or simply, tenderly, take time to reflect on your moments. Journal by allowing your thoughts to spread across the page. What is the fruit you are harvesting in your moments, your life? Perhaps heighten your awareness through silence, meditation or prayer, yoga or a walking meditation, music—whatever pathway that you find brings you into oneness, a presence—and reap the harvest of joy, happiness from within. Embrace your adventure in gardening.

Bringing this chapter to a close, I want to convey that nothing can steal (in stillness) my joy. I look back on my journey to acceptance, acceptance of my self through healing of me, reacquainting with my self. My childhood comprised countless playful acts of life, and I lived many dress rehearsals, playing an array of carefully selected characters, and at some point lost the flow of joyful moments.

When and why did my childhood become so much less fun and much more intense? When did I surrender to the scripts handed down to me, allowing them to take a hold of my authentic childlike spirit and form my new role, a me character, and a new chapter?

And when did I decide to retake and rewrite only when the drama became too much for me to continue with the scripting and constant failed dress rehearsals? I am forever thankful that my life made me so miserable that I began experiencing satori-moment awakenings early and have continued to do so for many years.

I left behind the recurring common play of life—different characters with the same ending, an ending of sadness, and of desperately reaching to find a reason for that sadness (it always was someone else's fault).

Yes, there was a time when I would live as a victim and became very good at it. It was always someone else causing my unhappiness. Yet always, in all different ways, there was a knowing that this was not who I truly was or am. My body, mind, and, most important, my spirit told me subtly yet loudly in my heart, as if I had turned down the scripting mind's thoughts long enough to hear what was a soft calling. I soon felt it strongly, and it drew me gently. Who I really am was always waiting patiently for my return. It was like going home, and I have never looked back in disappointment, because I am home!

I have often asked myself, "At what age did I lose the inner excitement of each moment—the heartstring to the love I felt connected to, the love that made my early years fun and free?" It was as if every day was a celebration of life.

What if every day, every moment, is a celebration of your life, a birth moment to rejoice and play with, something to be opened—the present moment waiting so patiently to be unwrapped with excitement? What a gift, and what an answer to so many prayers. When my beloved within was becoming very familiar to me, talk about a priceless birthday gift!

Every one of us wakes each morning and is given the opportunity to step out of bed and walk through the day's journey with courage, balanced with a loving heart, as Smilin' Rylan showed with every step of his life.

Yoga is life; life is yoga.

6

Breathe in the Space of Stillness between Thoughts

As we move on to the apostrophe of Rylan's untrainings, let me take a moment to explain. An *apostrophe* can be defined as space that indicates a missing letter. So think of the apostrophe in our lives as our willingness to pause, absent of mind chatter, turning off autopilot mode in our days. Yes, it may be tough or rough, possibly because of how we've lived our space up to now.

Shortcut to Happiness, Which Costs Nothing yet Is Everywhere

June 18, 2021

PLEASE TAKE A MOMENT TO WELCOME perhaps another satori moment. Imagine having never seen the outside. Assume you were kept inside (with no windows) for most of your growing years.

Now, visualize your first glimpse into this mystery of the natural world, which for the most part we take for granted. What would be your first experience stepping outside into this unseen fantasy of nature?

Would you feel it was a facade, an illusion? That someone was playing a trick on you? How could this be real? It's so different from the handmade, put-together structure of a dwelling—the only real environment, up to this present moment, you knew to be real.

This fairy-tale oasis of utter aliveness, where everything is so vibrant, seemingly so unreal—truly someone must be tricking you, presenting an illusion and playing to your vulnerability. Being vulnerable? Can you step out of your busyness for just a few minutes and discover the space of liberation from the mind's history of what is, even if just for a few breaths?

So ready, set, let's go ... enjoy the journey of simple awareness. I do this often. I can always count on it bringing me into now. It takes my mind away (my breath away too).

I act as if it's the first time I'm walking out my front door. In Cambria, it's often my porch I use for my connection to becoming conscious.

I do my best to quiet the chatter in my mind, emptying out everything I can so as to open the space between thoughts. Actually, it's when I neither act nor search—I simply open the door, and my breath is taken away as I take my first step into paradise, where I am nowhere yet everywhere. (Remember we've never seen the paradise of nature.)

It doesn't matter what time of day it is, but I usually step into awareness practice first thing in the morning and when the sun is setting. Although, now, I can do it anywhere I am. At times, I literally have tears just flowing. Other times I'm just aware. There are no words.

As I have mentioned, the experience has become easier for me to fall into. I have practiced often, moving (yet not) into the fantasy of reality, and now am able to step into the mystery often. When I stopped forcing, it became natural. We all have it. We've just become accustomed to making our minds habits to listen to, perceiving the thoughts as real.

So here's the best way I can explain it: I once again find my self in the space that is nothingness yet everythingness. In this space, I feel as if there's nothing in my life I can lose or that I need, and I feel such an overwhelming secure, all-loving peace. Nothing matters, just a contentment of being present in the now. And ...

Now just is.

As another week ends and we welcome each moment of the coming weekend, may we take a moment of life and find a new awakening presence as we open the door to the natural and take in our first glimpse: mesmerizing love to everyone!

May We All Unwrap Many Happy Moments as They Become Present

December 24, 2019

I was listening to morning songs of my heart, as I do each morning after meditating and before setting foot on the ground, to open and peek inside as if everything were new. The words hit me, flowing so beautifully, welcoming me to allow my day to unfold without expectations and reminding me to be open to the newness.

Sometimes that means my choosing to trust, even when I feel scattered and not together. And yes, I find the space through breath, allowing awareness of self to take the wheel so I don't return to autopilot (during which my mind might take me on an unwanted trip to the past or lead to another unwanted destination). I remind myself to choose patience toward myself and extend it out to others.

During one of Smilin' Rylan Kids Yoga classes, we presented a what-if to the kiddos. We started by sharing thoughts about the space, the apostrophe, asking what that would offer to the kids when they were faced with a what-if. We then invited them to take the time to breathe, go within, and use their inner video cameras to play what-ifs in the space of stillness. It was so much fun witnessing how the younger ones absorbed the idea—taking a breath and either playing things out in their minds before acting or knowing that it's OK to choose not to act (perhaps remaining within).

What if every moment were a celebration of life, presented to our souls as a gift, a present? Take it in. This present moment presides in our only lives. Actually, it's the awareness that is. So live. Live to the fullest! When I was present with Rylan, we lived *in* the moment. It was miraculous! Life would actually stand still in time. I was once again feeling like I was in a dream state.

During class, we would talk about Rylan and his life, his mission. Some of the children had met him in the physical before he took his flight, but most knew his energy, his spirit, from our discussions and loved him dearly in the spiritual. I would often remind them—and they would truly take it to the heart's space—"What each moment brings to you will depend on the energy you bring to each moment." When times are challenging, we can still

191

choose to allow the story to end and to be in observance of what is being presented to us. Oh yes, I know it's easier said than done, but once again, we have it with us all the time.

The little yogis celebrated and were open to feel how yoga, with its focus on breathing and being in the moment, can bring them to the now with each pose, can help them move through the space between each pose.

What will we bring to the next moment? We can use the space as a calm reservoir and allow peace as it carries the next breath, delivering our bodies into the chosen pose. Just as the breath rides into the next moment of our lives, so, too, we ride the moment, choosing to celebrate. Picture that as a what-if.

Celebrate! As we together practiced the gift of namaste, we were reminded to bring our chosen energy into each of the coming moments as well as our lives. What if a slideshow of breaths reminded us of the space, a pause, where who we really are lives—a picture of joyfulness present?

Please watch "Smilin Rylan Kids Yoga If I Had No Money" on YouTube: https://www.youtube.com/watch?app=desktop&v=yZFAK0VRrC4. These were a few of our volunteers. Kids are so willing to be free and just be.

They were asked the question, if you had no money, what would you give your parents as a gift? Listen how amazing children (within) are! If we would return as children—the miracles, the excitement. It's so much fun to just imagine a bunch of children running the world. I vote for that!

Breathe in Space: Therein Lies the Magic of Becoming Self-Full So as to Become Selfless

February 17, 2020

Rylan loved to lie on top of me, heart to heart—my heartstring to this day. Yes, we definitely paused in the space between thoughts.

In the space that we have allowed and welcomed into our busy lives, we become still, silent, and free from distractions. When I am in the space, I return to conscious. I know it without knowing it. Until I no longer am and my mind chatter tells me its viewpoint.

I am reminded of all the times I spent with Rylan (admittedly, it was often when he wasn't feeling well after treatment) taking the time to cuddle and just be love.

No words can adequately describe it—becoming so self-full you gain the ability to become selfless. For each of us, the attempt to explain how it feels to connect to this indescribable experience—well, our attempts would be detailed in so many different ways and never quite be enough to account for the magnitude of it, but I dare you to try!

193

In that space lives the freedom of our spirits to soar and reach for so many opportunities to serve others in pure love!

That's what the Smilin' Rylan little yogis experienced from the start of planning a surprise for Olivia (diagnosed with a tumor behind her eye at age five) two weeks in advance. The event, which fell on Valentine's Day, involved their decorating her home, demonstrating, expressing, their love from the driveway to Olivia's front door. Their actions were filled with selfless excitement, their hearts open and self-full for someone other than themselves. If only we all would be as children, playful and giving in the moment.

Their hearts were so self-full. Therein lies the space—the space to become selfless, open to expanding the love outward.

I find it so inspirational that children have not lost their innate spirit of compassion. I believe we all still house that compassion, although, as I have shared so often, we lose our desire, getting back to the dirty, smelly laundry we carry around. Out come the reasons, excuses of business, and justifications for why we don't have the space, the apostrophe, to acquire the time. What if we found the time in space instead of Facebook, Twitter, TV, our phones, and on and on? What if? Just imagine.

I feel and therefore think that there's a misunderstanding that the space has to be perfectly quiet, perfectly still in movement. I personally have experienced the calmness, the stillness, even while doing something active. It wasn't always like that. Yoga magnified my ability to sense this spacelessness and actually be fully in the moment, with a sense of serving, in whatever the moment brings—be it walking, singing, dancing, or even cleaning toilets.

I believe children have that ability. Yoga guides them to rediscover—or hanging on to—that beautiful gift that they were born with. We all were born with it, and we have it whenever we step into the space.

May we all breathe in the space to self-fullness, becoming more selfless, and be the change we say we desire.

Joni Kirby

Hey, Grown-Ups: It's OK to Disagree, but It's *Not* OK to Disrespect

October 9, 2020

Have you ever felt so out of place (out of alignment, not in the space of awareness) in a conversation, whether in a group or with one other individual, and you went ahead and agreed with what someone was saying, when, in your heart, it didn't reflect your feelings or beliefs? Perhaps you went along just to keep the peace because the alternative might have involved your chosen company becoming very strong (even rude and perhaps angry) in response to your sharing your honest feelings about the topic. You know certain people well enough to know that sharing and then agreeing to disagree is not an option they would go for.

That doesn't happen very often anymore to me because I choose my company whenever I'm able to—unless I'm thrown into a situation, which shouldn't happen too often. Back in the past, when I wasn't so aware and I'd be surprised, or would feel stuck, in those situations, it was because I wasn't feeling centered with my inner soul, my inner self; I'd lost the knowingness that my own best friend is I. Kind of like the old verbiage—"me, my self, and I," the one I am always with.

I cared more about maintaining temporary peace than about aligning with my soul's belief, but is choosing to go along, insincerely agreeing, really keeping the peace in the long run? Not an easy question to answer!

Well, there have been times that I'm glad I desired peace—well, not sure whether I felt the peace in my heart—but only wished I had just chosen to be silent (which isn't always the best choice either!). Once again, for the most part, we do choose who we spend our time with. During other times, we can practice becoming more aware by choosing in that space between what is happening and what our decision is going to be, asking the question, What are my intentions?

It's a good time to choose to redevelop the gifts we received on entering this world, unwrapping and using them more often: self-awareness, the conscious voice of stillness, inspiration to imagine, and freedom to be who we really are.

196

So perhaps when the next challenging situation comes along, choose to find the space within. There the four gifts are waiting to be unwrapped, celebrating you in gifts of presence. Choose responses that are healthy ones, made within the space of knowingness. Soon it won't matter who you're with or the conditions that surrounded you; you'll weather the seas with smooth sailing, calm.

Time we spend with our selves is time well spent. I am not in any way saying it's easy—we can get our lives so full of busyness—but in my life, it has become less stressful through the years as I have stepped back and honestly, self-fully spent more time with my self (I-ness) in silence, practicing meditation, yoga, and breath (prayers); journaling; and, after truly relearning to unconditionally love me again, making sure my choices come from my inner love for others.

I pray we are called to revisit, to truly look within, and heart listen to understand where someone else is coming from before feeling, and in some cases insisting, that we be understood. Instead, may we choose to be open, lovingly agree to disagree, and love with all our hearts! At times, we must make the decision to love from a distance—a statement I have done my best to honor and live by.

Heart Listen: Filter Your Thoughts to Truly Listen in Love

This is a wonderful way to listen, especially during times of intense emotions, with stress or beliefs possibly dividing friends and family. Hopefully we are finding our peace as we go within to the safeness of our hearts, to the comfort of our love for ourselves as well as others.

This is a place, space, wherein we find and feel stillness as we hold one another softly in our hearts. There's an inner lighting of hope and belief. Just imagine as we light the world on fire with our one love pulling together, replacing anger with compassion—a world where we choose to come together stronger for all humans in kindness! My butterflies are fluttering once again within my heart as I visualize and indeed know this to be.

We may ask our selves what our thoughts, actions, and words are speaking. Are they wrapped in the intention of love for all other human beings? Or are they labeled and put into categories or groups?

Consider the following and then journal: How is my garden of life lately? What am I growing, producing, and nurturing? Have I maintained my life's garden with the heart of a caring, kind, loving gardener? The harvest will produce what it's been given to grow; thoughts, actions, and words all carry the energy.

Have I developed my own fertilizer to nurture my garden, or have I followed, without questioning, the handed-down instructions that represent others' agendas?

Why not choose to care through the heart, grounded in soil worked with the hands of many coming together, growing the new earth's produce for our future families to benefit and carry on? They can carry on with so much less fear and fewer feelings of lack and entitlement. We create a newfound homestead of a deeper knowing of love, sharing with caring for all.

Believe me—I have asked my self many times, "Whose journal am I reading?" Now, here is where it's so very important not to pass judgment on that past person you used to be connected to, the person who wrote those words in *your* journal. I have said for many years—I'm sure someone said it, I read it, or I downloaded it from consciousness—that if you find you're judging, criticizing, and beating yourself up, stop it. How will you be able to begin to become that someone who feels no desire to judge others if you are constantly judging yourself?

I write at the end of all my journal entries—well, most—"I love me." Loving myself even when I don't feel very lovable is so very important to my moving into feeling and finding the connection of eternal love for all. Of course, *love* and *like* have two entirely different meanings in my book. I don't always *like* how I react, but I choose and feel unconditional love for myself, and I extend it out to others! I may just choose not to be around someone—at times I just don't like how that person acts. I still want to be the best humankind I can be, being a kind human and loving wholeheartedly.

Isn't that how we do our best to teach our children—that is, by example? (Or maybe not?) Come to think of it, you can witness families in which children are afraid to voice their feelings and opinions and often grow into versions of their parents in their own future relationships.

When our hearts are nurtured with intentions of the well-being of all, we can't help but listen, planting love as our seeds. Imagine how we would move through our moments with a lightness, our minds filtered from the heart, welcoming thoughts of peace and oneness. Listening with open hearts, we would just be, while giving space for others to breathe in, and perhaps (with time) listening would become a gift that we gave to not only others but truly ourselves.

Begin to feel the energy when you're in a room and there are differences of beliefs and opinions. Take a breath in the space. I've often been in a room and felt (well, at times) that different sides ultimately had similar beliefs but that people's choice of words and demands to be understood before first listening delivered a challenge to heart listening. Through heart listening, they could welcome, accept, other ways of looking at the situation, but as it was, individuals' behavior left little room for reaching within and listening from the heart.

You can almost feel the energy in these situations. People seem to find it easier—at least in the moment—to stand strong in their scripting of the past, perhaps with great fear of the possibility of listening, understanding, and, heaven forbid, agreeing.

If we would be still with the intention of listening from our hearts, perhaps a bridge over troubled water would provide the opportunity of a third alternative and synergy would become the beautiful rainbow. I believe, deep within my heart, that someday we shall overcome and love will lead the way. We will live as one, begin embracing and understanding, and acknowledge that we (yes, you and I) choose how to respond at any given moment. For me, that is empowering.

May we experience more love and faith!

Child's Pose with Smilin' Rylan
Kaleidoscope of Kindness

December 2, 2019

We are reminded that life is constantly changing, just like the colors and angles of a kaleidoscope. When we choose to bring forth the brilliance of the moment, as Rylan often did, a hospital room can miraculously change into a basketball court, transcending moments colorfully into magic. Looking through the lens of our awareness, we allow an ordinary experience—or perhaps one of fear or

lack—to become a vibrant, multicolored experience of plentiful blessings.

We experience firsthand what kindness will do to an ordinary moment. In my perception, the lens of awareness becomes, yes, a kaleidoscope of kindness to ourselves that extends outward to others in all different arrays of form and light.

Practicing just being still is challenging enough for most of us, but being able to combine this with our breath of awareness will guide us to and through appreciation. Gratitude and appreciation align our inner beings to one another. We are delivered into a kaleidoscope of colorful, beautiful diversification of our moments of life as they change into a landscape of unseen adventures. We are alive, fully and heartfully remembering we are all a continuous connection of the one; we are the one.

Such an old soul. Rylan, a rainbow of love, light, changed the space of a room into a gathering of all our light energy moving together as one. Darrell was taken back to who he really was (and is) when we were in Rylan's presence.

A kaleidoscope (reminds me of rainbows dancing) uses light and mirrors

We are connected at the seams of energy—a perfect pose demonstrating this.

to reflect objects, creating amazing, beautiful, colorful patterns. We can choose to use mirrors, reflecting ourselves so as to bring awareness of our

presence. Are we dark? Are we beautiful, enjoyable arrays of dancing light? We step outside ourselves and observe with awareness. We then have room to choose our response to any given moment or situation, the inner self reminding us that we have a choice!

Our light and energy is the by-product of that decision. Smilin' Rylan yogis experienced this last Wednesday as they celebrated our servicepeople by doing "Love Train."

Please watch "Smilin Rylan Kids Yoga Love Train & Kindness Performance" on YouTube: https://www.youtube.com/watch?v=JGtHmZhX8UI.

It was amazing. The energy and light was definitely a kaleidoscope of colorful smiles of kindness. We can find the space to bring light into any moment, celebrating no matter the pattern life is offering us. We do have a choice.

What a beautiful experience—not only within our own selves but feeling the love as it flows out and is received by others with such an openness. It's contagious! The Love Train moves through the hearts of those who watch, and everyone wants to join hands.

How about we all join together as a kaleidoscope that continues to change, the brilliance of light continuing as we move together, the magnitude of love exploding as energy flows beautifully out to all.

A Year in Time: A Breath in the Space of Now, Where Time Is Not

July 15, 2021

Anniversary dinner at Black Cat in Cambria.

On July 16, 2020, at 5:30 a.m., my best friend, partner in life, and husband took flight as I held him. Those final moments, my heart, spirit, and soul witnessed a peace-filled surrendering as his spirit, soul, and energy gradually, beautifully, left his body. There was a knowing that we are all connected as one to the one and only.

We do our best to put words to the unexplainable experience. Many have tried to communicate what their hearts held as their loved ones took flight into their nowhere yet everywhere of no time. I believe we all have something in common that brings us back to the understanding that there is no time but the now. And then the now is no longer real—was it ever? It's the mystery that's so darn exciting and beautiful to talk about, be about, and feel.

Challenges are portholes to our happiness when we believe. I at times feel Darrell's presence as if his body still breathes close to mine, his soul as if he's right beside me—as though the last year hasn't even happened, was a dream. Yet there are also times when I feel it's been many days, weeks, and months since he left and took flight from the physical. You see, time just *is not.*

What my heart is calling me to share today is this: I'd like to softly, tenderly remind all of us that we are gifted with the physical/material world as a stage, or a play of life. As we move through our stories of this life, the amazing existence we call a lifetime, may we live from the love in the heart's space, allowing it to gently and sweetly carry us through our thoughts to our actions or perhaps stillness. With such meditation or prayer, we experience happiness from within.

A moment in time (space) lived in the now.

Wherever present energy is, there we will experience a love light, reminding us that our energy, our light, is what continues on. We most often are welcoming bedtime, going to sleep, where the body and the mind are left and we're in a flight of nothingness as the body and mind are released. That was my experience as Darrell took flight for his last time.

Our loving forever family members Chuck and Susan. Susan also took flight, shortly after I moved to Cambria. I feel her often and talk with her also. This picture was taken to bring some lightheartedness to our moments. I believe Darrell was at one of several appointments at UCSF, and they set up their fishing line and lawn chairs in our front yard, which was directly across from their home. They are amazing friends—forever friends and chosen family.

I was contacted yesterday by Chuck about Darrell's and my home I sold last December to a loving couple and family. He was asking about the beautiful stream in the front yard, as it needed attention. It had decided to carry its symbolic life-flowing water past its man-made borders. My dear friend wanted the contact person, Joe (who, by the way, does all things through love), to care for it.

The kaleidoscope of energy from the neighborhood flows to and through communication with the new owners of the beautiful home I sold—energy that is never forgotten and never fades. Energy that is neither seen nor touched, that you can feel from an invisible presence. It's a gift, yes, a love light.

When Darrell's and my home was listed, it didn't move as quickly as other nearby homes did. I always knew in my heart there had to be the right connections, the right energy, and perfect timing for someone to move into our home. The home was so full of loving energy. Even though life brings challenges, love always wins. Love never fails and never ends.

When I met the couple who viewed and instantly fell in love with our home, who immediately knew it was their next beautiful living space, I, too, knew it was truly meant to be. This was the right time and couple, and I was ready—ready to move on and open the space for this amazing family to begin where our energy had left off. Our energy of love and light would always be a part of the space in their newfound home.

This reminds me how important it is to have faith. There is always a reason, and the secret is to become so filled with love and faith that there are seldom times of doubt and fear, and when there are, they're fleeting.

The couple who was destined to begin their next moments in our home—I knew as soon as they walked in that this was their home. I immediately fell in love with them both. We continue to keep in communication. But I use this larger example to illustrate the importance of simply *believing*, its own satori moment.

Believe that when your energy is aligned in the space of knowingness, it's OK to be in the space of happiness. Even when there are times you think life is going against you, rest assured that it isn't. I know this to be true. I also feel the argument in your mind beginning, so take a breath, and feel what the thoughts are bringing to your body through emotions. Don't resist. Say that you're choosing to bring awareness into this moment. Allow everything to be and feel.

Times can really be tough, making it even harder to keep the faith. But there is light; there are miracles in all moments. In fact, when we feel shaken up, we discover the kaleidoscope of energy, of light, in the presence of colliding emotions.

No argument from me: times may present themselves as very challenging and downright tough, making it tempting for us to give in to fear, lack of control, sadness, and so many similar emotions that compose the story of our racing thoughts. During these times, take a breath and choose your next moment: What is the alternative?

I continue to feel the emotions of missing the physical forms of my loved ones. I do my best not to allow that to still the moment I'm in. Krisi and I cry. We share and then move from a beautiful memory into our moment of now, welcoming the energy of inner happiness and joy. We love to laugh!

I also at times miss the physical structure of my beautiful home of twenty-five years. But the energy is always present. The energy I brought with me from the beautiful years and moments I spent in that space is also in whatever space I move into and celebrate.

I have asked that question so many times in my life: "What is the alternative?" When I choose the alternative, I feel the yucky, thick quicksand muck pulling me under, and I can't wait to climb out. "Breathe, Joni." The I reassures me, and I decide from that space, changing my energy and choice.

Our office family enjoyed teasing Doc on his birthday. Actually, it didn't have to even be his birthday. There was no telling what he would find out front. One Christmas, there was a huge blow-up fish. Darrell couldn't stand blow-up decorations,

One of the memories of energy.

so the family and extended family from all different neighborhoods joined in for the fun. It was a blast! The love and relationships were unique and boundless. We were and are there for them as they all have been for us.

I knew I would always keep them in my heart's space, but it was my time to follow my heart on a new chapter. I was ready to begin again in a new home, remembering my real home is within my heart's space. Nice, warm, and comfy with my self, the self.

And you guessed it: this analogy is about a physical material home—and I'm not talking about the material part of the house. I'm talking about the energy that is within the space, the energy that is flowing, filling in the space between the four walls of each room, the windows, the ceilings, and the floors. Those tangible elements are temporary and easily taken away. The energy remains and flows, expanding as it grows, touching hearts with no boundaries. That's when a house becomes a home. The energy is love.

The love energy of all those twenty-eight years that was present in the space of that material home can be felt and continues to expand. Hearing the new loving couple talking about how much they enjoy and feel the energy confirms once again my belief that energy speaks when you listen (feel) softly with your heart's space.

I believe we are connected forever. The couple's energy and the loving family and friends they will welcome into their space will continue to bring the fragrance of love through their living of each moment in time. Love is the breath.

It's similar to the way the scent of a candle will remain after the flame is

blown out. The candle is out of the space, out of sight, but you can smell its lingering notes. Taking in the fragrance of a rose with your eyes closed is even more beautiful. It's neither seen nor felt by touch, yet there's definitely a palpable fragrant energy.

I feel the unseen physical of Darrell, and even more Rylan's, through energy of love. They just left their physical, yet in the space of where I am now, they are permanent love lights. I am filled with so much gratitude for the physical time with Darrell. I'm grateful for the fragrance of his energy that remains, that reminds me how temporary our physical lives are yet how permanent our energy remains as it expands back to the one.

May we all take each moment and live it as present as possible. How? Well, we have choices, practices, to guide us into the presence of now, encouraging our physical bodies and minds to be open to, and more aware of, the fact that they are temporary. Why not choose to find the wonder and excitement in that? Choose to deliver more gifts of celebration of the truth of one's being? Feel the natural happiness that meets you openly at any time. Be the gift, giving freely through your energy. Find the joy awaiting. Love to everyone. Love, light, and namaste!

What Is My End in Mind? Am I Living It?

August 28, 2020

Darrell's physical body has been gone from sight since July 16, 2020. As I reflect (especially these past five weeks), I ask myself, "Was I deeply, intentionally, living in the moment? Were my intentions wrapped in the thought of having the end in mind present?" I always believed, intellectually, the end in mind is fused together with the now as one. If my mind is aligned, thinking with the end in mind, am I really present in this moment?

I love when I'm challenging myself to a deeper reflection, a quieter meditation.

We can use the right words—and I say *right* lightly (we are the gatekeepers of our own thoughts, intentions, and words)—we can speak them, but what do our moments, our lives, truly reflect?

We lived the moment! We were and are connected.

At times, others may view our present life circumstances and want so badly to come up with the right words, believing these events of sadness are tragic. But can these life moments be blessings when we live the moment of faith? Is it possible these events are blessings? Yes, they break our hearts, but can they not only break our hearts but break open a deeper awareness? There's the hidden gift, the blessing, the rainbows: becoming aware of the preciousness of every single moment.

So today perhaps take a moment and write out a statement of what you desire for you, your self, to "live by and with" as you travel your journey into the soul's flight and beyond.

What do you want to be remembered by after you leave the physical? *How* do you want to be remembered?

So we deeply and prayerfully ask, Who am I, and what do I really desire? Have living-in-the-moment experiences today, moving through each moment of today in celebration of being.

Hospice / I Chose Not to Heart Listen on May 19, 2020—Now One Year Later

May 28, 2021

Darrell and me enjoying the Pink Jeep adventure in Sedona.

HOSPICE: Honoring our special person in caring energy.

I don't believe in regrets. Having said that, I admit that this is one day, May 19, 2020 (wouldn't you know that despite Darrell, Doc, having been an optometrist for all those years, this is the first time I've made the connection between *twenty-twenty vision* and the year 2020?), Darrell's birthday, is one of those exceptions.

Yes, if I were given a second chance, a chance to rewind the clock and go back in time, I would consider making a different choice.

I believe with all my heart that regrets do us no good, and I also believe deep within my spirit, my soul, that everything plays out with the theme that all will be well.

I believe that there's always a deeper reason or meaning and that, at the very

So many wonderful memories.

211

end, Darrell's flight on July 16 was possibly made more beautiful because of my decision on May 19. So it's true: if we knew what the future held, we perhaps would really screw things up.

Why do I write the preceding text, when most everyone would love to have a crystal ball to look into to see what the future held?

Because there's no way of knowing what the alternative outcome would have been, and having Darrell home with me for his last five days in the physical gave way to a beautifully peace-filled flight with all those surrounding in love. What a takeoff.

Note from soul to crazy monkey mind:

The humans in us at times can be the tormentors of our bodies and minds. At every class, we would do a yoga song and routine with the Smilin' Rylan little yogis. They really related to the message. It told of the monkey mind, how becoming silent and meditating can help calm our crazy minds and thoughts, allowing life to be so much more fun.

The human in me played with my memory, rewinding during times I was most vulnerable. I insisted on viewing playbacks of the emergency visits, me taking a very sick, hallucinating Darrell three different times, spaced out a few days in between. This was the very end of April and the beginning of May 2020. Unable to go in with him (restrictions during COVID-19 pandemic), I would sit brokenhearted out in the car with the air-conditioning running for several hours.

Each time, he would get antibiotics (for reoccurring infections since he had no bladder) and sodium replacement, just enough to barely get him out the door and back home. I would beg them to keep him until he was much better, but because of COVID, that wasn't going to happen. Not until May 19, 2020.

So, on a day when we usually celebrated Darrell's birthday, I felt a real possibility that we would be celebrating his birth into the nonphysical. I truly felt I was going to lose him, and that send-off would have haunted me, even though my soul, my spirit, knew it would be fine.

This was the catalyst for my being devoted to helping others make a much more knowledgeable and informed decisions when they're confronted with very sick loved ones—perhaps loved ones who have recurring health issues—to open alternative possibilities. In my opinion, it's important to share a more natural, loving, caring choice.

We must become aware of how often we choose to simply put a bandage on what is causing a loved one's pain, thereby prolonging a life that I believe we as humans often hold on to so as not to lose the individual, preventing that person's natural life process from playing out.

I feel that if more people were presented, as I was, finally, with the true facts of hospice, they would experience, as we did, a choice. It was an alternative to lying in a hospital room (rehab facility), instead being at home with family and friends, elevating the human spirit in dignity and love.

It doesn't matter how many years our loved ones have been present in our lives. For me, my dad was seventy-eight. My husband had been in my life for more than thirty-five years (day in and day out), and of course, my heartstring Rylan had been with me almost seven years. The journey to the flight of release and beyond should be a memorable journey of love whenever possible.

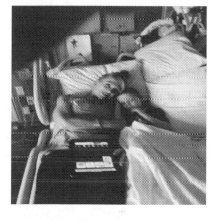

Once again, it doesn't matter how many years our loved ones have physically been with us. I know from the deepest part of my knowing heart that it's all a journey of acceptance and that hospice assists and supports patients as well as families with that transition.

I believe that we all should take more time, in the moment, the space of centerness, to breathe in awareness and listen. We must heart listen to all involved, with doctors, patients, and families coming together; take the time to step into the space between the moments; and remember we are all a family. I feel deeply that if more would take time in life to slow down, allowing the space to be present, it would make for a more empathic, loving human race.

I know I say this a lot, but we are humankind. So where does the *kind* disappear to so often? Busyness? Shame on us.

We are raising our children, our grandchildren, and they watch our actions so much more than they listen to our words. May we all make a vow to raise kind human beings, being kind as humans.

Back to May 19, 2020. Darrell, as I mentioned, had challenges with low sodium, which brought about hallucinations as well as recurring infections. He was literally out of his mind. I was locking my bedroom door at night because his infections and sodium levels as well as the sundown syndrome would cause him to become paranoid and at times act violently. This was not him, and I knew it. I even dread writing this, but I share it so that others may hopefully gain some insight into ways to take a different course and so they know they aren't alone. I did fear he would do something without being aware of what he was doing. This didn't have to be. There are choices I (or we) could have made to release Darrell from this torment, to help me so I could have helped him.

So, on May 19, 2020, I felt I had no choice (yet I did and didn't even know it) at this time but to call the ambulance. He kept pleading with me, telling me he just wanted to stay home and was tired. I wasn't educated and had very little understanding of hospice—at best, a totally wrong, ignorant view. He wanted to leave this physical body and fly; I just wasn't heart listening, truly hearing what he was saying. I felt I would be giving up on him, but it was quite the opposite.

If I could choose to rewind, I would have had hospice lined up. I now know Darrell was trying to hint to me about just wanting to die. Instead, I watched my husband, my best friend, being taken out by EMTs, begging me not to send him away.

I didn't see him for almost two months, and it took a lot to be able to get him home, where he (nonverbally) begged to be. Home, on the proper medication, to relax him and allow him to find the peace that awaited him. Those two horrific months could have been much more peaceful for Darrell and me. If only.

Now, what's a gift I'd like to give to others that I wish someone would've given to me sooner? The understanding of hospice. Or, at least in my experience as a loved one, I know Darrell wanted to take flight a long time ago. I believe the choice would have brought so much more ease to the family also. People should at least have the option. There are choices, and we can voice them without feeling as if we're giving up on our loved ones. Quite the opposite—it was an unselfish act on my part. We are loving them, not ending their lives. Their energy goes on as if a beautiful, long night's sleep. Waking to freedom from pain.

I don't know how hospice would word its marketing if you were to call for someone to come talk to your family. My childhood friend from San Diego, Carole, did that exact beautiful service, guiding others through the process of making a compassionate choice of life. That gives you a hint of how blind I was. Hospice gives you back the power to decide a love-filled celebration of life to flight.

I would mention to Carole about coming and talking with us, but when it came down to it, my fear of losing him overwhelmed my desire to help him. That's the truth. Ignorance on my (and our) part, yes, and stubbornness. I'm going to share what is tough for me to even say: I felt I would be killing him. It's so sad that we as humans are ignorant of what is natural versus human ways of keeping a person's physical body stuck here when the spirit is ready to fly.

I want to share this experience with anyone who's going through such a chapter of life with a loved one. Sharing those last five beautiful days was my rainbow, a miracle. Just think that I (we) could have had more time at home with Darrell no longer having to undergo treatment to prolong a life in a body causing him so much suffering, when there was no cure and he was no longer living.

The rainbow always appears, bringing so many miracles and, yes, satori moments. I am forever filled with gratitude. We were able to share Darrell's last days in the physical to freedom and now beyond.

Another miracle, or satori moment, amazing and yet not amazing; children get it. During Darrell's last few days at home on hospice, Maximus and Alissa were present—I mean *present*! Their understanding was beautiful, is beautiful.

I feel this gives them the opening to understand that death is not, or should not, be a time of fear and pain for our loved ones. Yes, another satori awakening, yet children like Rylan never felt the fear of taking flight from their bodies. I believe we generally convey to children, teach children, perhaps more with our energy and actions than with our words, that dying is to be feared.

Maximus and Alissa witnessed a beautiful way to take flight from this world to beyond in dignity. It was natural and for the ones present a beautiful time of sharing, remembering, and Loving. You know, I videotaped the two of them about their experience because there were potential buyers for our home who, when they found out someone had died in the house, had chosen not to make the purchase. The video is something so very special, and I wish others could witness the joy from these two, as it would serve to help them release some of their own fear. Although a lot comes from our personal faith.

I feel we can give our children and young people (of all ages) a greater understanding of options for loved ones as they come to a very natural life experience: death. Perhaps we could all start changing our fear of death to an experience of peace.

Once again, as our week ends, our life in the moment begins. May we cherish and live each moment with the understanding that, just as each moment has birth and will die, there will be a time for each of us to celebrate life as we take flight. How about having another kind of birthday, celebrating as we take our flight into the beyond? Let's wrap each moment in love.

Becoming Self-Full Opens Space to Being Selfless

April 16, 2021

In a typed (yes, using an old-fashioned typewriter) untraining in 1992, I opened with the preceding saying, soon to be my usual quote. To this day, I still say this is "my" quote, but I acknowledge I've downloaded it from above and it's likely attributable to several others.

We would do a "brain surgery" at the very beginning of each untraining in order to hopefully get the mind less active in the past, or the future, and become present in the now, open to awareness, awakening satori moments.

Whenever there were new attendees, I could see their minds dissecting the statement in the entry's title. With time, little by little, I saw satori moments happen. There was an evident aha radiating across each person's face, and people's eyes shone with a vibrant glow: a sparkle of joy.

If I found (felt) a struggle from anyone within our sacred, beautiful surroundings, our circle, we would continue to talk about the meaning behind that quote, the Joni-ism. I came to accept that I'm a little different but that we seem to gravitate to just the perfect setting and surrounding group of journey seekers. We are all the same in our unique individuality personalities—I love that!

When I look back on my teens through my midtwenties, I know I was spending more time trying to live with my unhappy person (me) and get through the days of the drama that I created. I'd be exhausted and have nothing to give to others, and I'm not just talking about time. I'm talking about the space within me that actually had room to care and love unconditionally.

Oh yes, we can pretend we're giving of our selves (and often, at the time, we don't even realize our lack of authenticity), unaware of the dishonesty behind our intentions. It's understandable why so many people are suspicious if we're kind and giving, because they can't imagine our actually freely giving through kind thoughts, words, and actions without having alternative motives. I can get that—I understand. They can't imagine being so self-full that they could actually be selfless and think totally about someone else even for a few moments.

I can remember back in the day being so full of my own story, jumping from job to job, relationship to relationship, so busy blaming and pointing the finger. Seriously, who could have time to really be able to care deeply for someone else? I wouldn't even take care of me. When you're lacking self-love, when you're lacking and not full, how can you sincerely be there for someone else, freely and unconditionally?

Once I started dedicating my moments to excavating the layers within me, my baggage started to lighten up. There was the birthing of the space, and it became so easy for me to want to be presently there for others.

Satori moments. I can't remember whether I shared in past entries what I did in the week following one of my most powerful, life-changing satori moments. I went to a therapist after my second divorce (I was about twenty-five—yes, I know, crazy) because I wanted to help my daughter handle the separation between her dad and me. The therapist asked me what or who the common denominator was in all the unhappy jobs and marriages. It hit—*bam!*—an amazing explosion, a satori moment that saved my soul (or I should say *me*, as my soul is already saved).

The awakening? *I choose freely all my life decisions; we all do.* As I've shared several times, I left that office crying all the way back to our practice. I believe I left the me, along with many tears of surrendering, to welcome openly to the peace of the satori moments. Tears can truly be cleansing, and within a week, I wrote long, transparent love letters to at least ten, if not fifteen, different people—from my past employers to ex-spouses, former friends, and family members—asking for forgiveness and apologizing from the bottom of my heart. From there, that beautiful act of love, I now could forgive me and love me back to my self.

What a beautiful return to home—so cleansing. I still feel the love of the swarming, fluttering butterflies when I remember that gift. Openly and honestly surrendering, I was reborn.

Yes, I felt reborn, a returning back to my self, as a child. If you're a parent, can you recall your little one when you would open your mouth and ask, "Can Mommy [Daddy] have a bite, please?" and the toddler would selflessly shove a bite of whatever he or she was eating into your mouth? Children don't yet know lack; they are self-full!

I wanted to be as a child, to hug everyone I came into contact with, and to this day, I hold that precious memory in my heart, in my soul.

Can you remember having witnessed subtle changes in children as they started pulling back and learning "mine," beginning to pick up the habit of guarding their possessions? They then grow up, maturing (immaturing) in a magical world that opens all of us to a journey of rediscovering (or not) who we truly are. We must arrive in the newness of now. The journey is so worth the times that seem to be made of unending struggle and pain. We arrive (blessedly) and remember we are love.

Through the adventure of growing back full circle, back into childlike innocence, we can all arrive through our own satori moments back to our selves, the I-ness within.

We can go from innocence to almost a subtle selfishness, to choosing and rediscovering the gift of being self-full, childlike. We can return to space of fullness so as to be able to put ourselves aside at times when we are needed, therefore giving ourselves the beautiful gift of loving others—and the love returns tenfold. Becoming selfless from a place of fullness, we then can give freely, unselfishly, to others through simply being.

Hmm, I can't tell you where that last paragraph came from. After reading it a few times, I'm certain it's what my heart is trying to say. Perhaps take a breath, absorb it, and see how it feels in your heart's space.

Journal: How does that resonate within me? Do I willfully give to others with no strings attached? When I listen with awareness, can I hear the subtle voice of my self, the I, answering that question? (You know the voice that when you hear it; your mind resists, thinking up reasons to go against it.)

So keep up the beautiful gifts to you. Wake at least twenty minutes earlier; find silence through meditation; and play music that moves your spirit to love and peace, taking it with you as you step out of bed.

With your first step, you'll feel the lightness of a child excited for the day to come. At least for this one day or moment, choose to set aside whatever fixed scripts or habits steal from the fullness of your self. Make a different choice. Never allow a kind word or action to remain within you; act on it.

Happy beginnings of new satori moments. May so much love come to all!

Does the Thought of Doing Nothing Scare You? Truthfully?

September 17, 2021

If I were to ask you to sit and wait for me to call, would you be willing to take a breath and find the space of now? Would you approach it as a gift, experiencing almost a calm excitement during this period of no time?

Or would you start becoming fearful, feeling irritated, waiting for the phone to ring because you have things to do?

Would you be still and present long enough to discover the space between those thoughts that dictate your to-do list? Or would your mind hop on the next train of thought—too many to even remember—perhaps leading you toward a train wreck of stress and frustration?

Journaling during an untraining session was a welcome gift to those in attendance.

Would you become aware enough to even notice you weren't aware? Follow this thought, arriving so in the moment you'd fall into the space, allowing the awareness to pull you off the tracks just in time—a moment before the mind and body totally took over you, inevitably heading toward another crazy train collision of familiar stress and frustration. They'd provide you with the same distractions, perhaps just a change in the train tracks, the scripting of this mind trip. But you're safe for now.

Perhaps you need a gift of a present moment to just be, where angels are heard singing in the silence of presence, their wings of fluttering awareness. It's the warmth of total love, a knowingness—in that space I is, and it is all one.

When I visit (wish I would be there more) that space of unchangingness, it presents nothing to do. Time doesn't exist. Even when I am doing, it is through a beingness of stillness. All just seems to flow together. No matter the activity in the moment, a calmness wraps the doingness in this nothingness of everythingness (I know, a lot of -nesses). Every moment flows to the next, and there's where the fluttering of butterflies, of Rylan's wings, fills my heart, extending throughout my entire being.

I was telling my daughter, Kristin, that our friend Nancy and her son, Benny, came to visit me. The joy, the love, that radiated from all three of us as we delivered the rocks and chocolate-covered pretzels to the neighbors was felt!

At first, Benny was shy; he wasn't sure he wanted to do that, randomly giving out rocks with *love* and red hearts painted on them. As we walked downtown, though, gradually, you could tell Benny was beginning to feel free again, free to be present with all his love and gratitude. He was excited to be a part of this random act

Nancy and Benny on my porch with me.

of kindness toward strangers (yet our family, our human family).

Just writing this, I can feel the warmth, the fluttering, begin. I'm in this moment, where all moments are one, and filled with so much appreciation.

Children move through their unsureness quickly when they feel open and safe to choose. It helps knowing their true inner kindness is still on the surface, for the most part. And, of course, *fun*! I live for fun! I love when children can rest and trust, knowing that they are safe. And they feel safe when the adults in their lives are no longer fearful of what others will think, or a number of other mind-boggling feelings and behaviors children's minds have picked up on and begun to store. Of course, Benny has an amazing mom! She's one of the most open and authentic people I'm blessed to call a close friend.

Adults tend to be more apt to visit the thought *What will people think?* and other similar excuses, often robbing themselves and others of so many wonderful life experiences. When we become so full of love for our selves, we are no longer the sort of selfish people concerned more about what others will think than about giving of our selves in love and sincere service.

Children are so open to express love and kindness when they are given the opportunity. It definitely helps when they continue to live it. It's so much easier when parents, family members, and teachers are also examples. Otherwise, it's likely to become buried, in need of excavation and later satori moments.

If we could be as children, the world would be ... You decide what to fill in.

I say often that I love all the changeable gifts we have in this lifetime. I enjoy eating, I enjoy my little home, and I enjoy getting dressed nice once in a while and going dancing—fun, enjoyable, and also fleeting.

But through the years and the gifts I've received—or the gifts I've always had within that became buried—I've had a wonderful life of rediscovering how truly amazing I am. Yes, there are practices that have guided me back, yet it's always been within, waiting for me to return to the space, that part of me that will never die.

I forget, often returning to the me, absent of the unchangeable I. Well, it's not an absence but rather a temporary move to the back, behind the driver's seat, with the caboose patiently watching and loving the me regardless.

For most of us, we are almost like robots, allowing the outside world to be our inside world in our everyday moments. We turn on our TVs, fire up our technology, and scroll through social media, and before we know it, we end the day without actually having lived one single moment. In line at the grocery store or waiting for an appointment, are you able to find, discover, the pause and just be, not allowing your mind to take you from past to present, unreal life? Just be aware. Feel your breath.

Does it scare you to have nothing in the moment but you and self? Are you able to become aware of your surroundings and find the inner connection to those standing next to you as you feel your breath, or are you unconsciously grabbing for your phone to check your email, Facebook, or Twitter?

I love giving. I love picking the perfect gift, writing the perfect poem for someone, but if I could give something nonmaterial, I would love to give the space of nothingness, the perfect in the imperfection of whatever the outside is providing in the moment. That's why I enjoy teaching private lessons so much (well, also large classes of kids as well as adults). I enjoy immensely what I feel from the presence, the space of allness from the nothingness—an unexplainable gift of presence, of now.

I remember when Darrell finally realized he could no longer go to the office and see patients. I began losing my best friend; Darrell's soul was harder to feel, to sense. He began to fill every waking moment with TV, mostly the news. We used to watch TV together, a good movie or a spiritual talk, but he found that the news began to be his scapegoat for his anger. He would move into feeling, acting, as if he were a part of all the drama going on in the world, actually in the middle of it. He would make me giggle when he would say, "I vote Joni for next president." You would laugh, too, if you realized how much I avoided talking politics. He knew how I felt, and he brought some humor to a world in which more laughter would be a blessing.

For days I'd hear the front TV and his bedroom TV, both often set to the same news station. I didn't stop playing my spiritual, beautiful, loving energy music. He even knew the words to some of the songs. Perhaps subconsciously we bring in what we are truly listening to.

I would feel the fear in him when there was silence. It was too uncomfortable to have that silence of peace. He wasn't ready to be still, to become free and know that he was not his mind. Yes, he was being stripped of what he thought he was.

For many years, he felt so strong in his IQ; people were marveled by his mind. He wasn't ready to accept that he wasn't his mind or his body. He was the I that remains, who he really is, that which is unchangeable—the part of him that wasn't dying. He was (and is) the self, the I-ness that continues on. We should all come to understand and welcome that because we are all dying. Yep, we are. Rejoice and celebrate.

When Darrell came home on hospice (I know I've written about this before—humor me), I hadn't seen him in about two months, and the moment our eyes met as staff wheeled him out, the love, the light, was that turning kaleidoscope. Through all the years, I'd seen a tear drop from his eyes only a few times. As I ran up to him, his tears were unstoppable. I could see his soul through his eyes. His body was so broken down, and his mind was gradually surrendering.

I'm trying to find the right words to best describe it. It's like his body and mind abandoned him yet opened up the space for his soul to fall through and take the front seat—the I that was waiting patiently in the background of the heart's space.

Right away, I noticed only his light, his acceptance and knowingness of the part of him that was dying and the part of him that would take flight. He was so ready. For so long, he had begged me to allow him to die, though he'd said it out of anger, frustration. He wasn't ready. Tears are flowing as I write this, not tears of sadness but rather tears of joy, of peace—his peace, my peace. I am so very blessed to have held him those last five days! Actually him. It was beautiful.

A living metaphor. Go within and rediscover that part of you that doesn't change in a world where a body, a mind, is always changing in all ways.

Ask, "Who am I? Am I aware?" The I is just waiting.

Be patient. Become very aware. Begin to realize how our feelings are constantly changing, our bodies are constantly changing, and our surroundings are constantly changing.

Now discover through uncovering the unchangeable within.

Find that which doesn't change.

When you become aware of the things that are changing, constantly changing, become silent and still, patient with the me. You'll be open and able to go within and find that which doesn't change. Don't force it. Ask, "What doesn't change?"

Please don't allow the questions to overwhelm your mind; simply accept what comes. When we get resistant and frustrated, that's when we push it again into the background. Explore the satori moments and rejoice in life. Enjoy, have fun, laugh with your self, and play with life.

It's truly a gift that you give to your self, to be able to release and understand what's temporary. My husband and my dad experienced it as they were on their last moments in their physical bodies. Rylan lived it. Wouldn't it be a blessing to live there now and not wait? Just a thought.

My loving energy extends out to everyone.

Seeds of Intentions: Plant Your Life's Garden

Seeds We Plant Grow

January 13, 2020

WE NEVER REALLY KNOW WHAT seeds we're planting, scattering into moments. I never had to invite Rylan to practice yoga with me. I just knew that if I spread two mats out, he would end up on the one beside me. He would just mimic whatever I was doing. Early on, he would join me on my mat. This was one of his favorites: side plank.

I remember getting overly concerned that he might hurt himself. I'm so thankful I didn't allow my fear to keep him from learning about how amazing he truly was (and is): courageous, strong, adventurous, accepting, and of course fun. He was always willing to keep on keeping on. I planted seeds of yoga, of life, without even meaning to, just by being and living my moments in love.

In his short life, Rylan inspired me to spread seeds of yoga to children. Smilin' Rylan Kids Yoga was planted and continues to bear loving fruit.

Just as the trees have seasons, at one time, there was a seed planted, with no knowledge of how the roots would take, how long the tree's life would be, what fruit and how much it would bear, and how much shade it would provide. The seeds were dropped, and life began. Seasons would bring constant changes. So magical. I am constantly reminded how life is so mysteriously beautiful. Change is exciting when we find awareness through our breath in the stillness of the now.

The winter season is breathtaking. I love all the seasons. As I walked Love and Faith this last December and admired the bareness of the trees, I found myself imagining the inner energy happening, anticipating new growth, making room for the new yet to come by discarding the old. I, too, felt my innermost calling to let go so I could make room for space in my life—to throw some seeds of intentions and let them go. Once a seed is planted, we must let go of expectations. Otherwise, as we tend to do with other thoughts, we latch on, determined to control what fruit the seeds will sow.

We share with the Smilin' Rylan yogis how important their energy is. We asked them to have very low energy and think negative, self-defeating thoughts so that Naomi could take a picture of them. When we take time to nurture our inner selves, through yoga and other self-love activities, we open our hearts and welcome peace and joy. We are better able to shed the old that isn't serving our souls and become open to dropping seeds of loving intentions without any connections or ties to their outcomes.

Our days turn into months, months into years, the seeds leaving our legacies just by our having planted intentions in a moment of love. In the photo that follows, the little yogis were asked to set intentions of love and of kindness. See and feel the difference in energy just from the picture? You could really feel the difference in the energy present in the room.

In the preceding picture, they saw the difference. They felt the difference. Which picture do you think they enjoyed looking at, not only with their eyes but with their broader vision? We talked about how, just by looking at the picture, they could feel the energy.

A fruit-bearing tree gives the most fruit in the last season of its lifetime. If we continue to give of our lives by nurturing ourselves and extending out, spreading seeds of life, perhaps every season we, too, will leave behind the most fruit; our legacies will be the seeds we plant, the seeds we spread throughout our lives.

On my last day, during my last breath, I will close my eyes knowing that I take nothing but that I left everything through my seeds of love. Happy planting, everyone!

Tree: Personality versus Character

September 22, 2019

A Smilin' Rylan yogi, Baily, and I doing tree pose with a character of support for Smilin' Rylan (Baily is rocking the custom Smilin' Rylan T-shirt worn by many).

Yes, there is a tree pose in yoga, and it's one of many people's favorites. Why? What causes us to have favorites and to avoid other poses, situations, and challenges? Rylan loved a challenge. His family and friends enjoyed presenting him with another obstacle to watch how he moved through it. Wow—wouldn't it be wonderful if we didn't allow life to rob us of that, instead welcoming the unknown as yet another adventure?

The following picture captures father (Jeremy) and daughter (Bella). I enjoyed guiding them in yoga. They are practicing a partner pose, holding each other in love, while in tree pose.

The imagery of a tree provides a wonderful example of personality versus character.

The branches and leaves, flowers and fruits, are vulnerable to outside conditions, easily swayed by wind, shaken by frost, and—we can't forget—transformed by humans. They depend solely on the environment, much like when we live out our personalities, our personal realities, rather than our I, the awareness of who we really are, the heart's space.

228

When we are living out (or from) our personalities, our choices and happiness tend to be based on our outside conditions. We consider what others will think of us, caring more about making a good impression, a good image. We're concerned whether others will accept how we act and look, perhaps hoping for acceptance in a prestigious group and fearful of being rejected, left out.

The trunk and roots of a tree represent character, a deeper belief, based on intuition or wisdom—yes, awareness! They're strong, able to withstand outside conditions. Both time and awareness are required for growth. Children tend to come into this world with stronger trunks and roots.

If only we allowed them to continue nurturing their character and placed less emphasis on the personality. How can we do that? Through our words and, more important, our actions, using the I-ness of awareness (and the other gifts we are born with: the conscious voice of stillness, inspiration to imagine, and freedom to be who we really are).

I am challenged every time warrior 3 is part of my practice. I often share how yoga teachers choose warrior 3 as their hot pose. Ironically, but not at all unusual, I choose warrior 3 variations for my clients also. For years, many have known it as a challenge for me, that I struggle with it. Yes, it's definitely not a love of mine. We were discussing that it's OK not to like it, but I definitely choose to love it for the challenge it brings me. I enjoy how it allows me to strengthen my awareness, feel the emotions, and hear the inner voice that sneaks in as I'm practicing that pose: "Joni, you are not your thoughts, not your body." And back to awareness I go. As I breathe and become present, I am set free in that moment.

Bella and Jeremy are practicing being present and breathing as they embrace each other, connecting heart to heart and through eye contact. Perhaps if parents would take time with each child and practice stillness and eye contact every evening—well, just imagine!

When I meet a challenge in life that I don't like, perhaps some gathering that I feel I should attend, I can relate to the emotions and attitude that can take over because of past history, past stories. That's a gift yoga has enhanced for me. I'm much more aware of how I'm perceiving something, the lens I'm looking through. I know, for me, the awareness delivers me to the present moment, and when I am, all else is fine.

I say to myself, "You chose to be here; choose to find the gratitude in each moment." My thoughts and body release me, and my character is strengthened. Now from the deeper wisdom of my character flows my personality. I fail often, but I'm continuing to choose to heighten my awareness and embrace the warrior 3 experience of life!

If I practice only the poses I love, that aren't challenging for me, I'm choosing to stay safe in life and not allowing my wisdom to guide me to my creative dreams! I have always found the ability to be out of the box. Yoga has taught me it doesn't matter what other people view or judge—it's all about how I feel about me. Our little yogis continue on the pathway of using yoga on the mat to strengthen their character both on and off the mat. It's so wonderful to witness how incredible they are!

This Is Your Lifetime, and It Could End at Any Time—Dance, Sing, Love

May 14, 2021

At any given time of the day, where are your thoughts? Where is your energy? What are your emotions and your body telling you? I find that check-in to be so liberating, as it brings me to my soul, my spirit. It brings me back to who I really am, back to I, my self, and I remember who I am.

I allow the moments to just to be, no stress of doingness, with a presence of newness, oneness.

Since you can say—and you won't hurt my feelings—I'm on the last chapters of my life (and, truthfully, any one of us could be on the last page, the last sentence, or, heck, even the last word of life right at this moment), you might ask, "What does your life speak of you? What does your book of life write of you?"

For me, looking back, I feel so blessed that I've had satori moments beginning early in my life and continuing to my last chapter, last pages. They've brought my self closer to me so that, living in presence much more often nowadays than not, I love my life.

People often say to me, "Joni, you use the word *love* so easily, yet it's so hard." I for one believe that thought is hard, that thought is what births the effort of love, yet love knows no effort; it just is. It's always present, regardless of the outside effort the body and mind reflect. Release and return to love.

Here's the question to ask: How often am I present and aware? The I is waiting patiently.

Believe me—I so understand. Our minds produce the fog, the mist that rolls into play, distorting our vision. Things just aren't as clear as they could be. Actually, what is clear? We begin to understand and view the illusions for what they are. During those times, we still enjoy as we go within the heart's space and feel the happiness within. Perhaps I roll out my mat, or take a walk, allowing the wind, the freshness, to carry me back into my faith, becoming clear once again. Yes, I do believe there is only love. It's up to us to discover (uncover) what that means deep within the heart's space and to believe.

Perhaps we have our own ideas about what love should look like, with everyone happy, smiling, hugging, partying. Perhaps our vision is living in a big home, driving a fancy car, and having all kinds of food at our fingertips, with no struggle.

What if love were moments of sadness? What if love were moments of struggles? A moment of fear as we waited patiently knowing the fear would dissolve? Perhaps a moment of fright, aloneness, or anger? This is the first time I'll

Rylan loved to feed his Jmom.

have shared two pages from my past personal journals.

As I moved here to Cambria, I found all my journal books—well, most of them. It was amazing how I would just open up and find a page that would remind me that the past is the past and that if we revisit it too often, it takes us back into time, which can either help us or hinder us. Being in the moment, I chose for it to help me grasp on to the love of each fleeting moment, remembering that nothing is permanent—well, except the I within—bringing even more gratitude. The I won't allow me to get stuck in a past moment. Quite the opposite. It reminds me (and I hope you) that life happens and, in the end, all that truly matters is the love we've given and received through our natural happiness.

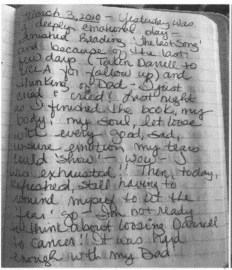

Take a beautiful awareness breath. What if the end result is always love? It's like creating a delicious batch of homemade cookies; you can't really smell, see, feel, or taste how wonderful that cookie is until you go through the effort of combining all the ingredients that, individually, wouldn't necessarily be considered yummy. Then, of course, the dough has to bake in a very hot environment. Sound familiar?

When I'm facing a difficult situation and it's becoming heated, I do my best to align my spirit with the knowingness that there is only love. Then my response can deliver or take away from that knowingness for myself and possibly for others as well. I would often choose to take out my baking supplies and make my well-known peanut-butter-and-chocolate cookies to deliver to neighbors, friends, and businesses. The joy and happiness of life would quickly return, yet it took my aligning my self to move into love.

More than twenty-five years ago, I acquired the nickname "the Cookie Angel" from one of my favorite places to deliver to, Jan, Kahn, and Soares attorney office in Hanford. I have loved spreading seeds of kindness through making cookies and would feel so happy as I sneaked onto neighbors' porches, rang the doorbell, and dashed off before being seen. That was the mission. At first, it was a secret delivery, but that lasted only for the first year. I still would continue escaping before they could see my body or hear my voice. They'd open the door to a surprise of love and gratitude, from my heart space to theirs.

Some would post on Facebook a picture of the cookie delivery, and someone would reply, "We know who that is." I would get warm, fluttering, loving butterflies when my daughter and friends would tell me about it. The love flowed from the beginning of my mixing the batter, to my baking and packaging the cookies, and well into the delivery and afterward. Although I wouldn't hang on to the past but rather feel it in the moment, remembering that we choose our actions and words and therefore happiness is right before us, within us, even when the exterior seems heated or stressful.

The intention behind any action defines that sentence, paragraph, or, sometimes, chapter of life. At times, sadly, someone's entire life's story, his or her book, ultimately ends up being tied to negative intentions—this can possibly play out when we continuously allow the past to be the present moment. Take a breath, pick up your pen, and make each moment a book of life by an author who is planting seeds, themes, of love. Be your own best seller.

So let's mix a batch of yummy cookies, stirring up as much love as possible, and may we choose to share them as we share our love as *one*. Amen.

Plant Your Life's Garden, a New Life

Happy Birthday to Every Being
Every Day, Every Moment

An Amazing Harvest as We Choose to
Celebrate One Another Daily!

April 23, 2021

Who among us doesn't enjoy celebrations, getting together with people we like and enjoy spending time with, celebrating one another? It truly does feel good to lift up someone else in love and appreciation just because, celebrating each moment with that person. I was blessed to be on the receiving end, being that it was my birthday, my date of birth. Believe me—I was celebrating each of them as well.

A birthday is the one day a year on which we celebrate someone's birth into this world. It's a wonderful life (also one of Krisi's and my favorite movies). Birthdays mark the physical beginnings of our plays on earth, the short periods of time we consider lifetimes.

Wouldn't it be just wonderful if we celebrated one another daily, even moment to moment? Hmm … sounds absolutely mesmerizing.

I used to send my mom flowers on my birthday. Anyone who's given birth knows it's one of the most sacred, beautiful experiences of life. I enjoy sharing with people the question, How could anyone not believe that there's a higher being loving us unconditionally? The miracles of life that happen so often go unnoticed.

My most beautiful experience of birth? A challenging choice, for sure! My self giving birth to Krisi (I laugh at the phrasing *give birth to*) or my experiencing the blessing of my daughter giving birth to both Rylan and Grayson?

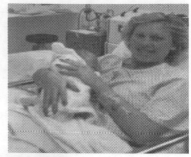

Proud mommy and daddy and Smilin Rylan

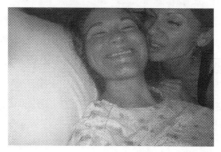

Krisi beaming. I'm sober—just high on love.

At times, when I was giving birth to Krisi, the uncomfortableness overtook me in the moment; I was not as aware at age twenty-two. I was actually able to be totally present in the now for every moment Krisi spent giving birth to both Rylan and Grayson. My awareness was so keen, so right on.

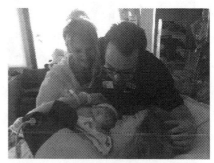

I'm blessed I was asked to be present once again, during Grayson's birth.

It's amazing that I began breath awareness more than forty years ago in Lamaze. Even though playing sports in school would bring more consciousness of breathing, it was (at least for me) fleeting.

It's fascinating that I began meditating back at age twenty-two without my even realizing it—that I was using awareness as I gave birth—not connecting that's what I was practicing. Breath awareness opens up a porthole of knowing, a knowingness of how sacred and precious the moment is. My breath moved me peacefully and calmly into the now. That was an additional side gift I received many years ago. Birth and flight days are gifts, never-ending gifts.

For many years, I've felt we would benefit by celebrating those we love—and perhaps even those we love but may not like very much—for no particular reason. Simply and beautifully for the reason of love and appreciation. We could choose days and moments sporadically throughout the year, and this celebrating could happen more often than not.

When my beautiful daughter was only six or seven, we used to make up a day *just because*, secretly planning a surprise celebration of one member of the family. The love and acts of kindness soon spread to our practice. Those are some of the most precious memories I have. Of course, I find myself saying that about all my memories.

As we continue to celebrate special dates throughout the year, may we also make it a moment-to-moment seat-of-awareness celebration of our brothers and sisters in life. Smile at someone. Offer acts of kindness, sporadically, sprinkled like confetti throughout the year—heck, throughout the day—especially when the expectation is nowhere in sight, even during heated times. "Surprise! We celebrate you!"

We must celebrate one another just because, for no reason except that, together, we are human kindness, called to love one another. We are one.

Garden of Life

July 10, 2019

In Rylan's short life, seeds of love and joy were planted in our hearts, in the world. The energy of the earth absorbed his joy, love, energy, and determined will to live in the moment, planting love seeds as he journeyed with wonder and excitement through life.

Maximus doing tree pose in front of Rylan's garden.

As I was planting yesterday, I felt Rylan's energy working through my heart as my hands worked the earth's soil, tenderly, inviting space for each plant to be a part of the wholeness. It's amazing that roots are always growing but that it's only the ground level up that's present.

How healthy are our roots—those deep roots that give us the strength to keep growing (or not)? Roots are the foundation. What seeds are we planting in life's garden?

What do our gardens of life feel like as we peer from our hearts' awareness? Are they joyful places to visit? I am the gardener of my life—no one else is. So do I take responsibility for the harvest of my life?

Take a breath, breathing in the calmness of the moment. Now feel from your heart. Ask yourself the following series of questions.

Is my garden a joyful place I'm excited to tend to each morning? Am I excited to begin again as I walk as the gardener of life—my life, my journey?

Do I continue to shower with gratitude as I water my life's garden each day? Do I at times spread tears of joy, and other times tears of hope and compassion, while lending a loving hand to assist another's garden? All the while becoming present, perhaps sending a prayer of healing or doing a dance of celebration?

Do I tend my garden through awareness, conscious of overgrown weeds that take root in the form of thoughts, actions, and reactions that tend to inhibit my growth, my journey within? Do I scatter seeds of fear-based thoughts, involving perhaps blame, criticism, judgment, or anger toward others, all the while damaging my inner being? A conscious life's garden feels no need, no desire, to cast stones of fear (except, if we're unprepared, during an occasional thunderstorm).

If we're present and open, thunderstorms are welcomed and in fact clear the air, the cloudiness, bringing healing and eventually rainbows of hope, tying together a knowingness that all is perfect in all its present imperfections.

As we become more open to look from within, our thunderstorms become a bridge that brings healing sunlight back to us as strength for our roots and garden to grow in depth and hardiness, aligning us with who we really are.

May we all choose to throw seeds of kindness until our gardens are so mature that an occasional thunderstorm will simply and beautifully bring a brighter awareness of enlightenment, allowing space for us to be present with awareness, spreading further kindness. After all, aren't we all in the big garden of life together?

Let's play, pray, praise, and appreciate. Happy gardening!

Nurture Your and Others' Spiritual Garden Reservoirs: Plant Love Seeds

October 23, 2020

I'm choosing to believe that, for the most part, our surroundings are met with friendships that are nurtured through the blessings of understanding. I believe that time spent planting seeds, making deposits in the emotional bank accounts of those we hold dear to our hearts (and honestly all others), is a valuable awareness activity we should practice daily and similarly hold dearly in our hearts' space.

Dr. Stephen Covey writing in my book during a weeklong cruise. It was a once-in-a-lifetime dream come true. Stephen Covey, one of my forever mentors, right there to talk with and hug and love on! He is amazing (and, yes, I know he took flight, but I feel him in my moments of stillness).

What seeds are you planting in each moment with your thoughts, words, and actions? More than thirty years ago (yikes), I was first introduced to the concept of the emotional bank account (EBA). Another satori moment. It was in fact a huge aha moment, hit me right away. I just got it! But I also knew deep in my heart that intentions are everything. Of course, there are definitely times when we just have to start with the habit—in this case, committing the EBA to memory and putting it to use. With the EBA as a habit in action, the heart will guide the intentions.

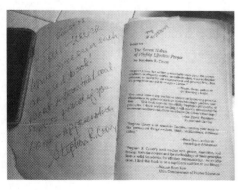

Of course, when I arrived home, I sent Dr. Covey and his family some of my famous cookies and received a phone call from him at the office. The staff were lost for words, which none of us ever lacked. They thought it was a joke. In case you're unable to read his written words (of course, you can see by the yellowed pages that I bought one of the first published copies): "Jan 2005, Joni—never have I seen such a used book …"

Through my words and actions, I started teaching my daughter at a very young age, and I've enjoyed doing the untrainings for years. The EBA has always been a welcome highlight, inspiring many a satori awakening. I love this analogy from Covey's *The 7 Habits of Highly Effective People*, the concept of deposits in others' EBAs. We talk about how important it is to deposit more than we withdraw (can you imagine trying to withdraw money you haven't deposited in your bank account?) from the people close to us. At this time in our (shared, external) world, it's even more important.

When we use our four birth gifts, we unwrap the beingness of awareness. Consciously, we become more aware of what our life gardens are producing. How generous are we with our deposits not only in others' EBAs but also in our own? Do we bring our compassion to reach not only people close to us but also those in need around the world?

Now more than ever, we need to choose to remember we are human beings having a human experience *together*, heart to heart, bringing a spiritual experience in love. We are truly one humankind as we spread reminders that we can choose to be kind humans. It's time for us to plant some seeds wrapped in intentions of love and kindness. Let's do this!

So as another week comes to an end, it seems to me a perfect time to reach out to someone, possibly someone with whom we share a strained relationship, and make a deposit in that person's EBA. But we must do so continuing with nonattachment, planting the seeds and simply allowing them to grow. Feel how the deposits, blessings, return tenfold. Happy depositing as we pray as one. Love will lead the way.

Kindness Is Cool / Now More Than Ever, Be Kind, Be Brave, and Be You

---

March 16, 2020

A beautiful fellow (kindhearted) yogi shared with me a couple of weeks ago that when she was younger, she thought and felt that kindness was *not* cool. Her daughter (whom I adore) helped her see how untrue that was.

And not through words but rather through actions.

For many, hearing that kindness is cool brings some discomfort. There's a kind of uneasiness, as our thoughts seem determined to convince us that kindness is weak and leaves us vulnerable. Me may think, *What if by being kind I miss out on something for me* [e.g., water, toilet paper, hand sanitizer], *something I deserve?* Or—how about this one?—*They never do anything kind for me!*

There she is, under the rainbow making a heart shape. She helped open the space for her mom to feel that love and kindness are cool.

I was sharing at the grocery store today how sad it makes me just hearing and seeing how people have been filled with fear, causing a scarcity mentality, resulting in their, yes, being unkind. Of course, many others are also saddened by this selfishness. But I mentioned more than once, "Next time you see a fight over TP or bananas, just go up and give them a great big hug." I totally believe this with all my heart because *being kind also means being brave!* We may leave with a black eye, but that's my loving advice, my choice. We are truly one! (And, FYI, I wrote this before the mask mandate was in effect.)

As thoughts convince us of those untruths, the emotions attached to those thoughts become familiar and comfortable and, with time, tend to lead us into the same crazy cycle: when anything stressful or fearful comes into our lives, those familiar emotions take us on the wild cyclone of sabotage and storytelling, farther away from true happiness and joy.

For others, our minds convince us that we *are* kind. But if we take the time to have conversations, one-on-one, with our inner souls, we may just find we could easily become much more authentically kind, with no strings attached. We could offer kindness that's dependent on nothing, just plain, true unconditional love—love that births inner peace, happiness, and joyful moments in our daily lives!

My beautiful, kind yogi sister shared how it took the birth of her daughter—her watching how innocently and naturally kind her daughter was—to silence her mind and create space for her to listen to her heart speak to her inner beautiful self, leading her back to her aligned love within.

But ... You know, one of my favorite things is that when you use the word *but*, it tends to negate everything stated before it. *And*, in this case, let's erase all the negative talk about fear and the acts that lack kindness, such as hoarding. Let's allow the breaking open of these moments of our lives. Yes, we must embrace a *real* breaking open of moments in our lives in the form of satori moments, which help us uncover the habitual beliefs that have been brought into our daily thought processes.

When emotions connected to those thoughts begin their cycles of storytelling, we have to make a choice. Perhaps, for example, the coronavirus is an opportunity for not only us but our towns and states and all countries in the world to choose love and kindness.

I was talking to one of my clients yesterday and shared with her that I feel like sometimes when momentum is going full force in the direction of fear, eventually something will break open and we'll have the opportunity to use our kindness and love rebuild, constructing something more beautiful than ever. A worldwide satori moment. Love always wins and never fails. We will make a big shift within ourselves and therefore extend out. All is well, and, yes, this, too, shall pass.

When we really get within our hearts, out of our minds, we don't feel good when we're unkind. Kindness brings us into who we are truly meant to be. People think that I live in fairy-tale land thinking this way, but I believe I live in reality. I believe there is so much goodness and kindness in the world already, and this gives us *all* the opportunity to quadruple the effect of conscious kindness!

I say, "You perform an act of kindness—share it!" Naomi and I were talking about how a loving man helped deliver water to an elderly couple and then shared his kind deed. There are so many acts of kindness happening. If you know of someone who's performed an act of kindness, or if you have done something kind during this time, share it! Why do we shy away? If we allow our light to shine, we give others permission to do the same—one of my favorite concepts from Marianne Williamson!

When we live only in our minds, we start finding evidence that there's no reason for kindness in this moment. And, truly, most "evidence" is false because we can never, ever really get into the mind or heart of somebody else. I believe with all my heart that if we could feel other people's heartfelt intentions, we would come together in kindness and all would be well!

So I vote for "Kindness is cool—be brave and be you!"

Rise Up and Join in Awareness of Love

November 13, 2020

I have enjoyed journaling through the years, questioning my experiences, thoughts, and feelings and asking my self for input.

Yes, I have to admit that sometimes I may feel that I could handle a certain project or situation more efficiently with my self, but I believe with all my heart that we were meant to come on this journey of life to work together, play together, laugh together, and join together in hope. We must nurture that hope of the knowingness that we have within an enjoyable, inner happiness awaiting as we experience our journeys of life—not only for the sake of ourselves but, most important, for everyone, as one.

At the end of Darrell's journey here, I chose a group of angels who together helped make Darrell's flight absolutely beautiful. I experienced firsthand how quickly (five days) strangers can become not only my angels but also chosen family, gathering together in love. Talk about synergizing! Hospice is an example of individuals coming together with and in a mission of love.

They will always be part of my chosen family. We know that our energy expands; research can't even measure the extent to which a kind thought, word, or action can affect energy. I witness all the time how synergy creates energy. Ours coming together will produce the energy we emanate.

It's so true that when they came together, they became one, magnified during yoga practice as their breath and awareness heightened.

My experience of life has shown me that when two or more gather and synergize together, it's almost like nothing's impossible. Of course, the possibilities may not always be exactly

One of the first small groups of Smilin' Rylan yogis. I love these now teens. Synergy into energy of fun, laughter, and so much kindness.

245

what the initial expectations are, yet there is a knowing through the gifts—of awareness, inspiration to imagine, the conscious voice of stillness, and the freedom to be—that the rainbows of happiness are delivered from within.

We may come together to do something that is almost impossible without support. Hopefully we become humble—humble enough to put aside our egos and listen first, going within, asking, "Am I aware?"; opening to and heart listening to what others may be offering as suggestions, paying attention to not only their words but the actions of their energy; and perhaps together giving birth to a gift that's better than what either side alone brought or could bring to the table. It is not compromising but rather synergizing to a higher alternative that exceeds all earlier expectations.

I feel that for most of us it's at times challenging to become humble. The me inside that often supports the personality can be stubborn, to say the least. This provides the perfect opportunity for journaling.

For me, being humble means that I'm becoming totally open, able to step out of the me of the personality and listen twice as much as speaking, heart listening with a desire to understand so as to do what's best for all. The big picture is that the end in mind should put an end to the mind. But, again, the mind is a wonderful servant—as long as the heart space, the I, is the guide.

Energy to synergy requires us to look within, becoming humble, seeking to understand others before we expect to be understood, and truly wanting to come together with a win-win mentality. Then there's the opportunity for a true third alternative: not my way or your way but a better-together way.

So another week is at its end. As we begin the weekend, may we join in one voice, understanding that our fight to be right is distinguished by the fire of the higher, by the flow of hope of a brighter future for all.

Being Kind to Our Selves Is One of the Greatest Kindnesses We Can Give

September 17, 2020

I believe we're all here to be fully present individually so that we can be present for others. We are here to serve—well, I'll add that I believe I'm here to serve. We can serve through our energy, a kind thought about someone or something, or even a smile or other action that delivers peaceful energy for others to bathe in.

If we're in alignment, love and kindness are flowing through us. Otherwise, how can we give from empty hearts? When we are self-full, no effort of action is required. When in alignment, we can't *not* radiate love and serve others. It just pours out, and then it's as if there's a current that waves the love and kindness outward, where they then return to the creator. Then the waves return to us, beautifully orchestrated, by no accident or coincidence. The butterfly wings begin their waves of warmth, and energy flowing, the gift returns.

I remember one of my spiritual mentors years ago saying that, ultimately, we're always doing for ourselves. At first that unsettled me. I was confused, a little uncomfortable. Back then, I couldn't fully bring that thought into my inner awareness long enough to understand it deeply. I do so now and have for many years.

At first, I took that to mean there was always a condition attached, and I didn't agree. To this day, I do hear that sentiment from people—those who are suspicious when an act of kindness is performed, when it's obvious to me it's been carried out with nonattachment. It's unfortunate and sad that we grow so suspicious. We can't believe somebody is being kind for no reason, with no attachment, giving unconditionally merely because that person is living with and through kindness.

It's a choice, yet in a magical current of waves, it's not. It's the only way the waves can return. They flow onto the sandy shoreline as a gift and will return to their source.

What I now believe the statement conveys is that the energy given will return, meaning we're doing for ourselves when we do for others! I love that! The energy of giving is the return.

247

It may not come in the package others feel is warranted, but there are those who give for no other reason than love, a desire to give, with no expectations. We feel when we give—it's from the space of oneness, and we're naturally giving to ourselves as well. We have no thoughts either way regarding the return, finding the space to understand that those who lack from within often do give from an emptiness they sense. Most likely, those people feel they need deeply the return—that it will fill them up. Yet returns that result from that type of giving are fleeting, ending in an emptiness, an even deeper void.

In that way, we're just like oranges—that is, when the orange is squeezed, what comes out is what was inside. That's exactly what happens within us; everything we do we're doing to ourselves. Squeeze us, and we'll quickly reveal what was marinating inside us. Just watch as it squeezes out. When we give from a place of lack, we receive lack, or at least the feeling of lack.

How I treat myself most likely indicates my intention behind my treatment of others. If I give from an emptiness, I can't help but feel I need someone, something, to fill me up. Again, what I give to others, I give to me. At times, the me is aware enough, therefore calling on my spirit, my soul (my inner self, the I-ness), to take the wheel. I feel that most of the time my energy is filled with love. If I at all feel that I have to do something, a service or an act, it's not coming from the fullness of who I am.

I can say from my knowingness that, most times, I am full and give only when I am. It brings such warming energy throughout my entire body; my heart feels the butterflies fluttering around. How can I not give, with the waves of energy flowing freely from me, unknowingly yet knowing, unattached?

When we serve and give of our selves, our internists (our internal doctors) know we're serving from who we really are and connected to all—set free.

"No One Has Ever Become Poor by Giving" (Anne Frank)

June 15, 2020

My beautiful daughter (every day I celebrate having had her) and I just hung up from our early-morning talk celebrating our relationship, our love, and sharing about life—the temporary life of the human form—with joyful hearts.

At Grayson's baby shower. I love my daughter, Krisi, so very much.

We discussed the knowingness that who we are isn't this form that so many of us put extra emphasis on—the walk of this form through life. Yes, it's beautiful. And, yep, the play of life from this form is what leaves the residue of our time here. Of course, it's from not the physical but the energy. It's the energy of who we really are that remains. That's what excites me; it breaks chains that I've placed on my existence. I release who I thought I was and become free to be my self.

Releasing the earthly binds of illusion, I become open and begin to take each moment as play, even in challenges, being present and knowing that in stillness, even in the busyness, I can choose my script for my next play of life. It brings a clearness, calmness, and freeness to me, and I enjoy my life's play.

And this brings me once again to the intentions behind the act of giving, which may incite mixed feelings of gratitude. We could consider so many reasons not to give in certain situations. I, for one, find that exercise unproductive. It really comes down to our hearts. What are our hearts speaking? They aren't judging, I'm sure. I'm not talking about the mind, the scripts we've been handed down from others (e.g., the scarcity mentality) or the judgments inherited from family or friends. Listen with your heart's mind, your heart's space.

My heart has shown me, when I listen softly, that I am able to let others' criticism or judgment regarding giving roll off my back, not influence my heart. I continue to feel good and comfortable listening to the inner voice of I. I listen softly and become silent as I am speaking to me. No longer will I feel any possibility of judgment. Yes, there is the argument—if you want to call it that—that some people manipulate by giving. I don't recognize that.

What I have noticed through all my years is that people who make those statements are usually people who have those very intentions when they're considering giving (just an observation, but I never claim to know what someone else's motives are). I personally don't call that giving—if there are any attachments or motives. I choose not to allow that to influence my decision. The intention is everything, but that's between you and your inner heart. And, as I see it, it's no one else's business.

Krisi is such an example of that. I have used her as an example for many years, often while I'm doing an untraining, explaining how during regular conversations (from when she was as young as four) we would talk about awareness and refer to the videotape analogy.

My daughter and grandkids have been raised with the idea of thinking about a videotape—a recording we can choose to rewind, having the opportunity to learn from those replays. We ask ourselves whether we'd be happy with our plays of life in those recorded scenes.

When I was talking with her on the phone this morning, and because of her beautiful giving heart, Krisi proceeded to tell me that instead of selling Grayson's outgrown bouncer, playpen, and so on, she wanted to give them away. I mentioned to her I knew somebody who would appreciate them. She and I both got so excited. Giving is a gift we give ourselves. May we all have a beautiful day giving, receiving, and watching as we feel the love circling all.

Make a Love Shot

July 2, 2019

Rylan loved to do love shots for his Jmom and grandfather. My beautiful daughter, Krisi, taped him one day and blessed me with this video. After watching this little basketball player, who would ever believe that cancer would win in less than a year? Please take the time to watch the video "Rylan's Love Shot" at https://www.youtube.com/shorts/_C_VhyeeDso. It makes my heart smile, and I feel yours will smile too.

Win isn't the right word; when do we ever really win except where love is the intention? And even then, it may not appear as a win. Rylan is and always was the winner. His love will always win and forever be love shots in my heart.

I'm not talking about a shot of anything but love, though what is the true definition of *love*? How would you define it? As for me, it's not about words. In my opinion, there are no words to truly express what love is.

It takes my accepting and being open to a relationship with my inner self—the deeper I-ness—unattached, unafraid, patient, and with a desire to go deep within. It's journeying to who I truly am.

The game of life can become so goal oriented that we often forget we do have a choice: we can play or sit out. We can maybe look at it a little differently to bring it around to home, remembering it's OK to sit on the bench and watch the game. There's no pressure to make a shot, a three-pointer. For me, it's my calling not to make a basket, a goal, but rather to return to my self. I begin again as the I takes the front seat—the coach within reminding the teammate of thoughts that I am the head coach. What do I desire? Perhaps I discover there's nothing, no objects or baskets, listed as the goal. Rather, it's about a returning to presence in each moment—and

251

from there, the desires are born. I (the thoughts) ask the coach to let me in the game, and it's about playing the game, not winning. I play the game and enjoy, happy with each breath, each part of the game. My happiness doesn't depend on met goals, external objects, yet they are part of the game, and I so enjoy them. So be a good sportsman; it's just a game. Where and when do I enjoy the game of life? When my heart is open and awareness is heightened, goals are just a part of the moment, and I can feel when I need to be in the game and when I need to sit on the sidelines, neither one being the reason for my inner happiness.

When the game of life is so goal focused, the thoughts in our minds can become so constant that there's no space to bring a clear presence to the mind. When we are still and focused—well, just in the moment—then look out, because our love shot is a slam dunk! We've won regardless of what the game of life's scorekeeper may show. We're winners of our plays of life.

Whenever There Are Challenges, We Hold the Promise of Change

June 25, 2021

Listen and feel the impulse from your heart. I'm sitting with Love and Faith. It's early Sunday morning, when I usually begin writing for the week. I have windows all around my tiny little home, and I'm peering out to the complete freedom of the outside, to the innocence of nature. There's a presence that's given to us any moment of the day, and we're free no matter our surroundings.

A contingent continuance from last week—contingent on what? Who? On breath, stillness. Hopefully another satori moment is waiting patiently to be uncovered

I write "Choose love" often during our walks on the beach.

as an aha moment. Once again, I feel the space as the exterior changes, and my inner I remains unchangeable. There's an inner question to contemplate.

What if everything were just right? (What if it is in fact just right?) We'd feel no inner need to judge, no desire to blame. We'd consequently hold within our hearts no feelings born from the desire to blame or judge anyone or anything. Instead, we'd operate from the desire to love, leading to acceptance and, in many cases, changes in our perception of the play of life.

Choose a time when you're feeling aligned, when your heart's open in the awareness of honesty, and ask your inner self, "Why do I judge?" Listen softly, gently, to the nudge from the heart. It should be a light tug of nonjudgment—nonjudgmental of the you inside. Feel the change of mind unwrapping as it opens and at times becomes the gift.

What if we had everything we needed within ourselves? If we held the answer? A soft nudge, an impulse, moving our next moment's decision to a flow of loving grace?

We'd move into the awareness, where we'd lose our personalities yet find our inner selves, complete, with no need or desire for anyone or anything to make us feel alive. There'd be no need to find partners to be our other halves in order for us to be, feel, whole. Of course, I find myself being pulled back into my mind's chatter of life, but not nearly as often as I did years ago.

I prefer the mind to be the servant of my inner freedom, my presence, changing my perception of the moment. I gain awareness simply by being the witness and falling away so as to be present. Truly, no words can fully explain it. Good job, mind! I love the mind, especially when it's not causing monkey-mind craziness, when my self, the one, is (nonverbally) speaking, delivering seeds of intention; I am who I really am.

My doingness is much more productive and less stressful. The mind becomes a partner in the fun play, and happiness just is, bringing so much more joy. I am resting in the presence of now, where there is no future and the past disappears.

The times when the mind pulls me back and I'm drawn once again into the circus of my thoughts, jumping back and forth from past to future, I feel a temporary insanity. I no longer feel I'm truly living. There is a perceived challenge, but in such moments, we are presented with the gift that opens the promise of change (or not).

When we feel the contrast of the peace-filled presence of now and the turbulent feeling of being ping-ponged between past and future, we then have the opportunity to receive (as we listen to the nudge, the soft voice from the heart's mind) the gift and the opportunity to unwrap it. It takes time and courage to undo the mind chatter.

There was a time when my mind, being uncomfortable with stillness, would relentlessly be carried back into the chatter. Back then, being present just felt too unfamiliar and uncomfortable, too still and quiet. It felt totally foreign.

Peaceful, seriously! As I began meditating, bringing awareness and still moments to my days, my mind chatter began to fall away and quiet down, bringing peace. I began to crave it. My mind began to ease into the change, from chatter into the nothingness of the now. Presence became comfortable and familiar. I chose to unwrap the gift. I truly hope everyone does.

It's been at least twenty years of committed daily meditation practice. It didn't happen my first or second experience summoning moments of silence and stillness, but I began releasing, little by little. At times, I felt my mind would never quiet long enough to receive the space of awareness—and then I would feel the nudge of change happening. My heart was not going to become discouraged.

These little yogis loved to do the monkey-mind routine,
ending in a seated stillness and meditation.
Please take the time to watch the little yogis practicing it: "Smilin Rylan Kids
Yoga - Monkey Mind," https://www.youtube.com/watch?v=Zlf9FZLWnls.

The vigilant mind puts up a struggle, trying to stick to the habit and known commitment to the monkey mind. But—and this is a big *but*—little by little, the mind loses the battle, and once again peace wins. The mind adapts begrudgingly yet willfully to the newfound moments of gentleness, though not yet enough to feel the happiness within. Perhaps not most of the time, yet it's perfect in the imperfection of it all. Each moment becomes a blessing in time of timelessness. Our minds become advocates for stillness more often as well as wonderful partners with awareness.

Now (I know—there's that word again) I am enjoying more now moments in nature. Yet I know the outer landscape really becomes less important and the ever-present love of this moment prevails innocently as the mystery that is living us.

Through the years, people have constantly asked me, "How can you be in the moment and be able to live your life without planning?" And for years, one of my passions has been to share my experiences with people through untrainings and to care enough to simply share when asked. Yes, I have a passion to help others discover the benefits of meditation and silence in prayer, stillness, breath, and yoga, vehicles through which my self has guided me back little by little.

You can plan for your future and then let it go. Choose to commit to what is important to do through your calm beingness. Then let what happens play out, unattached to the outcome, becoming wrapped in acceptance.

Otherwise, the mind will try to be the planner and the dictator while constantly ping-ponging you from past and future,

Naomi and daughter, Haley, being in the moment through breath of meditation.

sending messages continuously like a recording. It will demand at times in a threatening dialogue, claiming it wants what's best for your self, and then make sure you accomplish the task it expects you to get done. It's craziness, and once again, the challenges can bring the promise of change, the rainbow, the miracle. I know—I have witnessed it over and over again.

As another beautiful week ends, may we begin the weekend with the reassurance that challenges bring the promise of change. We must embrace and receive as we all come together, believing nothing is impossible. Enjoy your moments.

One Person's Junk Is Another's Treasure—but a Treasure Junk?

November 6, 2020

I had my first garage (treasure) sale. Well, I had a group garage sale years ago for donations to the Christian Home in Hanford. Why oh why would I now, after knowing the time and effort, have another? Why not donate? I kept asking myself those exact questions as I spent hours working on it during the days leading up to it. I had loving help from Naomi, Cyndi and Teresa, my beautiful friends and sisters from other mothers. They probably wondered too. Just think of all the seeds of intentions planted in that one day of gathering—yes, seeds planted to grow into gardens of love.

I have had several people ask me, "Was it worth the time and effort?" Probably not, if it had been solely for the money, but it was a journey of giving, heartfelt giving. I'll explain. There was releasing, mourning, and celebrating space of lightness, so it was well worth all the time, emotion, and surrendering.

I wonder whether you'll understand as I do my best to explain. It's like I wanted to see and talk with the people and feel the energy of my treasures—and possibly my junk—being transferred to people who'd hopefully treasure them too. Yes, I know I'm using the word *treasure* a lot; you see, treasures plant seeds of intentions.

I will be moving from a very large home into a very tiny, tiny, tiny house, soon to be my home. There was no other choice but to go through the mourning of not only losing my best friend, my partner, my love of more than twenty-five years, but also letting go of things, the possessions. Yes, there was junk that I'd accumulated over years and that, to some, I suppose, would be treasures. The items, objects, that had been my treasures—how could I just let them go without treasure maps to give the fortune seekers? They'd become our treasures from the years of travel—memories, gifts of love.

Darrell and I traveled so much. It was his release—truly one of his favorite things to do, from the very beginning of our shared moments together. We experienced this beautiful country but also other countries, other places. We always brought home at least one treasure, usually a piece of art (if you entered our home, you would see, and feel, several art pieces of hearts too). Darrell loved art, and I love hearts.

I never took for granted the home we'd made together. It was a very loving home we had for years during which close friendships turned to chosen family. The special gifts, or treasures, that we received, we cherished. I would bless my home on my departure as well as feel the energy as I left the space. Walking through the door on my arrival home was a blessing. Every little item that filled the space, our space, contained memories, and those memories filled the room. Yet it was more than the items—it was the fragrance of the space, the nothingness yet allness of love.

I would seriously, and I still do, walk through my home with awareness, feeling the preciousness of the past but not letting it take away from my living in the present moment. I'd celebrate how we can bring the love from the past and make our moments that much more precise.

So I'm feeling the blessing of all those years, now precious memories I hold dearly in my heart. On the day of that precious-item sale, I was able to see, feel, and welcome the transfer of precious cargo to its new wonderful owners. That's the gift that can be received at a garage sale. In fact, let's change *garage sale* to *transfer-of-precious-treasure sale*—yes!

Yes, the treasures as memories were very strong for Darrell, but there were also many items that held memories attached to Rylan's heartstring.

Now I can carry them in my heart and allow the possessions to find their way to becoming treasures to others. I just have to now let go. It was miraculously amazing being present and aware and seeing as the new owners left with their newfound gems. Parents and grandparents had bought for their grandchildren, anticipating the joy the books, games, and other items to would bring. They looked forward to time spent enjoying one another and making new memories as the transfer of blessings continued. What a gift we give as we receive.

My mom and dad shortly before my dad's diagnosis.

I noticed there were two women at the dollar table. I found out later they were mother and daughter. All of a sudden, I was hearing my voice talking to my dad. It startled me at first. After my dad took flight, I received some of the gifts I had once given him, and one was a voice-activated frame. I forgot my voice was still on there, so I had a conversation with this lovely mother-daughter team.

Of course they bought it for a dollar—who wouldn't? I could feel the new family was excited to rerecord their voices over mine and that it was going to be special to someone. Yes, it was someone's newfound treasure, and soon it would be making new memories. My heart was full. It's so beautiful planting new seeds of love.

So, once again, as the end of the week leads into the weekend, may memories bring treasures as well as reminders to cherish the moment! Enjoy!

Conclusion

Bringing New Beginnings

The end is the beginning. This is not the conclusion but rather the birthing of a new beginning. We're concluding the old, putting to rest the past scripts that no longer serve us. We're embracing that now is the only real time, and even it isn't exactly real.

There will be some happy endings, hopefully many, to your reading this book of love. The satori moments of enlightening practices will move you into the next moment, when the moment moves you. Hopefully you're even more open to practices of joy, of peace, discoveries and uncoverings. Perhaps there's a better word: hopefully you're ready to *recover* who you really are. Your aha satori moments will gift you with the realization of the joy present in your own play of life—the joy in each moment, right there, waiting to take you into a space to just be.

You now know, understand, what a satori moment brings. The beauty of it all is that when you allow awakening moments to guide you into the present moment, and you feel the peace of what life desires to bring to you, you're giving a present to yourself and therefore to others. These moments remind us that we are all connected—we are all one.

So as we begin again to fall back into loving ours selves and therefore others, may the awareness bring us together in the now.

When Was the Last Time You Looked Up to the Night's Magnificence?

June 23, 2020

Imagine perhaps that you stepped outside to do something, forgetting about your to-do list, and were delivered into the moment of now. Even though your external world is filled with activity, you're on a mysterious adventure in the present stillness of peace. You become the stillness of all the moving. You've arrived on an instant vacation of peace.

The ocean is such a natural balm for the soul. Hopefully you kick off your sandals to feel the sand between your toes, to feel the loving energy from the knowingness that you're right where you're supposed to be in this moment. Spontaneously happy. On an impulse, with no energy going to thoughts, without stopping to take off your street clothes, you run, even skip, into the ocean's tumbling waves. You're welcomed by the vibration of the salt water splashing, embracing you, and witnessing the dance of your playful heart, leaving yourself humbled and free.

Love and Faith; my granddaughter, Ava; and me taking off for the ocean's healing energy, having fun.

Perhaps you experience a kind of embrace as you take in the night's magical gifts, with nothing to do, no time, and pause in the living presence of space from the absence of time, absorbing the sky's play of light and energy. Why aren't we all sleeping outdoors?

How about times when you choose to turn off electronics, headphones, TV, and chatter from both your mouth and your thoughts? What do you owe your thoughts? Nothing! Breathing effortlessly, ask, "Am I aware?" Open up to a dream state, a soft awareness, and sense the wonderment within you—the sameness in all!

It's never too late to explore. It's always the perfect time, when you've released yourself of any steps required to arrive in your beingness. It's already present, effortless. Be in the now, with the one who is with you always (and in all ways you). Take a breath and believe.

It's never too late for us to discover the peace right at our fingertips. At first, there were certain practices I used to help relax my mind's habit of thoughts, to rediscover the unchanging one who is always ready to receive me back home. So, yes, we can call it a *practice*—a practice of being aware of how many of our moments are spent doing what we *think* we need to do to be happy, while it's all right within us, uninfluenced by the outside world.

The most real part of all of this is when I slow down my thoughts and ask, "Am I aware?" I've been choosing this more often these past few years, and it brings the preciousness right now—what I have right in front of me, within me. It's free. It's like the lyrics from one of my favorite songs: "Don't mistake the weather for the sky." It's so simple, yet we make it so difficult. It's all within, unchanging; why not take a peek?

So, once again, I am reminded not to mistake material items—that may be wonderful to experience—for the preciousness of the now. We are not our bodies; we are the awareness of our bodies, and it is temporary. Find that release so as to welcome the enjoyment of this play of life, with no attachment.

As I finish expressing my gratitude in this moment, I am sitting once again in nature, releasing any need to label what I'm taking in as appreciation, the nothingness yet everythingness, imagining thousands of years ago, when the backdrop of every day, every night, comprised the birds, the trees, and the sounds of nature, hypnotizing us into releasing into awareness of consciousness.

So the next time your heart speaks, listen. Drop your mind's chatter and join the dance of life. Live the moment. Better yet, *be* the moment and rejoice.

When Darrell and I danced, we were definitely
living the moment to the fullest of now.

Do You Believe in Angels?

February 19, 2021

And if you do believe in angels, do you believe they are among us? I am open to all the possibilities and allow my self to guide me so as not to miss these beautiful experiences. I don't put them in a box, or compartmentalize them according to old, handed-down scripts and beliefs. Everything is open, borderless, as old doubts are released. Why would there not be more experiences of angels? As we take flight from these vehicles, these earthly vehicles we call our bodies, our energy, too, will be released; where does it go? We share a lot about our feelings, experiences, including the presence of angels. But do you truly believe?

My most recent adventure, experience, with an angel was last week, while I was talking to my chosen sister Cyndi. We were sharing our feelings, which we often do—such a gift. It's a true blessing when you have a safe place to really go deep within your soul and share your emotions.

I don't have much biological family close. My chosen family members are precious treasures I cherish deeply. While we were talking on the phone, Cyndi reminded me that I have so many people who love me and are here for me. And, yes, I do know this to be true, but being the loving sister she is, she often reminds me, as I do her. Yes,

Cyn, me, Krisi, and Leaine.

we can say we already know this, yet sometimes it's nice to hear it from someone else's mouth.

My TV, which I've had up now for at least six weeks, was on *sleep* (you can see Darrell's ashes in the beautiful art pieces sitting directly below the TV screen to the left). As I hung up the phone with Cyndi, this is what appeared on my TV screen.

Of course, some people will say Siri answered. First, that has never happened to me, and if it did in that moment, then it was my angels bringing a message to me through Siri. I could feel the energy, the love in that moment. A million butterflies fluttered and danced throughout my heart, enveloping the space within me as well as without. The room was filled with peace.

I have no doubt Darrell and Rylan were getting a kick out of it. Darrell loved Queen, and I never really heard Queen's music unless Darrell put it on. I grew to appreciate it. Don't we do that with (not for) family, with hearts open and willing?

Often, people see only with their minds' vision, missing out on relationships with their ever-present inner selves, who they truly are, the space where angels find their porthole to communicate.

I asked a friend this past week, "How could you not believe that your spirit continues on after the body dies?" Note that you can call it whatever you want—spirit, soul, energy—it's just a chosen word that connects a person's heart with his or her mind to explain his or her feelings and beliefs.

Rylan was definitely behind Queen's message.

When you watch and are present as people take their final earthly breaths, their last human moments, and you're connected, silent, and consciously aware, you sense the presence of angels as they lift your loved ones into their tender care. This eliminates any fears, any doubts, you may hold about there being truly only love—how could there not be?

I believe in angels. We tend to get so caught up in rules that we feel compelled to outline our views of the experience. Why not encourage individuals to feel and flow in their knowingness, allowing their presence to take them for a beautiful encounter, and to share in their words—speaking it and celebrate it?

Here we are once again. I am reminded that as each week ends, we require nothing to celebrate the weekend. Angels really do exist, so hold on to your TV remote and believe. It is not what we see; it is the way we see and believe.

Effort and Ease: Yoga Reminds Us That Life Is Balance—Breathe It, Feel It, Be It

I so enjoy being a student of life. One of the primary reasons I also enjoy yoga is because it reminds those of us willing to allow our hearts to feel humble of the fact that life and yoga aren't meant to be stressful, hard, or straining in any negative-feeling way.

If there's anything we can label as *hard*, it's digging deep within and resisting, fighting against, what our hearts' nudges are expressing to our bodies through our senses. That's hard, very stressful—resisting and fighting what is, expecting things to be different. I believe we encounter challenges when we're not being present enough to hear our deep knowingness, our senses, and we remain unaware.

We miss the opportunity to allow, even welcome, this time to be the awareness in the now present moment. And, yes, I so understand and have experienced myself that it's not easy at times. But, as I often say, what's the alternative? I've learned that fighting against what is present in the moment brings unhappiness. When I'm in the place of seeing with acceptance, my action or inaction delivers me into the next moment freely and once again reveals inner happiness.

Become a child again. Welcome yoga through breath, posture, and willingness to be present. All aspects of yoga can guide us to remember how

Smilin' Rylan yogis demonstrating that the dancer pose takes strength and flexibility, effort and ease, to balance, just as life does.

important it is to feel strength through the acceptance of the challenges. Through conscious awareness, we safely move through the poses on our mats—and through life off the mat.

Yes, it's about strength through effort, with the balance of ease birthing flexibility. Life is about being strong, in a sense—moving in and through

love, not fear, as we meet challenges gifted to us. Strength and flexibility are key, especially when life presents times that call for us to be bendable.

My yoga journey has guided my soft side to welcome and become even more open, vulnerable, but also to set healthy boundaries. I was raised in a family in which being tough was very important and crying was weak, and of course, I failed miserably. I found it comforting to share my feelings. I love to cry, and there are so many beautiful things to cry about. I feel blessed for my family, the good times, the tough times, the healing times—sound familiar? If we're honest, that's part of growing up in a family. It's a journey of becoming, uncovering, who we are and continuing to rediscover our innermost selves, the I.

When I'm practicing yoga, each time I'm present on my mat, it's about me, my journey. Well, it's always about me; I'm the reason for my happiness as well as unhappiness. It's a mixture of sweat and tears, both symbolizing the chapters closing. But it's also a birthing space, opening new chapters, new beginnings. I open my heart and my arms, welcoming a refreshing pathway of freedom to be me.

Rylan and Darrell. You would never know these two had the love affair with cancer together: one dancing through the affair, the other most often fighting (the word fight never sits well with my inner self, the I).

I write when I feel a connection, an alignment. I tell people I feel, I believe, it's Rylan (and the light of others) moving my inner soul, spirit, to speak, and my fingers start flowing into words. I sometimes read it back to myself, not recognizing or remembering having written it. So, wow, thank you for taking the time to bring the words into your heart's space.

This writing brings tears; they flow as I wait in the car for my husband. He once again gets out of the car, masked and gloved up [remember this was during the coronavirus lockdown], and enters the doctor's office, confused, sad, broken, and in pain.

My strength is being called on once again. Otherwise, I would allow my fears, sadness, to take over, and I'd become defeated, unable to be there for him. I get that. I have been blessed with the knowingness (yes, knowingness within) for some time now. No, I'm not saying that it's easy or that I don't get pissed off at times—I just know it does no one any good to choose otherwise.

I try to be flexible as I'm thrown into crisis mode, and I usually manage this with relative ease, choosing to see—it's always about the *way* we see, not *what* we see—the vulnerable side of the man I married thirty-five years ago. I feel the ease of compassion's gifts. It's these times I choose to go back to the past and relive the joys of our marriage, adding loving fuel to my sometimes-depleted empty tank of me: companionship, friendship, and all the adventures we shared. Loving ease fills my heart, and once again, I feel the balance. Peace travels through my heart's mind, where balance is present, with effort and ease.

I am hopefully encouraging a practice of yoga (if you feel the desire). Yoga has guided me in my return to the part that never doubts (well, maybe almost never). I am forever grateful for this gift of yoga, for life. The moments I've spent on the mat have deepened my beliefs: I am stronger yet more flexible. Love leads my steps gracefully into effort and ease of life as I take a conscious breath and celebrate. In the end (there is no end), all passes, and we see by consciousness just how beautiful releasing can be.

The Cookie Thief

October 21, 2019

The Cookie Thief

Valerie Cox

A woman was waiting at an airport one night, with several long hours before her flight. She hunted for a book in the airport shops, bought a bag of cookies and found a place to drop.

She was engrossed in her book but happened to see, that the man sitting beside her, as bold as could be … grabbed a cookie or two from the bag in between, which she tried to ignore to avoid a scene.

So, she munched the cookies and watched the clock, as the gutsy cookie thief diminished her stock. She was getting more irritated as the minutes ticked by, thinking, "If I wasn't so nice, I would blacken his eye."

With each cookie she took, he took one too, when only one was left, she wondered what he would do. With a smile on his face, and a nervous laugh, he took the last cookie and broke it in half.

He offered her half, as he ate the other, she snatched it from him and thought … oooh, brother. This guy has some nerve and he's also rude, why he didn't even show any gratitude!

She had never known when she had been so galled, and sighed with relief when her flight was called. She gathered her belongings and headed to the gate, refusing to look back at the thieving ingrate.

She boarded the plane, and sank in her seat, then she sought her book, which was almost complete. As she reached in her baggage, she gasped with surprise, there was her bag of cookies, in front of her eyes.

Yogis doing a routine inspired by "The Cookie Thief." They are amazing young ladies.

If mine are here, she moaned in despair, the others were his, and he tried to share. Too late to apologize, she realized with grief, that she was the rude one, the ingrate, the thief.

Yes, I'm a cookie thief! This is a poem that I've used in the past, and a class of preteen yogis I taught did yoga poses they choreographed to it! It was magical! I promise it will be worth your taking the time to watch! Check out both "Smilin Rylan Kids Yoga The Cookie Thief" (https://www.youtube.com/watch?v=d8VibjfIKVA) and "Smilin Rylan Kids Yoga The Cookie Thief #2" (https://www.youtube.com/watch?v=0QDuAAYNrEQ).

Years ago, when I used this poem for the opening of an untraining, it set the stage for all of us in the room to revisit times in our pasts when perhaps we made assumptions or judgments about people over something we were absolutely sure they did.

Then we took the journey of stillness—rewriting, rescripting, summoning the present-moment awareness, and wiping clean the past as if it were a smudge on the lens of our vision, removing and replacing it with acceptance, a rebirth in this moment: the now.

I would then recommend what I've done at times in my past, making a decision and sitting with the person or writing him or her a letter of apology, asking for forgiveness. It didn't matter to me if I really didn't understand at the time, and it didn't matter whether the other person felt it was my fault. I gained such a wonderful blessing from communicating my feelings, such a feeling of freedom. I love these opportunities for growth and rebirth. I had no attachment to the other person's reply. It really had to do with my inner me, returning to who I really am, and I could begin again.

Part of my growth through the years is attributable to my using my heart more and my mind less. Once again, the mind is wonderful. Make it your servant, not your boss. I receive so much freedom to be who I know through awareness—I am. For many years, one of my forever favorite suggestions to our office family was "Think from your heart's mind. Allow it to speak, and you'll know."

I would include this message not only during the adult untrainings but also during the little yogis' funshop period of class. I have always felt that if we could help them hold on to their inner selves—well, that's it. They are so open to the energy of love and lightness. I see it and witness it all the time.

It was so wonderful during funshop when they'd act out the poem "The Cookie Thief."

We constantly remind the little yogis that it matters—it truly does. As we practice poses, we open them to witness that how they move in and out of poses, what comes up in their thoughts and feelings as they practice on the mat, can guide them to become more of who they truly are within. They talk and share their excitement about the visions they see.

We suggest to them that their practice on the mat often mirrors their practice of life, emphasizing that they shouldn't be hard on themselves when they're less that happy with how they choose to respond. We convey that it's OK to acknowledge that we don't necessarily like the people we were being during a challenging pose on the mat, and we share times in our lives when we chose responses we aren't proud of. There is the gift. Yes, being a cookie thief is not cool, but we can choose to be cookie angels at any time! Just enjoy the process.

Be Inspired to Be the Me That Never Changes: Inspiration to Be

May 11, 2020

Choose to become inspired, remembering to breathe in spirit.

Naomi made the comment as we both revisited the photo, "We look so young." Of course, that picture is from a few years ago.

There's a special gift I was given in my late twenties and early thirties, and I still remember the satori moments (and they keep coming). I would either look at a picture or look at myself in the mirror, and I knew within my heart that there's a part of me that never grows old. We live in that inner place so much as children, living in the moment honestly, being honest, and speaking with open communication, until we start learning otherwise. We begin duplicating what we see and hear from those around us. Their scripts turn into our scripts and become our lives.

Smilin' Rylan yogis would become so excited when I rolled out my mat.

I began a journey, and I continue on this exploration whenever I'm not in alignment with who I am, that part of me that never changes. It's in moments when I'm not trying but simply being that I rediscover I was seeing out of focus. I can't even express what it is that calls me back.

Yoga on and off the mat allows the present moment to guide me to the next, with no expectations or resistance, just (though not just) me loving the space where the I plays in the moment. No restrictions on my age, no (or very little) mind chatter, and I become awakened to the timeless.

Yoga as a practice (yes, practice) has reminded me that my physical body doesn't matter. Well, yes, I believe in respecting the vehicle my spirit rides in, doing and being aligned as much as possible with who I am, maintaining it so it drives and rides as smoothly as possible through the joy and the bumps that will come during this magical journey we call life.

The practice reminds me that any *body* can do yoga. But through breath, movement, and present-moment awareness, life becomes yoga, and yoga is life. Yoking as one, we unite in perfect harmony, mind, body, and spirit.

This gift, as I call it, becomes even more special the older I get in biological years. There's a part of all of us that never ages, and I believe that part always sees good, feels good, and chooses to love. That part of us doesn't fear the death of our bodies; it knows that our bodies are temporary housing for the self that never dies.

Unfortunately, we may start believing in what other people say—the beliefs of individuals and perhaps society—even producing evidence to back it, and if we aren't careful, we begin to explain away unkind behaviors or mindsets, find proof of their benefits, instead of listening to that inner part of us. It's the all-knowing part of us that serves as our innermost navigational system. You can use a different label (e.g., intuition) for that whispering voice within, but listen softly!

May we rejoice in the ageless I, that which is not dependent on external landscape, age, status, rank, education, sex, IQ, and so forth. May we rejoice in the innermost knowingness that we are just perfect in whatever our lives bring to the next acts of our plays. Therein lies a deeper sense of life's true meaning: the inspiration that inspired me to *be*.

Yoga Teaches Balance on and off Life's Mat

December 4, 2020

Maximus, Alissa, and Brayden demonstrating balance and ease.

A healthy relationship requires two, both conscious, to continue on a loving journey alongside each other. From time to time, we should check in with our selves by asking the question, Am I living a balanced life? Our relationships really do speak loudly about how aligned we are with who we are—about those relationships we have with our selves.

When I'm practicing a standing pose, my effort meets my ease as my breath carries me through the moment. I am at one with me, and my life is a reflection. My breath will fuel the experience both on and off the mat. Connecting with breath can be a powerful first step in finding balance when the world requires so much of your effort. Yet practicing breath without awareness is like driving your vehicle with no gas and your windshield thick with dirt (of drama), meaning your ability to feel, see, be the ease, the peace, is nowhere in sight.

What does your life's journey speak? Is there a relationship that's continuously taking you down a dark road? Allow me to reframe that question: Is there a relationship that you're choosing and allowing to take you down, into unwelcome territory? First, I look at the me and ask, "Why am I in this relationship?" I ask what I'm getting from it. Is there a heck of a lot more effort with very little ease when I'm with this person? Am I feeling constantly out of balance in my life?

My mom loved yoga.

275

I believe that if you're complaining about a person, you should first point your finger back at yourself. What are you getting out of the relationship? Does it give you fuel, drama—drama that you can (willingly) marinate in? Talk about to other people? Have you grown accustomed to and comfortable with being out of balance, often gravitating toward others living in a similar parallel universe?

Perhaps you engage with a group, a tribe, of people who support one another's stories and often challenge one another—who will receive the trophy for the most out-of-balance life?—addicted to surrounding themselves with others who enjoy and thrive on drama. I used to win the trophy quite a bit, until life jolted me during one too many real-life tragedies. I chose to wake up! Hallelujah!

I feel that we all fall out of balance at times. The difference is we feel out of balance. We feel uncomfortable being in a space where we aren't at ease and the effort sends us into chaos!

It's scary if in fact we become comfortable in the chaos of drama and feel out of our comfort zones when faced with possible ways toward more peace- and love-filled lives.

This is where journaling every day can become an awareness magnifying glass. If you're desiring to rediscover who you really are, journaling can be an awakening as you reread what you've written, a soul-full satori moment arriving as your present-moment gift. In the evening, before I go to bed, and sometimes in the morning, I reflect and allow my pen to get to it, recording my thoughts. I recommend that you choose and journal with honesty. Here's a tough question I used as a journal prompt years ago: What are my payoffs for being a victim? Do I get approval and even praise from others—the group I'm attached to? Do I enjoy telling and retelling my stories of why I'm so miserable to justify my unhappiness? What do I get in return? This is where your soul meets you; the rebirth back to who you really are is just waiting in the background.

So what is our payoff? We can get addicted to yucky energy (we're almost afraid to live without the drama of negativity) if we're not aware.

From awareness grows the willingness to move into being more conscious, living from our inspiration and our willingness to be free. It gives us a freedom to be who we really are! Aren't you ready to feel ease

276

more? Ready for a new beginning and adventures to experience? So release the baggage and feel the lightness, the freedom!

I've found that when I bring the gifts of journaling, yoga, and meditation into my life, I feel much more open and balanced. My awareness heightens, and more often, I'm living in the now. Yes, I now find ease in choosing to look within.

Another week comes to an end and once again begins our weekend. May we all make the choice to find more ease in our moments. May we take time to ask our inner selves, our spirits, "Is it time to choose another road, companion, or tribe?" I have a feeling many of us would answer with a resounding yes! Maybe being with only our selves for a while gives us the perfect tribe. Enjoy. Life is truly amazing.

Satori Moment: Not Two Halves but Rather Two Wholes Coming Together to Gather as One

Darrell and me loving sweet Krisi at her wedding to Jason.

Years ago, it really struck me after my second divorce, when I was twenty-three—take a breath, Joni—that I had to look within myself and do the work and return whole. Yep, I had to do this before I could totally be with someone else, without needing or expecting that person to complete me. That wasn't anyone else's job. My spouses didn't sign up to come into my life to be scapegoats—people on whom I could blame my unhappiness. Well, I met Darrell as I was beginning my journey, and he was willing to support my excavation adventure of returning. You know what? I never looked back in regret!

Here's an experience in time I can giggle about now—but at the time? Not so much. This particular satori moment brought many blessings of my rediscovering my self. I was asked to write a poem and read it at the wedding of one of my most favorite people.

My knowingness, the satori moment, I knew I wanted to share. The theme of the wedding poem? The main point was and still is that it's not about two halves coming together to complete each other but about two wholes joining as one. The wedding was the perfect opportunity to share.

Well, despite my excitement to present an awakening moment, it didn't quite go as I'd hoped at the wedding. But, as I believed then—and it has definitely come to be—the bride not only is a whole person but also helps so many people in all areas of her life. I believe all chapters, and more so the challenging ones, help to bring rainbows of miracles not only in our lives but to others through their difficult times. For me? Anytime I can play a part in sharing a satori moments is a gift to me.

A Love Poem

On this special day, your day of unity,
A man, a woman, a decision to love ... *believes*
Not just for this time, this moment, the wedding day,
But the marriage and the gift your love as one ... *leaves*.

For this day, as all, will pass, dissolve—memories remain,
Another gift to cherish, to live by.
Your vows to one another today, forever,
Through good times and struggles, remain *alive*.

As this new chapter begins, leave your past stories,
The ones that no longer work.
Rewrite on your soul's heart, each one starring
You both as one. Your love story, your book.

Carole, an example of beauty—oh, no, not just in form.
Also in spirit, your light shines through the day's sun or storm.
David, your significant chosen other, whole—
His smiles of joy, commitment, shared from the soul!

We here rejoice in this union, a union so sacred.
Cherish each moment remembering you two are as one,
So make it

A coming-together not as two halves demanding completion
But rather as two wholes synergizing, making a difference,
Writing each chapter with dedication!

When challenges rear up—they will—turn your eyes,
Your souls, toward the love within!
Your gift sometimes lost in judgment—observe you, your energy,
Because if love is a decision, then love will not end!

The good within comes—it never fails—when both choose to look
toward each other's light. Your marriage, friendship, will shine.
Be still, know your heart, pass by the pettiness of the ego—
Make the decision to leave it behind!

For marriage is an instrument from God to grow as individuals and strive.
Learning to love outside the lines, learning to forgive,
Cherish this gift, the person you have chosen as your partner,
as you continue this beautiful journey through life!

I will end by saying a line from one of my favorite songs. It sings:
"For you can have all the riches of the world, but without
Love, do you really have a thing?"
All my love, Joni

I'm letting you in on a secret: that was not the first time I wrote and read that poem at a wedding. Just an FYI ahead of time. This is from the second wedding, which you'll read more about soon.

I loved the energy I felt as I wrote the poem; the words just flowed. Unfortunately, the first reading was not received very openly. In fact, nothing was mentioned to me except from my close friends who'd read it. Along with so many of us, the beautiful bride already felt that she was an incredibly strong woman, and with time, her mind listened to her beautiful heart. She wasn't in this life to attempt to complete someone else—not possible. After the fact, I discovered there was already stress the day of the wedding. The bride would be the first to say it (thank God). She is one of my favorite people. We share a lot of pasts (and the present) and have become that much more complete.

I am a firm believer that God doesn't intend for us to be in relationships that aren't nurturing our true selves—relationships in which we feel we've lost our spirits. Yes, I know—I have so many people damn me for that belief—but in my heart, I know it's the truth, for my self. We are here to be of service to others, and if we're in a toxic relationships, we're too drained to put any goodness out into the world.

I was given several opportunities to write poems for weddings. When another came, this time from my childhood friend Carole (engaged to David), I used the basic outline and made adjustments to customize it. I just couldn't (wouldn't) allow that poem to die, and I knew that for this wedding the poem was a perfect match. It was received beautifully. I love her and her husband and had known them both since our teens, many, many years ago. They are both friends and partners in their marriage. I smile with love as I write this. Hi, Carole! Love you both!

Yes, for a lot of us, we were raised hearing that phrase, "two halves coming together as one," as if individually we are half of a complete self, waiting to find the second half to complete us. Well, I finally got it. When I had one of my huge satori moments, another of my awakening, I knew within my inner self that I am a whole me.

Somewhere within me, my self was hiding out. Actually, I just wouldn't connect with my self. Too much baggage. But back then, I was determined, my goodness, to start rediscovering her, the self that is unchangeable, the I that I always, in all ways, feel at home within. One of my mantras is "Be still and know I am God." Listen and be present to feel the peace, to be free.

This satori moment is not only for a couple getting married. I believe it is true for families, friendships, and organizations. When we look to other people to complete us, bring us happiness, and blame them when they can't, we're doing ourselves a disservice, and we're doing everyone else a disservice. It truly begins with me—well, actually, my self.

I had to stop making excuses and blaming. Many of us don't want to point the finger back at ourselves. It means we have got to go within and take responsibility. Yep, we are response-able for ourselves and our lives. We're the cause when our lives are wonderful, and we're the reason when they're filled with unhappiness. I know. Believe me—I do. Breathe. It's tough to take in and even tougher to accept.

We must come to acknowledge that we have the power to decide (and often it's a decision we make moment to moment) to live knowing we are our own happiness. And it's not an easy task to endure, but it's oh so rewarding and wonderful.

I'd much rather live the consequences of being my own self than the alternative: continuing to spiral down, riding on fleeting (exterior-based) moments of happiness (exterior based) and feeling the blame and anger flow to and from outside sources, forces. Take another breath, hold it, and make a lion's roar and let it go.

Perhaps you might just decide to get out your self-made tools and begin again, excavating through the layers and layers of quicksand, muck, and s——that stink, smelling up your and others' lives.

It may seem like a long, exhausting journey, yes, but it's so liberating. There will be times—I know, I experience them—you must begin again as soon as you feel the muck oozing back. Begin again and bring the satori moments to life. Live them and feel them as you are once again moved into freedom and happiness, who you really are!

Each time, I feel as if a few bricks have just been lifted off my heart. (And you thought I was going to say *shoulders*.) I am able to love that much more unconditionally, not looking to others for my happiness.

We may attempt to cover up the malodors of our lives by putting in place temporary air fresheners, perhaps convincing others of our superficially happy homes. (At eighteen, I had a white Corvette and a brand-new home and walked in on my then husband with someone else.)

Reevaluate what you're spending your moments focusing on. I feel that many of us focus on work for status and approval and hang with like-minded friends who reinforce our unhappiness and confirm our reasons for it. Such friends often assist and rub our backs as they support our finger-pointing blame and our perhaps constant drive to win no matter the cost. At the end of the day, we're exhausted and empty, and the baggage continues to fill up.

If we're honest, we can all relate somewhat. What if all the outside things, objects, were suddenly taken away? How attached have we all become to our stuff and even to what others think of us?

We must all take a breath. No one twists our arms, choosing our choices. I take all responsibility—of course, sometimes not in the moment. I may initially think, *It was outside forces to blame! Why should I take the blame?* But it's not true! Bottom line: I choose my partner and my life.

What a wonderful feeling when I did begin taking responsibility! Amen and amen. I wouldn't change one thing about my life. I love my life—another daily mantra of mine for years. It has nothing to do with the things in my life. I may love and enjoy them, but I'm not attached. I have grown even more in that awareness this past year. My life as I knew it was no longer.

With time, and often misery, drama comes to a peak. The air fresheners no longer work, and the smell becomes so intense. Be aware.

It's unbearable most of the time. The cycles become normal and familiar to us. The miracle, the satori awakening? It's never too late; past is past and no longer real. It's always the perfect time to choose to move forward, one

Forever family: two wholes joining together as one.

step at a time, and begin the excavation once again. Hooray!

We can move forward when we get sick and tired of being stressed, on edge, and sad, of looking over our shoulders, trying to find more reasons as to why we aren't able to calmly, lovingly, greet a moment with a clear response. During these times, we find our happiness is fleeting and dependent on outside things, objects. In fact, unhappiness seems to be the norm.

It takes courage. It takes humility. It takes kindness and forgiveness toward yourself.

It's not that life is always supposed to be wonderful—as the saying goes, "Life happens"—but you begin to see and feel the difference. You see how you've unknowingly been sabotaging your own happiness. You begin to remember that what happens in life, with the exterior of self, no longer determines your response in the moment. There is freedom again. You choose and begin to feel whole again. It's magical.

I so happen to believe within my innermost self that truly happy people have no desire to bring misery to anyone, beginning with the self. They have no reasons—no *desire*. We all have reasons we can choose to be miserable and to blame. Truly happy people, people with inner happiness, don't have it in them to be hateful.

Every single satori moment (and there've been tons) was an epiphany, like a miracle exploding right in front of my eyes, right within my heart's space. The love just poured down. My life became less and less about what was going on around me and more about my innermost place of knowing.

Of course, as I have shared in the past, along with the joy of returning come the subtle (sometimes not-so-subtle) comments: "You're not being real," "You're not facing reality; what's going on?" and—how about this one?—"What are you after?" Very seldom do I hear these things now; this was mostly years ago. But I knew that they just didn't know. They not only didn't know me but were unable to see in me what they couldn't see within themselves. (In such situations, distance may be the open option for a time.)

It's just a part of the awakening. Allow it to be as the mist, evaporating, filtering through space. So often, people just don't understand what I've found to be my truth. They simply don't believe it's possible. The sad thing is that they have it right there within their selves. Question: Are you ready to receive?

I don't give anyone else power over my inner happiness. I haven't for a very long time.

It doesn't mean that I don't have times I revisit my boundaries and make sure I'm putting them in place and being very up front. I'm not about being "nice." And certainly, if it's done with and through love, it's about setting boundaries and respecting all parties.

Don't confuse being nice with being loving and caring, with boundaries, of course. I believe the word *nice* has received a bum rap through the years, leading it to become almost a sort of label for those without boundaries; open to being taken for granted; or manipulative, with inauthentic intentions. What I've found is that "nice" people often do have another agenda—not always, but often. I've heard one to many times, "Call so-and-so. They are nice and will do it." So, on both ends, that word lends itself to unreal judgment calls.

Once again—I say and write it often—we must first love and respect ourselves in order to be self-full, therefore open authentically to be there for others selflessly. Within boundaries, of course, we must be open and willing to be of loving service.

Just because you don't hear me yelling, screaming, and throwing fits, or being rude or angry with somebody, doesn't mean I don't respect myself and have boundaries. Quite the opposite. You can still be assertive with and in love. I pray others begin to understand the difference.

May we choose to stand up for love, for oneness, as whole, loving individuals, ready to be present for others. Enjoy this weekend, choosing to be a treasure, a gift to others. It's priceless. So much love to all.

May We Experience a Piece of Peace as We Become Present in the Moment of Now

September 24, 2021

"Peace begins with me."

Here's another analogy I'd often share and play with both at untraining sessions and the little yogis' funshop: I personally would imagine the thoughts of my chattering mind as waves on an ocean surface, allowing them to come and go, watching them, playing with them. Most important, I wouldn't allow them to become tidal waves and drown my I, my self. My thoughts and emotions were as waves on an ocean, rolling in and rolling out.

What we resist persists! I also believe that our energy follows our attention. I feel so much peace and joy when my energy is light and wrapped in love. Most of the time, I'm aware of where I place my attention. Not all the time, but I feel the difference so much sooner and easier now.

Back to the ocean analogy. I would at times allow my mind's waves to play with me, knock me down, tumble me, shake me up, and

Guess which beach girl is me at ten years old?

roll me around, and I'd possibly watch as the tide delivered to the shore of my soul another satori moment, waiting patiently as the I within awakened me once again. I would be delivered to the calm waters floating above my thoughts.

Growing up by the ocean and living in the water, I learned through experience not to fight, struggle, with the big blue, as the waves would knock me down. If I struggled and fought the ocean's waves, it was chaotic. Panic would set in, and deep within my mind, there'd be nonstop chatter: "You're going to be taken out by the ocean," "If you don't get air soon, you're going to die"—just a mix of the playlist.

When I'd let go and allow the ocean to play, roll, toss, and move me without resistance, I'd usually be taken back to shore calmly. How beautiful it was during those times to not struggle and just allow my body to fall below the waves and find the calmness until the waves passed.

So often in life, we must let it go, flow with it. When our lives become rough and the waves in our lives knock us down and out, then the labels, identities, entitlements, and expectations fall away. Those can be some of the most awakening moments, satori

Yep, a beach girl all the way. No makeup, but sunscreen I should have been better at.

moments, blessings. They're the rainbows I talk about, bringing light and love for self and others to fill the space as the water becomes calm. That's where freedom begins. Miracles happen when we let go and simply (yet not necessarily without difficulty) allow.

It still boggles my mind why we latch on to whatever hint of difference someone has indicated, or something we take offense to. Why do we choose to react by yelling or fighting through angry words to be right, heard? Why? Is being "right" that important? Is drowning and taking a loved one with us worth being right? And, by the way, what is our definition of *right*?

We all have times during which we fight with the tide of life in our relationships with others, but we can also save ourselves and others before we drown, even if we have to use CPR to resuscitate the relationship by means of a heartfelt, sincere apology. Why? Well, why not? Why is that so hard for us humans? My fur babies never hold a grudge or judge me. Why do we?

If we're truthful, we all have struggled with the rough tide of life and almost drowned a few times. At times, we've taken someone down with us. How about we put our pride aside and bring relationships back to life! Life is truly precious. Friendships are so enjoyable.

I so enjoy deep discussions with my chosen family as well as those in my family who communicate through their selves, through love, and not their fight to be right (egos).

We must be willing to take the friendship out even if the forecast is showing a rough ride. There are times when the turbulent waves (emotions) get high and the forecast looks very scary, but I believe there's always a way to work through even the most challenging discussions without taking someone down with us, or capsizing the friendship.

I really am at a loss for words when it comes to our feeling it's either our way or the highway. The thought of forgiving? For many, no way. I believe some feel they'd be admitting they're wrong if they forgive someone and choose to agree to disagree. I personally would much rather be happy than be right. Or than fight just to win the battle and lose common ground, territory, for future gatherings. Don't we all truly desire the same thing—going for a true win-win? We all just want to be heard, respected, and loved. At times, some feel communicating for a win-win seems too turbulent. Well, why not at least agree to disagree in love?

And, by the way, what's so awful about admitting we're wrong? It truly isn't about who's right and who's wrong. We all are looking through our own lenses at the moment. We all have different paradigms we adhere to.

It would be a blessing if more of us opened to seeing the other person's opinion, side. That's in no way saying we are wrong. It's being copartners; friends; loving, caring, passionate people who truly care about other people. It's about the world as a whole coming together, scooping out the water from the deck, and saving the friendship before it sinks.

So may we all find a piece of peace and enjoy the smooth sailing or a swim in life's unpredictable yet beautiful array of waves. Let's ride them and have fun discovering more about who we really are. The sunrise and sunset are beautiful looking out on the waves, especially after a storm has passed. Enjoy! I am floating with so much gratitude for you! Truly we are all one! Smooth sailing into the now and beyond.

Always Safe in the Lap of God, I Don't Have to Earn His Love

October 8, 2021

My myopic view of life slowly changed, opening to more aha moments of clarity, which often delivered me, kicking and screaming at times, into the realization (and still awakening) of blessings not yet seen. They were blessings I would soon receive by turning my outward focus inward. Please read on.

Every once in a while, I choose to do some spring-cleaning in my home, clearing out an accumulation of stuff that's truly unneeded, serving only to clutter my space. It would be freeing if we would also do some deep cleaning within ourselves, clearing the cobwebs built up from past stories still housed in the overactive mind. Journaling is a wonderful way for us to uncover some of the stuck items left in drawers of the mind, using up our space to be in the moment. When I do this, soon fear begins to soften and fade. A knowing replaces doubts, and all the while I remember I am always in the lap of God and God is always within me, loving me. there is no score keeping or need to earn His love. Amen.

As I have shared before, I have always known, ever since I was a little child, that everything is going to be all right. Well, not always. The amnesia began for a few years. Can you relate? Yes, and that darn amnesia often sneaks back up on me and goes within, taking up space. Go figure. As for me, the knowingness of love and faith brings me back to the present moment of now, and I am once again a believer.

Rylan lived and breathed the consciousness, awareness. We talked so often about God, about energy, using imagination to visit what our hearts believed as real. Most often we'd do this through play: God could be a superhero coming to rescue us. At times, Chanel or

Rylan and Satori were inseparable.

Satori was the superhero, soaring through the sky with Smilin' Super Rylan to save the world. How? Well, with Rylan, it was and will always be with a song and dance of love.

We knew, deep within, that Rylan had been sent as an earthly angel, an old soul. He had direct communication with God, and the silver cord—the one that connected his heartstring to God's—was never cut. His super love power would daily stream kindness, love, and fun, and he'd often be dancing. Bottom line: Rylan enjoyed life no matter what the outside presented in each moment. He lived his insight inside out, with all his soul.

I will never forget the hard-to-move-through Friday that Satori took flight to save Darrell's soul. I'd planned to visit Krisi, Jason, and Rylan that Saturday (yes, the next day) on the train, and I wasn't going to go because Darrell was doing so poorly—guilt was eating him fiercely.

Two of our good friends, Dr. Jeff White and his beautiful wife, Dianne, told me to go and that they'd look after Darrell. Jeff and Dianne live their faith! Darrell was in God's hands and always in God's loving lap.

However, because of all the treatments and medication, Darrell lived most of his moments in fear. The amnesia took over for much of the last six or more years, until those last days when he was wrapped in my arms, a blanket of love, and of course in the lap of God.

When my train arrived, Rylan ran to me, and everything was all right. He was very open to talking about Satori, his partner against bad guys. Rylan was still in remission, so we were able to go to lunch, where he shared his wisdom, his love, as he always did, through his kindness, smiles, and superpowers. And everything was perfect in all its imperfections.

For many, as we begin to move through the play of life, our doubts start to set in, deep within. We often have a hard time forgiving ourselves, and we experience a more challenging time going back to the child, remembering the gift we bring in every moment.

Satori was an angel. We would dress her up. Here she is dressed for Christmas as we leave for the office. She was (is) such a kind spirit of love.

How are we able to truly forgive others unless we've first healed from the deepest part of the me within? If we are to truly have the space within to fully forgive others with no resentment or conditions, we must first have done the work. We must listen softly to be able to have clear, guilt-free hearts of compassion. Guilt loves to hide in the background until we have the courage to meet fear face-to-face and forgive. Cleaning house can actually be very exciting and freeing, adding so much clean airy space to breathe and believe.

I love cleaning house from within, the space from all the years of satori aha moments. Isn't it just beautiful when we can realize the blessings, the miracles, coming as we receive and believe it to be possible? The perfect message, experience, at just the right moment.

Of course, there are things that, if I could go back, I would like to change, or that I feel I'd make a different decision about. However, there's a deep knowing within me that realizes I'm here because of every choice I made, every fork in the road, and I'm good with that. I'm at peace in the knowingness that everything is perfect in this moment; I love my life.

I've done my best to ask forgiveness of everyone I feel I've ever hurt, although I know there are some who I don't even realize I've hurt. I want to be able to live my last chapter of life before I take flight knowing in my heart of hearts I have done everything I could to make amends with all my brothers and sisters, all the lives I've touched, for any unkindness I'm conscious of having directed toward them.

While going through Darrell's drawers after he took flight, I came upon some papers that indicate, I believe, he was writing a song for me. He often was up at night, especially toward the last days, before the ambulance came to take him to the hospital on May 19, 2020.

That's how he proposed—he wrote a song and sang it for me on his guitar. I still have a tape of it. December 1984, he had me sit and got his guitar and started singing me a beautiful song he'd written. Tears are flowing in this moment.

I just know he was writing words to sing to me again. He knew how much I enjoyed to hear him play the piano and guitar. The last couple of years, his mind just wouldn't hold the memory, the note, the music.

After this blog entry was published, I went back in to add this very important part: After I corrected a misspelling that I found, there was a satori moment deep within my heart: Darrell was writing this song to *God*.

Yes, perhaps while he was writing the words, he thought he was writing it for me because he was going through so many challenging times, often feeling a distance from life and from me, but he was writing to God.

"Heard a noise comin' down the hall. When I looked, there was nothing at all. But pictures in my mind, a breeze passin' right on by. When you came into my life, you brought a joy that will never die. Always right there by my side, and I thought forever this will be."

"Tho our time was not enough, and time could never bring that anyway, you gave to me more than anyone could. Took me away from a crazy life, changed my heart from what was wrong."

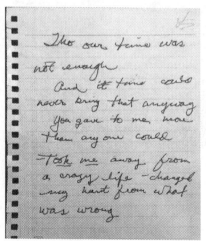

I believe this is page 2.

We begin to truly, clearly, and wholeheartedly see that love is not love when it's controlled, when it has to be earned. Love knows nothing. It's like the air we breathe; we can shut the air off by holding our breath, or we can allow the air to cleanse our lungs and fill our hearts. We fall in love inward, toward the self. We rediscover the joy of life, and once again, we find space returning to knowing love, life, is precious, amazing, and unconditional.

As I write these words, I continue to be in awe. The fluttering butterflies once again fill my heart space, flowing as they fly, extending outward.

Love doesn't demand, and love isn't based on performance or appearances. Love is. It's fresh air in a stuffy, hard-to-be-in room. Love is present, but absent of any judgment guiding our emotions to thoughts, possibly thoughts into action.

Love will bring our souls to an action that will be the most powerful answer to whatever the moment has delivered, making room for light to come in the space. Now shine your love light. Allow it to shine brightly. Don't hold back!

We can choose to stop the patterns, break the chains, that no longer serve our and others' souls. We can begin again, opening our hearts, remembering we are always in the lap of God, held tenderly, safely enveloped in His love. So may we all shine our light in love, giving others the space to do the same. Once again, we're reminded we are one.

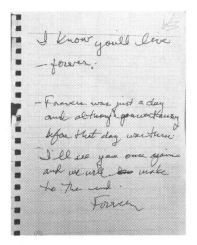

We are a blessing to the world. Be who you really are, and shine on. Love, light, and namaste.

Careful What You Bury Within—
It Will Grow and Reemerge

October 21, 2021

That's another statement I have used in my untrainings for years. So, yes, I would never tell people they shouldn't be angry or voice how they feel. If we allow that energy to come out (do the work), it's less likely that it'll be buried and pushed down, only to reemerge as an even more furious monster, wearing the mask of fear, anger, and blame, fire-breathing and leaving destruction in its trail. We may possibly slip into depression. It's a no-win when we constantly push down and bury feelings. But ...

I would add that the intention of expressing those thoughts is a thought in this moment to possibly open to receive—a satori awakening. I'd much rather ride on the breath of God than on the fire of anger.

I'm all about sharing how you're feeling but not about yelling and screaming or attacking. I'm sure you've heard that courage wrapped in consideration is a choice of action. Unfortunately, most seem to lean heavily on extra courage fueled from anger.

The times I've chosen the path of heated fire (fortunately less traveled now), the mind's scripts have echoed to me, "I have a right." At that point, or soon after, I'd immediately regret my thoughts, words, and actions. I never felt good in the aftermath. I'd be left with that mucky, yucky feeling in my heart, even if my mind's thoughts tried to convince me it was justified.

I believe that we can't retain our light when we're holding any anger toward someone else. It darkens and dims our light. No, you don't have to continue to be a part of any darkness; if you've chosen it, return to your light. Offer love in the moment toward you and others. Don't allow this darkness to remain in you. Release and accept the awakening.

Life will offer us contrast that we can choose to see as a blessing, using it as motivation to uncover what we've forgotten—you know, the times amnesia sets in. Once again, we return to the presence of who we really are. We aren't fear or anger; we are the vessels it moves through. Allow such feelings to be the waves, and bring the calmness of the underneath to the surface as soon as it's clear.

Again, our minds definitely try to convince us that it's the right choice to attack back. I feel, yes, we deserve to be heard but, again, meeting anger with anger just causes a larger fire of emotions—explosion time—often leaving hearts broken, with pieces fragmented and separated for years. At times, they're never mended back together; hearts remain broken, a piece missing.

Take the time before the blessing, the miracle, is no longer present. There's always a way to the other side. Yes, always, and it's never too late to heal!

I received many rainbows, miracles, from having been teased young. Of course, at the time, I didn't feel that way. What rainbows? you may be asking. Well, after the storm, years later, a loving, colorful bow of light wrapped around my heart. I didn't want anyone to feel like I had when I was teased. It doesn't serve our souls no matter how we try to justify our actions. I'd much rather have my heart, my soul, at peace.

Even when I feel I didn't text with the intention the receiver perceived, I desire always to do my part to make peace and heal the hurt, although there are times it's just best to love from a distance—a choice that at times can be the best option for all.

During those amnesia moments, when our habits of reaction take over, leaving the awareness lost in the background, I do my best to return to the scene and retake. Unfortunately, once the words are out, it's like trying to put toothpaste back into the tube; once squeezed out, it's hard to but back in.

I continue to have faith that we all truly desire the same thing. Why wouldn't we choose to have a better world, a better place to live? If not for us, for our children, our grandchildren, and all future beings.

It seems that emotions heighten, too, when family members are going through disease or illness. There is extra stress. Quite often, anger is a by-product of their fear, of their swimming upstream in desperation as they lose who they think they are, feeling threatened, becoming almost naked.

On the other end, I have witnessed disease bring so much unease that it opens up space, allowing for a sudden satori moment of awakening, ushering in the knowingness of just how precious each moment is. Some people allow these moments to shake loose many of the identified labels they've embraced that have disconnected them from who they truly are. As the labels fall away, these family members arrive back home again.

With my dad, we never were allowed to communicate, or, I should say, I was never able to communicate with my parents. I was always scared of my dad's disapproval. It was a time during which you didn't question your parents—ever. They weren't bad parents at all. Like many, they just didn't know any different. They grew up at a time of marinating in those beliefs, transferring them down from family to family. It's OK to break the chain! Is it easy? No, but it's so freeing.

This was one very strong change, choice, I wanted to make as a parent. I knew I didn't want to transfer it to my children, chosen or biological. Communication is so important, starting at a very young age.

I believe we are all responsible for giving voice to children—to listen to them and value their opinions. Yes, I know I need to add that we should also keep our boundaries safely in place.

With my dad, it was his way. We weren't raised to share our opinions, or any perceptions that would in any way question or threaten his beliefs. Back then, children were to be seen and not heard. That's just how it was in many families.

After a few months of treatment, heavy chemo, he still wanted to keep who he believed he was alive and heard. He had been through a lot growing up, and I believe he never worked through those hard times. He hid his vulnerability behind his ego.

One time, when I brought him home from the hospital, he was still high and feeling good from the drugs. I mean, he was *really* feeling good, and his guard was down. He shared with me, holding back tears, some of his childhood. He even opened up about life with us kids and his navy experience.

At times, we can definitely view a disease as a blessing of enlightenment—a wake-up call, a breaking-open, for all! Versus when tragedy is an instant flight to the afterlife, often leaving some unhealed hot spots for those left to continue in the mysterious play of life.

I was taken aback by how open he was, and I hugged him. This time, I didn't receive the usual halfway hug. It was an emotional-release hug with tears. I often wondered if he felt good the next morning or somewhat embarrassed. In our family, we didn't share our feelings much at all. It was perceived as showing weakness.

That was why I earned the "emotional child" label—and learned to live it and love it.

Here is one last time that delivered a rainbow bridge of connection before my dad took flight, another example of a miracle in the making, delivering patience and love, leaving pride in the dust.

We were having a family card night—my dad loved to play cards. It's not that I don't like to win, but it's never been important to me. It was about having fun. Well, I didn't play the hand he thought I should, and he just basically verbally attacked me, threw his cards down, and stormed to the bedroom.

I was dumbfounded. It wasn't even a conversation; it was his frustrations coming out, and he was using me as an easy, safe scapegoat. Of course, my heart was crushed, but I felt so sad for him and wanted to wrap my heart around his suffering.

As he left, storming to the bedroom, my mom put her hand on mine, asking me not to leave. I began to cry. Here I had my husband, Darrell, sitting across from me, going through testing—possibly the cancer was back, as his PSA was rising—and my dad was looking so weak and vulnerable, having been stripped of the layers of labels and accomplishments, the perfect house and yard, and so on.

Leaving was how our family was raised, and that's how my parents had been raised. Just walk out or, after an outburst, leave and turn to silence, noncommunication, for at times years. It was unhealthy, and such behavior is how we keep alive nonloving ways of control. Run, and don't talk to each other for days, weeks, months, or years! The toughest, meanest wins. I don't believe that at all. Leaving is a good choice to calm down, a temporary separation (a day or so), but not for keeping the anger within, sizzling.

My surprise fiftieth birthday party. It was the first time I'd seen my parents in three or four years. They were in attendance thanks to my brother, and it was truly the best gift.

Happy ending—you know how a miracle can happen if you allow anger to melt into the hurt, and love to sponge the residue, absorbed in a heart that is open and ready to receive the blessing of the rainbow bridge to the other side. Amen.

My dad actually came out of the bedroom, put his hand on Darrell's shoulder, and said something like "That cancer can really mess us up." In his own way, he apologized. I melted in so much love for his release, knowing that it really had nothing to do with me but that I was the bridge to his own awakening.

There was the blessing for my dad and everyone present in the presence. My dad had never even halfway attempted to apologize through all the years. I was bawling because of the relief for him, and my heart was as open as it was ever, for I knew, I just knew, that he'd had a satori moment that was meant to be born to release him. It truly is never too early or late to find those times to heal and embrace the I of who we really are, sometimes meeting our selves face-to-face for the first nonthreatening moment of release.

So, from my heart space, I ask, "What good does it do to get angry in response to someone else's anger?" One of my missions in writing these entries is to perhaps give at least someone another way of looking at responding to his or her challenging times. I want to show that we can all relate and we're here for one another.

If we do choose to walk away for the moment during a heated situation, or amid turbulent waters, we must take a breath and choose to be wrapped in the knowing that while troubled water may develop and continue to flow, there is always a bridge to the other side hand in hand. The rainbow bridge is awaiting, and another satori moment is ready to emerge. Celebrate during and after the crossing.

I know I say it often, but enjoy another excavation and discover another hot spot—melt it with forgiveness through awareness. What do you really have to lose? I have found that the only things I lose are sleepless nights, sadness, anger, frustration, and so on.

Those of us who live with handed-down fear, let's all begin refusing to feed that fear. Instead, let's feed love, allowing each moment to be ushered in with a heart filled with gratitude and appreciation for this beautiful play of life. May we come together and enjoy as we celebrate one another! And sleep tight.

Where Words Fail, Silence Wrapped in Love Prevails

September 30, 2021

And, believe it or not, oftentimes, as you let your hair down and become more aware, it's like a bad hairstyle you had in the past and now can't believe you actually liked. *What was I thinking?*

Or it's like a style you wore just to go along with the majority to be cool and fit in. When you begin to start wearing your hair how you like it, or clothes that feel good on you, you feel a freedom within you. You arrive back home, with who you really are, and you're free to be.

I will continue to share the beauty that was present on Darrell's last days. If there is just one more person who becomes aware, it will be worth another mention and every word typed. His coming home was surrounded by Love and Faith (literally). There already have been miracles happen because of our experience of caring by sharing.

Others have shared with me their decision to look into hospice—the love and freedom through their experience filled with beautiful memories instead of hospital rooms. The loving care that hospice provides for a loved one (and family and friends) is beyond words.

After our process of demanding Darrell come home, the help from his physician of forty years to get him released, and hospice, a miracle appeared, and we all embraced each moment of his coming home. I am writing not just about the material home but about, most important, the home within him and self.

Darrell no longer used the noise of words to camouflage or bury his readiness; he released the struggle and rediscovered His love, always waiting there patiently. Through awareness and time turning within, he welcomed and was ready for the truth of that part of him that doesn't die, will not die, and God's love. His peace filled the room.

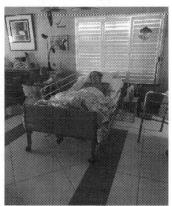

Word-free silence was our language those last five days to flight.

Quiet. You can feel it—listen softly. It's waiting in the background for more time with you. Why wait?

Darrell came home with no desire for TV, any outside or inside noise. I would play music, and I'd always sing to him. But mainly I would lie quietly and cuddle. I wish I would have had more time, but I am forever grateful that he was physically home—and returning home within, whole, before taking flight.

I am giggling right now, and I have to add this. It was beautiful: I was lying with him the night before his flight, and he started talking to somebody up in the corner of the room. Krisi was FaceTiming us.

He'd done this before, but at this time, he went from total silence and no strength to even sit up to full-out excitement, and he insisted we get out of bed and leave with Rylan and others. They came to take him, we believe. Darrell kept repeating, "I am ready—let's go," and then he quieted, becoming calm, peace filled.

Please don't put it off. If you or a loved one has decided to stop medical treatment or stays in hospitals to prolong a life that is no longer being lived, barely existing (and only because of continued procedures and/or drugs), there is never any pressure. A call to hospice will answer any and all questions and concerns. They truly are earthly angels.

During those last five days, when it was me and Darrell, there was stillness, quiet. Seldom was a word spoken; rather, in its place was the language of love through silence. There were no words that could have filled that time as well as the silence and the energy of love delivered in their space.

Darrell had left our home two months earlier (very sick, with extremely low sodium and reoccurring UTI infections) not wanting silence. He was nonliving through distractions and almost scared if there was quiet. He'd filled every moment with TV and returned desiring only the peace of stillness, soundlessness.

My heart goes out to all who are experiencing or have experienced what I

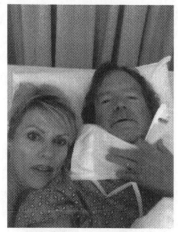

We did our best while he was at the hospital.

went through because of the COVID lockdown: having a loved one in a hospital or facility and not being able to be there to help take care of him or her. I lived as a part-time loving nurse to Darrell for thirteen years, day and night, as well as during the hospital stays.

The doctors and nurses would often comment that they'd never seen such love from a couple, especially when they found out how long we'd been married. And Darrell's health history of hospital emergencies and stays. It's funny—when I look back, I really don't know how I did it. Actually, yes, I do: love and faith.

So Darrell, on his last chapter, had a crash course in truly what is real and what is temporary. I say we all have the satori moments awaiting. Why not surrender and open them up in awareness? Let's allow the journey to become an adventure of love.

The labels and identities you used to think were you fall away; they no longer resonate with your true inner self. The healing begins, and the freedom to be is amazingly welcomed. Little by little, you lose the desire to be a certain way to fit anyone's else's idea of what you should be.

You begin turning the light switch on and realizing how you became so accustomed to seeing and living through much of your moments in darkness.

When you begin to feel like you've had enough of the mucky-feeling moments, look out—satori moments begin to bring awareness. Consciousness brings the

Christmas before his flight. I loved asking him to help with dishes.

lightness, oh so welcoming, comforting, and for at least that moment, everything is just perfect.

There's a feeling of perfection even though, on the exterior, it still may seem very chaotic and imperfect. That's what I love about the phrasing *perfect in our imperfection*. It's faith. We begin allowing room for light to shine as well as a stillness of silence, where love is the language absent of words—words that often present barriers to understanding.

Although, when we can finally look back honestly, we realize there were times we would have rather had a reason to curse and get upset than make a change, a decision to love as our foundation. Once we begin to choose love, it's almost comical to look at the past. Our choices of the past stay in the past. It is no longer real.

Often in anger, we tend to feel we have a right to let someone know how pissed off we are. At the time, we might even feel as if it'll make us feel better. Can you truthfully say it does? I can speak for myself, and the answer is a resounding no.

Do you hear (feel) the words of thoughts playing over and over in your mind, bringing some sleepless nights, or often just uncomfortable times during the day?

Can you imagine the innocent thoughts going on in these three minds? If only we could, or would, be more like children, animals— living more in the moment. I'm sure they have very few, if any, sleepless nights.

Perhaps you often revisit the overplayed drama, at times even missing a beautiful moment because of the fog of illusion from the past. Now is the perfect time for a breath of awareness and a desire for a change of scripting, a choice, a change, wrapped in love.

When words fail, silence wrapped in the energy of love can communicate a beautiful ending to a challenging time of miscommunication. We must allow the words to fall from our lips in silence, the silence of the present moment of now. Eyes that are windows of loving hearts need no words—use them at times. Marinate in the beauty of energy; replacing words at times is just the perfect choice.

It's amazing yet so natural when we begin to run toward compassion, kindness, and love and perhaps only baby-step, or barely even crawl, toward hate, judgment, and fear. We become gentler with ourselves, more quickly choosing awareness so as to stop short of any choice of words or actions and hightail it in the other direction, back to what the heart space is guiding us toward.

Our inner light, patiently in the background, waiting to be turned on, to shed some light as awareness, becomes present in the now. It's as if everything is light and so clear, radiant. And so often words aren't needed. A smile of acknowledgment, perhaps a hand reaching for the others? Perhaps a gentle hug, if nothing else, a soft loving presence of silence with no reason for words—words that often break the feeling of gentle perfection in the no-words presence of silence.

OK. Enough for now. I just have this song in my heart that wants to be sung, and my fingers don't know how to stop writing the lyrics. Forgive me.

May we bring a bit of silence into our presence as we move from the week's end into the weekend, remembering to speak with our loving energy of silence more often. Perhaps practice more silent language, enjoying the peace of the end of the week into the weekend.

A perfect ending to a story of love, beginning New Year's Day 2021 and ending New Year's Eve.

Joy Is Peace Is Unconditional Happiness from Within, Not Without

December 31, 2021

My neighbors Miranda and Jim— such wonderful, loving people.

As we prepare this week, celebrating the end of one year and welcoming the beginning of the next, we should contemplate how it would be if we celebrated our moment-to-moment movement with the same anticipation and excitement that we reserve for end-of-the-year festivities— celebrating, hugging, toasting all the good times, living each moment consciously in the now.

Consider taking it a step further: It's a common ritual to put on paper New Year's resolutions. How about new moment's resolutions?

New moment's resolutions could be written on the awareness scroll within the heart's space, instead of the usual New Year's resolutions, written on paper, often carrying guilt, and conveniently forgotten so as to ease any labor required of doing.

Consider one of those new moment's resolutions: "Being, rediscovering (uncovering), the joyfulness." It's already present in the heart's space, awaiting the awareness.

Appreciate everything you have. Look within, look without, but look for all the things (nonthings) that are not based on outside conditions. You'll know it,

Love and Faith with their pack leader, Renee.

feel it, when you find them. And while I keep saying *find*, I mean *excavate back into awareness*, patiently and willingly, rediscovering the natural inner happiness.

My family. I miss and love them.

Softly appearing the moment, you're no longer searching or excavating. Instead, you're playing and living in the moment of now, in the space where you are joyful, peaceful, and unconditionally happy.

Yes, of course, you may celebrate things that happen outside your inner self, but focus on what is unconditional, remembering how temporary the exterior happiness lives, survives.

What would be a reason not to end this year by celebrating and welcoming new moment's resolutions to take more time in no time, being present in stillness, meditation, prayer, and yoga and discovering the joyfulness that's already present in the heart's space?

The screen displaying your life's play will indicate times when the exterior landscape is good and not so

Evelyn and Renee, new friends in our community of kindness.

good. You are able to work through them all, finding joy. There may be times you choose to push the reset button and begin again, with no stress or guilt, no monkey mind of resistance fogging your inner vision and making it difficult for you to see and feel just what a wonderful life it is.

Here's a thought: I know it's the year's end, but humor me. Here's to everyone having a beautiful weekend playing in the moment's end, being so present in the moment that love and appreciation are all we know to be real. From my heart's space to yours, happy new moment. May we all rest in peace before we actually shed our physical bodies. Rest in peace in each moment of 2022.

Before I bring this message of love to a conclusion, I want to add two beautiful stories that warm my heart, to possibly ignite the birth of new beginnings.

I met an amazing couple, Carl and Luwan, while on my morning walk with Satori. We became walking acquaintances. I enjoyed their energy and the love they showed to each other.

My first encounter, around 2014, I will never forget. Satori was so excited to see people, so I asked Carl and Luwan whether I could "train" her as I walked past them. The young Satori was so full of love she wanted to express and had difficulties restraining herself from jumping up on people.

In our family neighborhood, when people had challenges, everyone stepped in. A neighbor in need? All pulled together, at least in prayer. The "walkers" would talk and spread news through their loving concern for their neighbor. I wasn't seeing Carl and Luwan and was told by a mutual friend that she'd had a life-changing experience. I won't give away her amazing story. I really didn't feel I would see her physical form again.

Here is Luwan's story, in her own words.

Prayerful Yoga Made the Difference
Luwan Duma

Restorative yoga lessons from Joni renewed my hope and strength through her encouragement, music, and the meditation selections she played at the end of her class. I realized the deep breathing she always made me do throughout the entire class took more oxygen to my brain to uplift and calm my spirits. No matter how I felt when I arrived, I left renewed and strengthened by her enthusiasm and spirit. Joni brings grace, strength, understanding, and hope to everyone. She makes children and adults stand a little bit taller—literally! LuWan Duma

The transformation I experienced through yoga can give hope and courage to anyone who has experienced life-changing health problems or severe loss of physical strength.

On February 15, 2015, I stopped breathing for fifteen minutes. My husband learned CPR at three o'clock that morning from the 911 operator. My hospital records said, "Sudden cardiac death."

At each stage, they didn't know if I would wake up or breathe on my own, if I would have language to express myself, or if my brain would function at all. I did, and it did! Could I walk?

Would I be able to eventually take care of myself? After two weeks of rehabilitation, I did. Slowly, slowly, at first. One step at a time—literally. Visitors did not realize the severe struggle I was going through because I looked so healthy. Everyone said, "You look great!"

They didn't know how dizzy I was or how I struggled with just punching a phone number on my phone. I didn't talk about it because I didn't want that to be my story. After two weeks in rehabilitation, I then struggled to walk in my house.

It was a wonderful day when I was able to use my walker to walk to the curb forty feet away. It was a long, lonely journey, eventually down the street, then around the block. Slowly, slowly. The doctors didn't tell me my heart was enlarged or that my ejection factor, the pumping strength of my heart, was a big concern. On January 3, 2016, I was admitted to the hospital with congestive heart failure. My ejection factor was 30 percent, a severely critical reading.

The cardiac surgeon told me I needed a mitral valve replacement but my heart was too weak. Therefore I needed a heart transplant. *What! Me? What!* I asked for a referral. They said there was no point in that.

I pushed for a referral to Stanford. I got it! As I left the Stanford Heart Failure clinic, I had hope. I asked if I could try to work up to walking a half mile. They encouraged me to do what I felt I could. Walking and exercises at home got me started. I loved swimming, but I just wasn't strong enough. It took determination to convince my doctor to order physical therapy for me in 2017.

I was slowly getting stronger when the physical therapist decided I was strong enough. With five weeks still left on the doctor's order, she decided I was strong enough to swim. She didn't believe me when I tried to explain that my all-over core strength and legs weren't strong enough to swim more than one or two laps. Out I went! I was so discouraged. Dismayed. Sad. But I couldn't give up. She had no idea what I had overcome already! On my walks in the neighborhood, I heard about Joni's yoga.

My last class was March 2020, when California shut down due to COVID-19. In those two years, I was transformed from a weak, discouraged, determined seventy-one-year-old who "looked great" on the outside to a strong, confident, calmer meditative woman.

My doctors have told me I am a miracle, but all I am is myself. On your journey, you will see the places along the way where people give up. You will say to yourself, "How can I do this anymore? I'm not improving." Think, *Oh, this is where people give up!*

There are many places along the way. Do not stop! Stay determined. Stay cool. No one else is going to do it for you. There is no one coming to save you. There are plenty of people who will help. Sometimes it takes a while to find them.

Namaste, Luwan

I started private lessons in restorative yoga on August 10, 2017.

This was a last-minute request to ask a couple of my adult yogis to share how breath, stillness, and meditation (what we did in yoga) helped them to feel back to who they really are. Of course, I had the blessings to guide many through their lives' practices on the mat. I miss and love them all. I know they feel our forever connection, our energy alignment, heart space to heart space.

I believe there are blessings through practices of breath and stillness, aligning conscious awareness, oneness. We are all connected at the seams yet seamless.

Luwan was a miracle to many. Those of us who know her were not surprised that she was brought back to the physical life and would be an inspiration to so many. She looks so young, both in her physical body and from her energy, her radiant, childlike spirit.

Luwan soon introduced me to Mark and Judi.

Judi: Although our time with Joni was cut short by COVID restrictions, the hours spent in her yoga studio were transforming. We started our first session on my birthday, August 7. Originally, I

When Mark did his first warrior 2—wow! It's a day, a moment, I [Joni] will never forget.

thought this would be something helpful for Mark, whose Parkinson's was progressing, and I only came to that first class to observe.

However, no one is just an observer in Joni's presence, and that same hour, I became a participant and a wannabe yogi. For me, yoga became an oasis. The movement was both soothing and stimulating, but it was the meditation at the end of the hour that brought such satisfaction.

It was the ultimate me time. I heard Deepak Chopra, experienced the melodies, but I was deeply alone—and in the best-possible sense. I was refreshed, body and soul.

I have done yoga since then but have never been able to fully recapture those moments, but I will.

Mark: I was a reluctant yogi at first. I was an athlete in my younger days, and now, at seventy-one and in my fourteenth year of diagnosed Parkinson's, I was out of condition, my muscles weren't cooperating, and my balance was precarious.

I'm not sure why I even agreed to try yoga, but I will forever be thankful that I did. For me, yoga was renewal. I practiced chair yoga, and it was good. I gained some confidence and I like to think some skill and ventured into the poses my wife and Joni were doing.

It was challenging, but, Joni, you always kept me focused on what I could be successful doing and never made me feel yoga was only for the well-coordinated and lithe.

The first time I was able to go into warrior pose, I felt I had made it. I could *do* yoga. Yoga improved my balance, my stamina, and my confidence to go on longer walks and rely less on my cane. I am taking yoga again because of the time I spent with Joni. It is more of a struggle today, but I have felt the rewards, and so I will keep at it and earn my warrior status again.

When I read their experiences, I wasn't prepared for their words of love and kindness toward me. I was expecting their experience of yoga, yet these yogis get it: yoga is life, life is yoga, and we are all together, yoked as one.

As this entire book hopefully displays—and I have come to embrace and live it most moments of the play of life—what you see in me, I can see in you. We are connected at the seams, yet life is seamless, a beautiful tapestry. May we continue to simply be part of it according to the untrainings:

> Remember Who You Are
> You Are Energy
> Love the Moment, Live the Moment, Learn from the Moment, and Laugh Often
> All Is Well: All Are One
> Nothing Can Still Your Joy
> Space: Breathe in the Space of Stillness between Thoughts
> Seeds of Intentions: Plant Your Life's Garden

It's really bittersweet coming to a close (there is no end). I'm feeling your openness as you finish the words yet carry (I pray) satori moments, guiding you through the coming presence with so much love, joy, and unconditional happiness within your inner space of conscious awareness.

A perfect ending to an ongoing story of love, beginning New Year's Day 2021 and ending New Year's Eve 2021.

Love to all, and I mean that from the bottom of my soul. We are all together—connected and resting in the lap of God. So continue to be tender with your self, your heart, and you'll do the same for others. Together we are the mysteriously beautiful handiwork of God. We will never end. Amen.

Printed in the United States
by Baker & Taylor Publisher Services